SIBERIA

ON

FIRE

Northern Illinois University Press   DeKalb, 1989

Selected,
Translated,
and
with
an
Introduction
by
Gerald Mikkelson
and
Margaret Winchell

S I B E R I A

O N

F I R E

Stories and Essays by

VALENTIN RASPUTIN

© 1989 by Northern Illinois University Press
Published by Northern Illinois University Press, DeKalb,
Illinois 60115
Manufactured in the United States of America
Design by Julie Fauci

Library of Congress Cataloging-in-Publication Data
Rasputin, Valentin Grigor'evich.
    [Selections. English. 1989]
    Siberia on fire: stories and essays / by Valentin
Rasputin; selected, translated, and with an introduction
by Gerald Mikkelson and Margaret Winchell.
        p.   cm.
    Bibliography: p.
    ISBN 0-87580-152-8. — ISBN 0-87580-547-7 (pbk.)
    1. Rasputin, Valentin Grigor'evich—Translations,
English. I. Mikkelson, Gerald. II. Winchell, Margaret.
III. Title.
PG3485.5.A85A2413   1989   89-16024
891.73'44—dc20   CIP

Frontispiece photo courtesy of Vernon Craig Sands.
This translation was made possible (in part) through a
grant from the Wheatland Foundation.

"Vasili and Vasilisa," "French Lessons," "You Live and
Love," and "What Shall I Tell the Crow?" were first pub-
lished in the United States in 1987 by Vanguard Press, Inc.
in the collection YOU LIVE AND LOVE & OTHER
STORIES by Valentin Rasputin, translated by Alan G.
Myers, with a foreword by Richard Lourie.

10 9 8 7 6 5 4 3 2

Dedicated to Antonina Rasputina, Jane Mikkelson,
and all the other children
who will inherit the earth
in the condition in which we leave it.

CONTENTS

Introduction i x

FICTION

Vasily and Vasilisa (1966) **4**

French Lessons (1973) **2 5**

Live and Love (1981) **5 2**

What Should I Tell the Crow? (1981) **8 4**

The Fire (1985) **1 0 2**

Auntie Ulita (1985) **1 6 1**

ESSAYS

Your Siberia and Mine (1984) **1 6 9**

How Did They End Up in Irkutsk? (1984) **1 8 0**

Baikal (1981) **1 8 7**

What We Have: A Baikal Prologue Without an
Epilogue (1987) **1 9 4**

Your Son, Russia, and Our Passionate Brother:
On Vasily Shukshin (1984) **2 0 2**

The Truths of Aleksandr Vampilov (1977) **2 1 9**

Appendix **2 2 5**

Bibliography of Major Works by Valentin Rasputin **2 2 9**

CHAPTER 1

INTRODUCTION

Valentin

Rasputin

and

His

Siberia

In March 1985, when Valentin Rasputin was a guest of the University of Kansas, we traveled with him by car for one week, covering 2,600 miles on a trip through Minnesota, Wisconsin, Michigan, Indiana, Illinois, Missouri, and Kansas. The writer was curious not only to see the Great Lakes and a part of the United States that reminded him of Siberia but also to learn as much as possible about American society. Various Midwesterners—medical and business people, teachers, farmers, builders, retired folks—welcomed us into their workplaces and homes. We visited an Indian reservation and a logging museum in northern Wisconsin, Tahquamenon Falls in Michigan's Upper Peninsula, Amish country in northern Indiana, Abraham Lincoln's residence in Springfield, Illinois, and Mark Twain's hometown of Hannibal, Missouri. At Rasputin's request, we discussed what it means to be an American and tried to define the distinguishing features of the American character and way of life. A keen observer, he was most impressed during our travels by the system of paved roads, which, he pointed out, make the most remote areas accessible any time of year; by the efficiency of family farms and the wholesomeness of farm life; by the Amish communities' cohesion and adherence to tradition; and by the range of choices available to students in our public schools. He noted that resourcefulness, a pioneering spirit, concern for the land, social egalitarianism, and love of freedom are qualities that Americans have in common with Siberians, whom he often contrasts with the more oppressed and alienated European Russians. The American genius, he concluded, is most consistently displayed in the realm of inventiveness and practical enterprise.

What about the Russian people? we might ask. Russians certainly have not excelled in road building or democratic government. Their most durable positive achievements have been primarily cultural. The national genius of Russia expresses itself most fully in the arts—in musical composition and performance, in dance, in the theatre, and especially in literature. Over the centuries, every generation of Russians has produced a few authors who combined extraordinary talent, integrity, and remarkable vision—who had within them, to use the Russian phrase, a "divine spark."* The images they created are etched permanently in the historical memory of their own nation and have often had an impact on foreign cultures as well. And despite the hardships and persecutions of the Soviet period, Russia continues to produce great literary artists. Many agree that foremost among them today is Siberian prose writer Valentin Rasputin.

Valentin Grigorievich Rasputin was born on 15 March 1937 and grew up in Atalanka, a small peasant village on the middle reaches of the Angara River in the East Siberian province of Irkutsk. He was raised primarily by his mother and grandmother while his father, who worked both as a farmer and as a logger, served in combat during World War II and then later spent several years in prison after receiving a harsh but typical Stalin-era sentence for the loss of public funds through negligence. The author's childhood was further shaped by the ubiquitous postwar famine and by the heroic communal coping efforts of his hardy fellow villagers. What his family lacked in material amenities the young Rasputin made up for in native intelligence and ingenuity. In 1948, when he was eleven and had excelled in Atalanka's four-year school, his mother sent him to live in Ust-Uda, the county seat, about thirty miles from their home, to finish his education. After he graduated from high school in 1954, Rasputin moved to Irkutsk, the provincial capital, where he enrolled in the School of Humanities at Irkutsk State University with the intention of becoming a teacher.

---

* *Iskra Bozh'ia.*

Rasputin worked his way through college as a part-time reporter for the Irkutsk Komsomol newspaper *Soviet Youth* (*Sovetskaia molodezh'*), and, after receiving his diploma, he became a television editor in Irkutsk. During this period, Rasputin first tried his hand at fiction writing. From 1964 until 1966 he was a correspondent in Krasnoyarsk for several East Siberian newspapers. While traveling extensively on assignment, he gained valuable experience and knowledge about construction projects and about the indigenous peoples in various parts of Siberia. In 1966 he abandoned journalistic writing and returned to Irkutsk. Rasputin explained this transition in an interview at the University of Kansas: "Journalism was interfering with my development as a prose writer. There was a certain narrowness about the topics I wrote on and the language— only about 2,000 words are considered appropriate for a journalist—was limiting." As a prose writer Rasputin acquired the freedom to choose among the 200,000 words in Vladimir Dal's *Dictionary of the Russian Language* and even to coin new words when necessary. "My imagination," he said "was restricted by journalism. After [I became a prose writer], my imagination just began to go wild" (*Oread*, 29 March 1985).* One might add that in Russia prose fiction and poetry have been for hundreds of years the principal forum for discussion of the life-and-death issues of society and human existence. Journalists have traditionally been more timid and more fettered by censorship than have other writers.

Today Rasputin and his wife, Svetlana, a mathematics instructor, live in Irkutsk, although he spends considerable time alone at a cottage on the Angara River near Lake Baikal. They have a son, Sergey, who teaches English, and a daughter, Maria, whose main interest is music. In March 1980 Rasputin was nearly beaten to death by muggers at the entrance to his apartment building. After undergoing surgery and after months of painful recuperation, he recovered without permanent impairment. He has often been asked whether he suspects that the authorities arranged this attack. The author answers with an unequivocal "no" and says that he provoked the attack by "buying jeans and wearing these jeans" (*LJW*). His attackers were subsequently arrested and sentenced to prison.

Since 1982 Rasputin has made several trips to Western countries at the invitation of his publishers and admirers. While a guest lecturer at the University of Kansas, he spoke about Siberia, past and present, and

*The *Oread* is a publication for employees of the University of Kansas. Subsequent quotations from interviews with Rasputin are taken from an article by Chuck Twardy, "Author Calls for Responsibility," *Lawrence Journal-World*, 24 March 1985 (identified in the text as *LJW*), and an article by Michael J. Farrell, "Rasputin: Siberian Writer Confronting the Price of Progress," *National Catholic Reporter*, 17 May 1985 (identified in the text as *NCR*).

about contemporary Siberian literature, emphasizing the works of Sergey Zalygin, Viktor Astafiev, and Vasily Shukshin and his own works. His most salient personal qualities are shyness, a wry, self-deprecating sense of humor, kindness, and unfeigned modesty. He is an accomplished and profound public speaker. After returning to Irkutsk he was frequently invited to talk about his experiences in the United States.

In addition to being widely regarded as the greatest Russian writer residing in the Soviet Union, Valentin Rasputin is one of the most influential leaders of his country's environmental protection movement. Despite his frequent skirmishes with government authorities over environmental matters, Rasputin has little use for politics, at least as a subject for fiction. For years Soviet literary officials have tried unsuccessfully to persuade him to move from Irkutsk to Moscow, where, they imagine, he would be more susceptible to their influence. He is not a member of the Communist party.

Rasputin's first published short story, "I Forgot to Ask Lyoshka" (*Ia zabyl sprosit' u Leshki*), appeared in 1961 in the journal *Angara*. It portrays three young men who work on a road-building project in the taiga.* One of them, Lyoshka, has been struck by a falling tree and desperately needs medical care. When their foreman refuses them the use of a truck, they decide to evacuate Lyoshka on foot. Along the way the three friends discuss the competing priorities of building communism and of looking after individual well-being. Lyoshka dies before they can get help. Despite the unusual psychological twists and poetic language that set this and other early stories apart from those of his contemporaries, Rasputin remained a writer of only regional significance for several years. Then, in 1965, he participated in a seminar for young authors held in Chita. There he was discovered and encouraged by Vladimir Chivilikhin, a prose writer with a strong interest in ecology and Russian history, whose best known work is a novel entitled *Memory*. In 1966 two collections of Rasputin's early stories and essays were published almost simultaneously—one in Krasnoyarsk, the other in Irkutsk. The second of these, *A Land Next to the Sky* (*Krai vozle samogo neba*), is a mosaic of tales describing the way of life of the Tofalar people, a small nomadic tribe living in the Sayan Mountains. In several of these stories the protagonists are old women, a distinguishing feature of Rasputin's mature fiction. During this time he also began to develop a distinctive authorial presence, to

---

*Taiga—sub-Arctic, mostly coniferous forest, dominated in Eastern Siberia by the larch and the nut pine, that spreads thousands of miles from the Ural Mountains to the Pacific Ocean.

assimilate creatively various folk speech patterns and beliefs, and to describe the organic connection between nature and human existence.

The first two collections of stories attracted the attention of literary critics in Moscow and were mentioned favorably in such journals as *New World* (*Novy mir*). By 1967 Rasputin had joined the Writers' Union and had become a professional writer. He gained national stature that year with the publication of another volume of short stories, *A Person from This World* (*Chelovek s etogo sveta*), and his first novella, *Money for Maria* (*Den'gi dlia Marii*). The former work contains the best of his earlier tales already in print (in some cases Rasputin revised and improved his stories by eliminating the conventions of Socialist Realism) as well as several new stories that clearly mark him as a mature writer with the distinctive voice and set of attitudes that readers and critics associate with his literary work as a whole. The most important of these new stories are "Mama's Gone Somewhere" (*Mama kuda-to ushla*) and "Vasily and Vasilisa" (*Vasilii i Vasilisa*). The latter story, somewhat longer and more complex than his earlier tales, contains most of the elements of character and setting, the interactions of people from different generations, and the themes that predominate in his later masterpieces in his principal genre, the novella (*povest'*). "Vasily and Vasilisa" is about a Siberian peasant couple who, after raising a large family and enduring numerous hardships together, become estranged. Their final parting words express forgiveness and acceptance of responsibility, two themes that recur repeatedly in Rasputin's later works.

Rasputin also received wide recognition in 1967 for the publication of *Money for Maria*, which caught the attention of the critics even though it initially appeared in provincial periodicals (*Angara* and *Siberian Lights* [*Sibirskie ogni*]). In early 1968 it was published in Moscow, in the journal *Young Guard* (*Molodaia gvardiia*). *Money for Maria* was the first of four novellas written and published between 1967 and 1976. The others are *Borrowed Time* (*Poslednii srok*, 1970), *Live and Remember* (*Zhivi i pomni*, 1974), and *Farewell to Matyora* (*Proshchanie s Materoi*, 1976). Each received more critical attention than its predecessor, and there was general agreement among readers and literary specialists that a writer of major talent and importance had emerged. All these tales are set in Siberian villages along the Angara River. They depict unforgettable peasant characters in family and social situations during times of crisis. *Money for Maria* relates the disappearance of a substantial sum of money from the local general store, run by a woman named Maria, and the valiant efforts of her husband to keep her out of jail by borrowing the missing amount from his fellow villagers and a brother who lives in the city. In *Borrowed Time*, an old peasant woman is dying, and her children are summoned to their

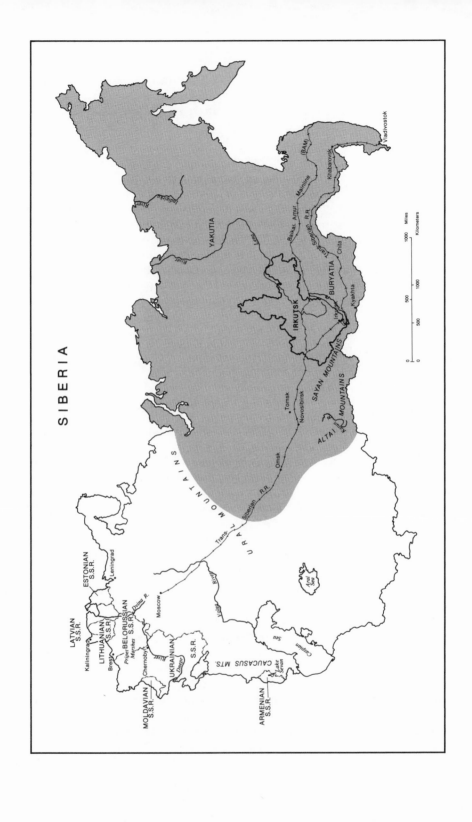

SIBERIA

native village to pay their last respects. In the process, old hurts and ani-
mosities come to the surface and the children quarrel even as their
mother recollects her entire life and experiences a bittersweet epiphany
of sorts. "The old woman [Anna] talks about her own death as if it is the
simplest thing," said Rasputin in an interview, adding that this is a characteristic of "people who believe," who practice their faith, because non-
believers and those who feel they have "lived badly" worry about death.
"She has to do as much good [as she can] . . . while she still has the
time" (*LJW*). When she dies, only one child is at her bedside; the rest
have returned to their distant homes and separate lives.

In *Live and Remember*, a thrice-wounded Red Army soldier named
Andrey Guskov deserts at the end of World War II in order to return to
his village, his wife, Nastyona, and his parents. He lives in hiding on the
other side of the Angara River and comes into the village only after dark,
gradually drawing Nastyona into a vortex of dangers and complications
from which she can extricate herself only by committing suicide.

In *Farewell to Matyora*, a village located on an island in the middle of
the Angara is scheduled to be submerged with the completion of a huge
dam and hydroelectric power plant downstream. The inhabitants of
Matyora (the name of the village and of the island itself) are ordered to
move to the mainland, where a workers' town (*rabochii poselok*) is being
built for them. Those most attached to their native soil and to the way
of life inherited from their ancestors, principally older women led by
Darya, strive to rescue the graves of their forebears and to maintain a
measure of dignity in the face of sweeping disruption and change.

Taken together, these novellas chronicle the breakdown of Siberian
village life from the 1930s to the 1970s caused by the excesses and brutality
of Stalinism, by the losses and deprivations during World War II and the
postwar period, and by the gigantic construction and modernization
projects of more recent decades. Rasputin's criticism of contemporary
trends and conditions has made him a controversial writer—some critics
suspect him of subtly rationalizing Guskov's wartime desertion, and he
clearly sides with Darya in her diatribes against the party and government authorities who enforce a decision destroying the islanders' cherished traditional way of life. Despite the critical polemics surrounding
these works, Rasputin was awarded a State Prize for Literature in 1977
for *Live and Remember*, which many readers regard as his best novella
to date.

After *Farewell to Matyora*, nearly ten years passed before Rasputin
published his next novella. The reasons for this hiatus are complex. The
injuries he sustained when he was mugged made normal literary activity very difficult for several years. Equally important, Rasputin was
experiencing a creative crisis. *Farewell to Matyora* seemed to have ended

the cycle of novellas describing the gradual but inevitable extinction of the Siberian peasant village he had known as a child. Moreover, Rasputin had lived in a big city for more than twenty years by then, and, although he returned periodically to visit his mother in the relocated Atalanka (itself a victim of the Angara's transformation from river into vast reservoir when the Bratsk Dam was completed in 1961), he considered himself out of touch with village life. Rasputin foreshadows his personal and artistic dilemma in a fictionalized travel sketch of 1972 entitled "Downstream and Upstream" (*Vniz i vverkh po techeniiu*).

During this period of transition, Rasputin was refining his art and moving in various directions. He completed a series of highly autobiographical short stories in which the protagonists, each of them introspective loners, delve deeply into their psyches and even experience altered states of consciousness, flights of pure fantasy, and mystical communion with spirits. In these stories, particularly in "Live and Love" (*Vek zhivi—vek liubi*) and "What Should I Tell the Crow?" (*Chto peredat' vorone?*)—both published in 1981—Rasputin gives free rein to a metaphysical tendency inherent but understated in his earlier fiction. The interactions described in these stories take place not so much between separate human beings as among various levels of the hero's own being and between the hero and voices coming to him from the depths of nature, from the past, and from a world beyond the here and now.

During the early 1980s Rasputin became intensely involved in the Soviet environmental protection movement, especially in the campaign to save Lake Baikal and its surroundings from devastation caused by industrial development. Several essays written during this period call on the public and on the authorities to stop the pollution before it is too late. As soon as he was able to travel long distances, Rasputin made several trips to various parts of Siberia and wrote a series of essays reviewing the history and present condition of his native region, which appeared in the journal *Our Contemporary (Nash sovremennik)* in 1988 and 1989 under the title "Siberia, Siberia" (*Sibir', Sibir'* . . .). He also wrote long tributes to several writers, notably those with whom he felt a sense of kinship, including Fyodor Abramov, Vasily Belov, Dmitry Likhachyov, and such fellow Siberian authors as Vasily Shukshin, Sergey Zalygin, Viktor Astafiev, and Aleksandr Vampilov, a playwright and close friend who drowned in Lake Baikal in 1972.

Meanwhile Rasputin's reading public and the literary critics waited impatiently for his next novella. Some speculated that he was finished as a serious writer. Finally, in 1985, Rasputin published one of the longer works of fiction that he had been working on during his recuperation and creative crisis. This novella, *The Fire (Pozhar)*, appeared in the July 1985 issue of *Our Contemporary*. Though shorter than his earlier novellas,

The Fire generated more critical commentary and public reaction than anything he had written previously. The setting is no longer a Siberian village but a workers' town formed in the early 1960s by the combination of several villages destroyed during construction of the Bratsk Dam. The hero of this tale is Ivan Petrovich, who works for the logging operation that has replaced farming as the chief economic activity in the area. His and the other characters' reactions to a fire that destroys the warehouses containing all the town's food and other supplies reveal human nature at its best and worst. It becomes clear that the time-honored communal support systems characteristic of life in the old villages have broken down because of modern developments and because of an influx of people with little or no commitment to the long-range interests of the region as a whole. *The Fire*, appearing just after Mikhail Gorbachev was named General Secretary of the Communist party, has become an emblem of glasnost and perestroika. This fictional yet highly topical work* sets new limits in Soviet literature through its overt criticism of the status quo, particularly of the excessive exploitation of Siberia's vast resources in the name of progress and alleged economic necessity. In *The Fire*, we see what has happened to rural society as a result of the rapid changes and dislocations in recent decades. This novella returns to the patterns established in *Money for Maria* and is widely regarded as a direct continuation of *Farewell to Matyora*.

Rasputin's early writing remains well within the accepted boundaries of Soviet reportage and the aesthetics of Socialist Realism. Throughout the 1960s and the early 1970s, he was often associated with a literary movement known as "rural prose" or "village prose" (*derevenskaia proza*). Village-prose writers present an unvarnished view of life in the Russian countryside that contrasts with the utopian and basically dishonest presentation of reality characteristic of most Soviet writing during the Stalinist period. Rasputin's first works differ from those of the new movement only because their Siberian setting gives them a slightly exotic flavor. With the publication of each succeeding novella, however, it became clear that Rasputin was developing a distinctive literary voice and his own thematic interests, narrative techniques, and stylistic peculiarities along with a universal appeal often lacking in village prose. His most cherished themes are the earth as a unified ecosystem, including soil, air, water, plants, animals, humans, and spirits, all of which are subtly and inextricably interwoven and interdependent; a nation's history as a unified and unbreakable continuum made up of past, present,

---

*In Russian, *publitsisticheskaia proza*, literally, "publicistic prose"; this refers to fiction dealing with issues of current public urgency in which the author's attitudes are clearly revealed.

and future generations, all of which are connected by a common place of birth and by the same cultural and ethical traditions; the psychological motivation of individuals, whether ostracized or accepted by society; the clash between modern and traditional mores, especially as it affects the earth, one's sense of historical roots, and one's behavior during a crisis; the perils and ecstasies of solitude and introspection; and the harshness of Soviet law, particularly when applied arbitrarily and without regard for mitigating circumstances. His often complicated narrative stance ranges from an autobiographical first-person narrator to a perceptive, if not always omniscient, third person whose point of view and mode of expression are strongly influenced by the consciousness of the protagonist, with frequent excursions into a character's psyche and adoption of his speech patterns along with lyrical digressions about nature. His stylistic peculiarities include Siberian peasant vernacular in dialogue alternating with impeccable literary Russian and complex, even ornate sentences side by side with elliptical phrases. Standard Russian is often embellished with archaisms, Siberian dialectal expressions, and highly inventive neologisms. Since 1975 Rasputin has shifted his focus to the recently formed workers' towns, to characters involuntarily displaced from their native habitat, and to the inner depths of memory and imagination. Occupying a unique place in contemporary Russian literature, he presents a way of looking at the world that contrasts sharply with the view of most Soviet writers and even with that of his village-prose compatriots.

Rasputin's writing is permeated with a consistent and coherent Weltanschauung. Most important are his attitudes toward Siberia, toward human behavior in its individual and social forms, and toward the role of the writer in culture and society. Rasputin believes that the land of one's birth is precious and has been entrusted to its people for safekeeping. It may be used for sustenance and enjoyment but must be passed along intact to descendants. The author feels that human behavior should be based on the time-tested principle of voluntarily assuming responsibility for one's actions; should demonstrate courage and resourcefulness in times of hardship and adversity; and should be seasoned with love, tolerance of diversity, and forgiveness. The writer discharges his responsibility to society only by depicting psychological and social reality with uninhibited truthfulness. "The main task of literature," Rasputin said in a lecture, "is to facilitate the improvement of humanity and to correct the disfigurement of humanity. To say that we have the best of all possible worlds is the task of propagandists rather than of writers. The writer is obliged to look upon life in a somewhat more complicated and profound manner" (NCR). He must not only entertain his readers but also educate them, provoke their sympathy (and

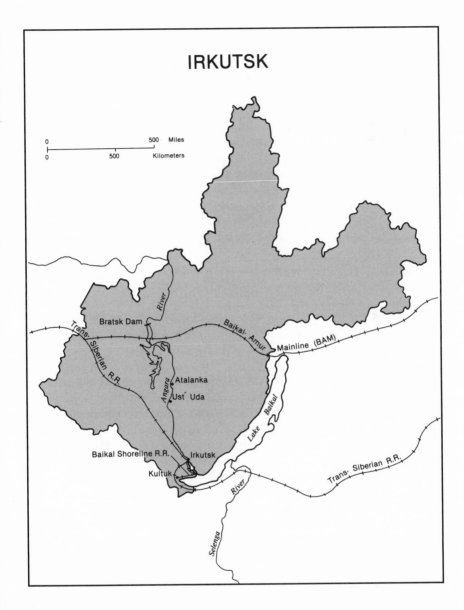

IRKUTSK

0   500   Miles

0   500   Kilometers

River

Bratsk Dam

Trans-Siberian R.R.

Baikal-Amur Mainline (BAM)

Angara

Atalanka

Ust' Uda

Lake Baikal

Baikal Shoreline R.R.

Irkutsk

Kultuk

Trans-Siberian R.R.

River

Selenga

antipathy), and raise the level of their awareness, especially regarding matters of conscience.

Rasputin's works appeal to readers of all ages and transcend national boundaries because their thoughts, beauty, and ethical values are universal. He portrays unforgettable flesh-and-blood characters whose lives are twisted by events often beyond their control but who struggle to preserve their integrity and self-respect. Such characters include the eleven-year-old boy in "French Lessons," the old woman in "Vasily and Vasilisa," and the middle-aged Ivan Petrovich in *The Fire*. Rasputin deplores harmful trends in contemporary Soviet society that have parallels around the world—the wasteful use of natural resources and the despoliation of the environment, including historic buildings and sites as well as the soil, water, and air. And he laments the abandonment of traditional standards of human decency and social cohesion (see, for example, *The Fire* and the essays in this volume). He describes both nature and human endeavors with such originality and insight that their subtlest interconnections become apparent and leave indelible images in the reader's memory. Rasputin has said, "I like to agitate the minds and hearts of the readers, not to frighten or to create a sensation, but simply to stir up what's going on inside them, so it would be painful for a while, but some hope would emerge" (*NCR*). He plumbs the depths of the human soul, searching for the origins of personality, conscience, and creativity and exploring mystically altered states of consciousness, as seen in "Live and Love" and "What Should I Tell the Crow?" Using both fiction and nonfiction, Rasputin illuminates matters of concern to everyone and provides new insights through his unique perspective and talent.

Although Rasputin's literary world is unmistakably his own, it is not strictly private and incomprehensible to the reader. His literature is firmly rooted in the Siberian earth and taiga, and the powerfully coursing waters of the Angara River are its life blood. Rasputin's characters speak from the depths of what he calls "spiritual memory" (*dukhovnaia pamiat'*) and "spiritual experience" (*dukhovnyi opyt*). His message is highly personal and yet drawn both from the communal lore of his ancestors, who were transplanted primarily from the northern parts of European Russia, and from the beliefs of the indigenous Asiatic peoples with whom they lived and intermarried. Rasputin's emphasis on history and mythology stems from his sense that some great catastrophe is about to happen in Siberia, and perhaps even worldwide. In his words, "When a person has no reason to be certain of what will come in the future, then there is a natural tendency to look back into the past. . . . I look for support to what I imagine existed in the past. I want to figure out what made me the way I am today. I lean over as far as I can to pick out the roots of my own ancestry. I am convinced that the deeper these roots have penetrated into the past, the more likely it is that my life will continue into the future" (*NCR*).

Rasputin's religion, as implied in his works, is an amalgam of Orthodox Christianity, pre-Christian paganism, and Siberian shamanism. When asked whether the frequent religious references in his works merely reflect Siberian culture or also suggest the author's own point of view, he replied, "Both one and the other. The heroes of most of my works are older people. If I denied them their faith, I would be going against the truth in depicting these people. Interest in religion has increased a great deal in our country in recent times as well, and I cannot ignore this." Regarding his own religious beliefs, Rasputin said, "I'm somewhere in between. I'm sort of vaguely religious. I don't follow the rituals of the church, which one ought to do if one were a true believer" (NCR). With a smile he added, "I am much closer to the philosophy of these old women" (LJW).

All his major characters, if not strictly autobiographical, are based on actual prototypes from Rasputin's life. His chief protagonists represent the generations of his parents and grandparents, who experienced most painfully the dramatic changes brought about by industrial development and social disruption. And yet everything in Rasputin's fiction and essays is viewed through the particularly acute and idiosyncratic lens of his perspective and system of values. Reading Rasputin, one is continually aware of being in direct contact simultaneously with a rich historical tradition and with a wonderfully fertile and creative mind.

The selections in this volume represent the range of Rasputin's thought, passion, and creativity. The first four short stories are, in our estimation, the best that Rasputin has written in this genre. *The Fire* is not only his most recent and perhaps most polemical novella but also a genuine masterpiece not yet sufficiently appreciated for its literary merits either in the Soviet Union or in the West. It ranks, along with *Live and Remember* and *Farewell to Matyora*, among Rasputin's finest novellas. Taken together, these novellas constitute a Siberian rural epic depicting the demise of a whole way of life that continues to survive nonetheless in the fiction of this devoted and loyal native son. The short story "Auntie Ulita" provides a poignant echo from the grave of the author's grandmother, reminding us of what has faded into the past in our hectic times and of how important it is to "live and remember" and to "live and love."

The essays survey Rasputin's main interests as an amateur historian and ethnographer, as an environmental protectionist, and as a colleague and critic of his fellow writers. They provide an intriguing glance into the author's ideas about his native Siberia, the city of Irkutsk, Lake Baikal, and issues addressed in contemporary Siberian literature including historical truth, regional patriotism, humankind and nature, women and families, the breakdown of social civility, and the aching of the human soul. While Rasputin's views on these matters may not please all readers, they do stimulate thought and discussion, and they deepen our understanding of his prose. His fictional world and philosophy of life are drawn from the rocks and soil, the forests and rivers, the skies and seas, the peoples and spirits of Siberia. But they are also clearly stamped with the author's personal insight, value system, and imagination. This book will give the reader an overall view of the mind, heart, creative consciousness, and homeland of Valentin Rasputin.

For the translation of Russian words we have followed J. Thomas Shaw's *The Transliteration of Modern Russian for English-Language Publications* (Madison: University of Wisconsin Press, 1967), using System I for personal and place names, except for those names with well-established English forms, and System II for words as words and for bibliographical citations. The appendix lists all Russian names cited in the book with accent marks on stressed syllables to aid the reader in pronunciation. All footnotes are ours.

When differing versions of Rasputin's original text were known to exist, we used the most recently published edition, except when we knew the author preferred an earlier one. Two of the essays are slightly truncated. "How Did They End Up in Irkutsk?" was written as a foreword to *The Art Treasures of Irkutsk* (*Irkutskie sokrovishcha*) by Aleksey Fatyanov. We have omitted a few phrases that refer exclusively to the book and are not relevant to Rasputin's fundamental ideas about Siberia, its art, and its inhabitants. Our translation of the article on Vasily Shukshin contains minor omissions, mainly long quotations from Shukshin's stories. In every case we have tried to remain faithful to the meaning and style of Rasputin's prose and to bring his world to the English-speaking public with all its richness intact.

Gerald Mikkelson and Margaret Winchell

SIBERIA

ON

FIRE

FICTION

VASILY AND VASILISA

Vasilisa wakes up early. In the summer the roost-
ers wake her up, but in the winter she doesn't trust the roosters. They
might oversleep because of the cold, but she can't oversleep. She lies in
bed for some time and thinks that today she must do this, that, and the
other—it's as if she's weighing the day to see if it will be heavy or not.
Then Vasilisa sighs and lowers her feet from the wooden bed to the
painted floorboards—the bed sighs, too, following her lead, and both of
them relax. Vasilisa gets dressed and looks at the opposite wall. Thank
God, she thinks, she has finally gotten rid of all the cockroaches—
there's not one in sight.

This half-sleeping, half-waking state does not last long. She doesn't
notice it; for her it is only one step from sleeping to working, one single
step. After getting dressed, Vasilisa snaps out of it and gets busy. She
lights the Russian stove, climbs down into the cellar to get some potatoes, runs to the shed after some flour, puts an assortment of cast-iron
pans on the stove, prepares mash for the calf, gives the cow, pig, and
chickens some feed, milks the cow, strains the milk through cheese-
cloth, and pours it into all kinds of bottles and jars—she does a thousand things and then gets the samovar going.

She loves setting up the samovar. The first wave of work has broken and receded, the earliness is gone, and now out of habit Vasilisa feels thirsty. Her day is divided not into hours but into samovars: the first samovar, the second, the third . . . In her old age drinking tea replaces almost all other pleasures.

She still runs around and fusses with the pans, but she keeps one eye on the samovar at all times. By now it's breathing heavily; now it's starting to huff and puff; and now it's begun to mutter and gurgle. Vasilisa carries the samovar to the table, sits down close to it, and sighs. She is always sighing; her sighs express a great number of nuances, from surprise and joy to pain and suffering.

Vasily doesn't get up early—he has no reason to. The single small window in his shed, like the one in the bathhouse, is covered by a curtain at night. Vasily doesn't like moonlight. It seems to him that the moon brings in the cold. The head of the bed points toward the window, and on the other side of it stands a little table. Hunting and fishing gear hangs on nails near the door, with sheepskin coats and quilted jackets piled on top. When he wakes up, Vasily pulls the curtain back from the window, squints at the light bursting in, and, after adjusting to it, looks out the window. What's it like outside? Snow, rain, sunshine? He gets dressed in silence, complete silence—he doesn't puff or grunt or groan.

When Vasily enters the cottage, Vasilisa does not turn around. He sits down at the other end of the table and waits. Without saying a word, Vasilisa pours him a glass of tea and puts it in the middle of the table. He moves the glass closer to himself and takes the first swallow, which burns his throat and goes down like a hard lump.

Vasilisa drinks tea while holding a sugar cube in her teeth. Vasily drinks his without sugar—he doesn't like it. He believes that everything should be used in its pure, original form: vodka with nothing added to it and unsweetened tea. He finishes his tea and puts the glass in the middle of the table. Vasilisa takes the glass, fills it, and puts it back in the middle.

They remain silent. Pyotr, Vasily and Vasilisa's youngest child, is curled up asleep on the bed by the wall. His bare knees stick out from under the blanket—it's always like that, winter and summer.

Vasilisa sighs and pours herself another glass of tea. Vasily puts his glass in the middle of the table, gets up, and leaves. Vasilisa does not turn around when he leaves.

"Hey, you slug," she says to Pyotr. "Get up or else you'll get bedsores."

Pyotr opens his eyes with displeasure and hides his knees under the blanket.

"Get up, you slug," Vasilisa repeats good-naturedly. "You haven't struck it rich yet. Drink some tea and get going."

Tanya, Pyotr's wife, wakes up, too, but she doesn't have to go to work—she's expecting a little one.

"You stay where you are," Vasilisa tells her. "You got no place to rush off to. We have to get this slug up."

In her view all lazy people fall into three categories: someone who is just plain lazy—a mere beginner; a loafer—a lazy person with experience and a long record; and a slug—someone who is incorrigibly lazy. Pyotr does not deserve to be put in the third category, and Vasilisa knows that she is being unfair to him, but she needs to grumble a little.

"A slug—he's a real slug," she mutters.

She's already back in the kitchen again, where she finishes her frying and cooking. The day has just begun. Vasilisa sighs—the whole day still lies ahead.

It has been almost thirty years now since Vasily began living in the shed, the middle one of three sheds that form a single structure. His shed is small and clean, contains no grain bins, and has a well-made floor, like the one in the cottage, and a fitted ceiling. The children used to sleep in it during the summer, but that was long ago, very long ago—back when Vasily was still living in the cottage.

When winter comes, he sets up an iron stove inside his shed. Five years ago Pyotr installed an electric light for him, but ever since then for some reason the swallows have stopped building nests over the shed door and have moved somewhere else. Vasily mourned the loss at first, for he loved to watch them, but then he got used to being without them, too.

Vasily stops by at the house only once a day, when the young folks are still asleep, and Vasilisa pours him a glass of strong hot tea. She sits at one end of the table, and he sits at the other. They remain silent—not once have they spoken a single word, as if they don't see each other, and each knows of the other's presence only from the glass that is put in the middle of the table. They remain silent, and it is not a strained silence or even a silence at all, but just their customary physical state of wordlessness in which no one expects words and words are unnecessary.

Vasily eats lunch and supper in his shed. He has a few utensils, and he learned how to cook a long time ago. True, his concoctions are pretty unsophisticated—more and more it's kasha and macaroni alternating with canned food, but sometimes, if he has good luck hunting, there will be fresh game. On those days Pyotr comes over for his share, too. Time and again he runs back to the cottage for a frying pan, some salt, one more fork, one more glass—that means they've gotten out a bottle of booze to celebrate.

"If you get drunk over there, don't bother coming home!" Vasilisa yells after him. "What a slug!"

She pronounces "slug" in a singsong voice and takes pleasure in it. Some kids are hanging around the shed: there's Pyotr's Vaska, named after his grandpa, and all three of Nastya's. Nastya, Vasily and Vasilisa's middle daughter, lives in the same house but in separate quarters—the house is divided into two parts, and Nastya has the smaller one. Their older daughter, Anna, lives four doors down and is married to a teacher.

Vasily is not stingy. He leaves himself only a little of whatever it is he has caught. He doesn't need a lot. The largest chunk he gives to Nastya—she has a harder time than the others, being without a husband and saddled with three kids. Pyotr chops off a chunk for himself and takes it to his own shed right away, so as not to be a nuisance. Vasily divides the remaining meat in half and has the kids take one portion to Anna. The kids run off, all in a pack. And only then does the frying pan of fresh game make its appearance—with the splattering, crackling fat still quivering from the heat and big chunks of flank cooked all the way through. They shut the door and open the bottle.

Vasily cannot live without the taiga. He knows it and loves it as if he had created it with his own hands, as if he had filled it with all its riches and spread them around himself. In September he goes out after pine nuts and knocks down cones right up until the snow falls, after which hunting season immediately begins. Vasily goes squirrel- and sable-hunting twice, once before New Year's and once after. In the spring there are pine nuts again (fallen cones roll around underfoot after the snow melts), in May you can pick wild garlic, in June it's a sin not to fish for the red-and-black grayling that live in the taiga, in July the berries get ripe—and every year it's the same thing.

The men come and try to pump him for information.

"What do you think, Vasily? There gonna be any nuts this year or not?"

"If the nuthatch don't eat 'em all there will be," he replies slyly.

"Well, sure," says one of the men, still not satisfied.

"I'll go on a scouting trip next week and take a look," says Vasily, who can't stand it any longer. "Then I'll be able to tell. But you can see for yourself that right now I'm sitting in my shed—can't see from here."

He does not have a job. The taiga feeds and clothes him. He turns in more pelts than anyone else, and in good years he fills five to eight gunnysacks with pine nuts. Starting early in the winter he gets letters from foresters in Lithuania and from geologists in Moscow and around the region asking him to go on expeditions with them in the summer as their guide. He gives preference, as a rule, to Lithuanian foresters—he finds it interesting to observe people of different ethnic origins and to memorize their strange words. Getting up after a rest break and not holding back a sly smile of satisfaction, he'll say "*ainam*," and the Lithuanians will laugh and follow him. Vasily also likes foresters because they've been specially trained to clean up the taiga and will never let a fire get away from them in the woods. But geologists feel like transients there and might leave trash, fell a bountiful Siberian pine for the sake of a dozen cones, or fail to stamp out their campfire.

When he goes off to the taiga, Vasily locks up the shed, and Vasilisa, watching him from the window, mutters, "As if he might get robbed, as if those trunks of his are crammed with stuff. If he'd only buy some pants with all his money. He runs around with a bare butt and makes people laugh. No shame, no conscience."

They sit opposite each other, Vasily on the bed and Pyotr on the low child's stool that was slapped together for him about twenty-five years before, and Vasily, who's not tipsy yet, is complaining about his lower back.

"It's started aching, the damn thing. You bend over, but then you can't straighten up."

"High time it should ache." Pyotr snorts. "You're still trying to run around like a young buck when you're sixty-five. Even so, with your health—everybody should be so lucky."

"Nowadays I'm afraid to go squirrel-hunting by myself. Have to find a partner." Vasily says it almost with pride. This is the first time, he's saying, that he has ever needed one.

Pyotr concentrates on poking around in the frying pan with his fork.

"Maybe you can go with me?" asks Vasily, knowing that his son won't go anywhere.

Pyotr raises his head. His face is snub-nosed and unshaven.

"I'd like to. But who's going to give me time off? The kolkhoz won't."

"No, they won't," Vasily agrees.

"Well, there you are."

The matter is settled, and Vasily fills up their glasses again.

A friend of Vasilisa's, seventy-year-old Granny Avdotya, has come to see her.

"I'm walking along thinking, 'I'll drop in and see Vasilisa!'" she shouts, as though announcing her arrival to the whole cottage.

Vasilisa takes off her apron—she has been doing some laundry and isn't finished—goes up to Avdotya, and holds out her hand.

"Let's shake hands, Granny Avdotya."

Granny Avdotya's hand is as limp as a rag.

"I'm walking along thinking, 'I'll drop in and see Vasilisa!'" she shouts again. "But you got no time to set down."

"How can I sit down?" Vasilisa readily replies. "I'm on my feet the whole day. First it's one thing, then another."

"You'll never catch up in a thousand years!" shouts Granny Avdotya. "Just remember, Vasilisa, the work'll still be here after we're gone. Even if you use a horse, it'll still be here."

"That's for sure." Vasilisa nods her head. "If you carry it over from one day to the next, you just have to keep carrying it farther. You're always on the move, like a gypsy with a bag."

"And no way to get out of it!"

"No way at all."

"Nope, no way."

They nod their heads at each other in agreement for a long time. Then Granny Avdotya asks, "Where's that Pyotr of yours—at work?"

"At work, my foot! Afraid not." Vasilisa snorts. "They locked themselves up in the shed over there and I daresay they're drinking like fish."

"That's how it goes!" shouts Avdotya joyfully. "Same story with my son-in-law. One son-in-law don't touch the stuff, but the other one never wants to dry out."

Vasilisa nods understandingly.

"And you, don't you never go over there?" Granny Avdotya motions in the direction of the shed.

"Listen, old woman, are you out of your mind or what?" Vasilisa takes offense. "I'm not even about to sit next to him in the same outhouse. What a dumb thing to say! I don't know whether to laugh or cry."

"Heh-heh-heh," Granny Avdotya laughs. "I got curious, so I asked. Thought you might've made friends in your old age and I didn't know nothin' about it."

"Don't talk nonsense, Granny Avdotya."

Vasily shakes up the rest of the vodka and pours it into their glasses. Pyotr finds it uncomfortable sitting on the child's stool, and he moves over to the bed.

"It hurts me, Petka, that you got no respect for the taiga," says Vasily. "All our kinfolk lived off the taiga, but when I die you'll have to sell my gun."

"I got respect for it," Pyotr feebly objects. "But who's going to give me time off from the kolkhoz?"

"Nobody, that's for sure."

"Nobody's going to let me off. If I didn't drive the tractor, that would be different. But the way things stand—it's like beating your head against a wall."

"Don't sell the gun," Vasily says sternly all of a sudden.

"Oh, that's terrific. What would I sell it for?"

"Don't sell it. I only got a little time left to live—let it be a reminder of me. Never know when you might meet up with some wild animal. It's a good gun."

"All right, enough. I said I won't sell it—that means I won't."

They fall silent. The last of the vodka in their glasses hasn't been downed yet; it shimmers a little, and in the electric light from overhead it seems covered with a thin film.

"Petka," says Vasily. "Let's sing."

"Okay."

"What should we sing?"

"I don't care. You start."

Vasily does not begin for a long time. He picks up his glass and holds it in his hands. Then, leaning way over the table, he makes up his mind.

The apple and pear trees were blooming . . .

He turns to Pyotr, who joins in. Then they do not look at each other anymore.

Out onto the bank came Katyusha,
Out onto the steep, lofty bank.

Vasilisa raises her head and listens. Granny Avdotya has gone. Vasilisa sighs, but even she herself doesn't understand what is in that sigh.

▲   It happened two years or so before the war. At that time Vasily suddenly started acting foolish. First every other day and then every single day he would come home drunk, and once he tried to beat Vasilisa. He chased her up onto the top ledge of the Russian stove, from which there was no escape, and climbed after her. At the last second an oven fork* fell into Vasilisa's hand. She grabbed it, aimed the prongs at Vasily's upraised neck, and struck with all her might. Vasily fell, and, not letting go of the fork, she jumped down and managed to pin his neck to the floor. He twisted and turned, sticking out his neck like a rooster on a chopping block just before its head is cut off. He wheezed out some obscenities but couldn't get away from the fork. Vasilisa let him go only when he promised not to touch her.

Remembering this incident when he got drunk, Vasily would become furious over the realization of his disgrace and would go after Vasilisa with his fists. She'd calm him down; it wasn't hard to deal with him when he was drunk. But once—Vasilisa was pregnant again at the time— he grabbed an axe lying under a bench and raised it menacingly. Vasilisa was scared to death. She began shouting at the top of her lungs and tore

---

*A kitchen utensil resembling a large horseshoe on a long handle that fits around the base of pots to remove them from a Russian stove.

out of the cottage. That night she had a miscarriage. When she returned home, she shook Vasily to wake him up and pointed at the doorway.

"Get out!"

Half asleep, Vasily didn't understand a thing. She repeated it more forcefully.

"You hear me? Get out!"

Vasilisa carried Vasily's clothes to the back stoop herself, and he took them to the shed, walking on the little wooden sidewalk he'd laid not long before. He tried to enter the house that evening, but Vasilisa stood firmly in the doorway.

"I'm not letting you in!"

They'd lived together for twenty years, and they had seven children. The two oldest boys were already working, and the youngest, Petka, was going on five. When the war broke out, the town chairman sent a special messenger around to all the houses so everybody would know about it and so nobody would make plans to head for the taiga. Vasilisa's family had just sat down to the table. The messenger, a snot-nosed kid who imagined war as a game for grown-ups, began drumming on the window and shouting merrily.

"He-e-ey! War's begun! War!"

Vasily arrived immediately, and Vasilisa did not drive him away; she wasn't up to it. He sat down on a bench by the door, put his hands on his knees, and remained silent—it was obviously unbearable for him to remain silent all alone in his shed.

He came back three days later already packed, carrying a bag. He left the bag in the doorway and went on in to the middle of the front room. Everybody stood up, and so did Vasilisa. Frowning, Vasily made a gesture that showed his embarrassment and began awkwardly thrusting his face into the children's shoulders. Then he went up to Vasilisa and stopped in front of her. Their children watched them and waited in agony.

"Vasilisa," said Vasily hoarsely. "Don't be hard on me no more—I'm likely to get killed. You and the kids . . . uh . . . "

Vasilisa offered her hand to him first, and Vasily shook it and left without finishing what he'd started to say. He shut the gate softly and carefully behind him and began walking toward the town hall, where horses and wagons were waiting for the soldiers headed for the front.

Later the wagons would pick them up in front of their houses. Vasilisa saw her two oldest sons and her daughter Anna off to war. Each of them got into a sleigh or a wagon waiting in the yard, and Vasilisa—opening the gate herself, pressing her apron to her lips, and crossing herself—watched how one after another the wagons left people's houses and moved slowly down the street and out of the village, how the

drunken men sang, and how the women clutching them wailed. Vasilisa
didn't accompany her children out of the village. She stood at the gate
and then shut it behind her as if locking herself away from any more
wagons.

One of her sons never came back at all, and the other one returned
but left right away for the city and stayed there for good. Vasily arrived
later than everybody.

It was already autumn and the villagers were digging up potatoes.
Vasilisa had just come in loaded down with a sack of potatoes and was
about to empty them into the cellar when Nastya came running up.

"Mama, Father's here! He's coming."

Vasilisa straightened up.

"So he came out of it alive," she said unhurriedly, reasoning out loud
to herself. "But Sashka got killed."

She threw the sack down into the cellar without untying it and shuddered when it hit the hard ground. Growing more and more irritated,
Vasilisa went into the front room. She didn't change clothes—no point
in that. By the time footsteps could be heard on the back stoop, she was
ready to let him have it. Vasilisa couldn't decide if she was sick to her
stomach or just tired.

"Vasilisa, it's me," said Vasily from the doorway, and she shuddered
again because she hadn't heard his voice for a long time. She remained
silent, but her face, all set for a reply, could not stay calm and, giving in
to her desire to respond, she said, "Sashka got killed."

Vasily nodded.

She said nothing more. The children came running up, thank God,
and she could escape into the yard and go about her own business. Then
guests arrived, men who had also returned from the war, but Vasilisa sat
in the kitchen until she got tired of sitting. Then she lit a lamp, climbed
down into the cellar, and started sorting potatoes.

The men sang in unfamiliar voices acquired somewhere out there,
during the war, voices acquired during cries of "Hurray!" and also cries
for help—it seemed to Vasilisa that they had gotten together only to
completely drown out the strange voices in themselves by singing and
shouting, after which their real voices would take over.

The songs were drunken but restrained, without devil-may-care bra-
vado, and the men who were drawing them out in their off-key voices
seemed to be looking over their shoulders the whole time to see if something had happened behind them. Each of them seemed to pull himself
up short so he wouldn't drift off into a daydream and be lost. And the
loud, drunken conversation was restrained, too, and was quickly interrupted by singing—all this was like a dull disturbing pain that would
flare up first in one place, then in another.

Vasilisa got tired and climbed up from the cellar. She didn't want to do anything anymore. She called Nastya and told her, "Go clean up the shed for your father."

"Mama!" Nastya's voice was full of reproach.

"Go on," said Vasilisa. "This is none of your business."

Vasily came into the kitchen almost immediately.

"So you're not willing to forgive me?" asked Vasily, standing right in front of Vasilisa. "You're not. But I brought you a present, Vasilisa. Just didn't know how to give it to you."

"We're not going to live together," said Vasilisa. "Once I was made this way, Vasily, I can't be made over again."

"The war made everybody over," Vasily countered softly.

"The war, the war . . . " Vasilisa repeated. "The war—it's a tragedy, not a decree. Even so, it made all us women into men. Now when are there going to be any real women? We need to bury it fast, this war of yours."

She sighed. Vasily tried to give her a hug, but she stepped away from him and his arms fell on thin air.

"It's no use," she said, moving away. "I was burnt once, Vasily. No point in trying to warm me up no more."

When he left, she was afraid she would want to cry, but she didn't want to at all, and she remained satisfied. She fell asleep quickly that night, and her sleep was untroubled, but when she got up in the morning, Vasilisa saw a thick, impenetrable fog outside and felt like going back to bed and falling asleep again.

After the war, Vasily did not stay at home very long. He waited until summer and went off to the Lena River, to the goldfields. When he was saying good-bye, he let on that he would not be back anytime soon, and maybe he would not come back at all. Who knows whether he wanted to get rich or whether it had become unbearable for him to live next to his family, completely separate from them, like a leper? Before his departure, Vasily gave Petka all his medals and decorations, instructing him not to let them out of his sight. First thing that evening he washed his field jacket and went into the village to say good-bye. He was merry and talkative that day, and he promised to send everybody money, but the next morning he was silent, as if he had left ahead of time.

Nastya and Anna accompanied Vasily to the steamboat and saw him off. Petka had run himself ragged somewhere and didn't get there in time. The gangway ladder was lowered and Vasily began to get agitated. He shook hands with his daughters rather absentmindedly and walked away. They spotted him on deck a minute later, but he wasn't looking at them anymore. The steamboat tooted its whistle three times and cast off,

and, as he was leaving, Vasily still stood on deck and seemed to be looking nowhere and seeing nothing.

Nastya went ahead and got married without him. Nastya stood out
among her brothers and sisters, who were all equally deliberate of movement and sensible, for her impetuousness and her amazing energy. "An
eager beaver," Vasilisa said about her. At twelve Nastya was the confi-
dante of practically everybody in the village who was in love. They sent
notes to each other through her, and twenty-year-old girls confided their
secrets to her. At fourteen Nastya went to work on the farm, at seven-
teen she got married, and a year later she had twins. She was in a hurry
even when there was no reason to be. And her domestic happiness apparently couldn't take such haste and it burst: four years later Nastya's
husband was killed in a logging accident, leaving her with three little
kids. Life slowed down after that.

Vasily returned the very next summer after his departure. He'd had
no luck in the goldfields—and hadn't earned any money either—and he
came back emaciated and crawling with lice, wearing only his field
jacket, which Nastya spent a long time steaming and ironing. Vasily
stayed in the shed and caught up on his sleep for a week, not going anywhere or talking to anybody, and then he got his gear together and took
off into the taiga.

It is July, the second half of the month. Summer has subsided,
but the days are sultry and oppressive. The roads raise endless dust,
and the dust settling on the rooftops makes the houses look small and
insignificant, like last year's haystacks. Smoke hovers over the Angara
River—there's a forest fire somewhere.

The kolkhoz is already through with the haying, but it's still too early
to start harvesting the crops. The kolkhoz workers make every possible
use of this short breather for their own purposes—now they can begin
mowing hay for themselves. In the mornings the villagers row out to the
islands in the river or go off into the taiga. Only a few stay at a home,
and they diligently water their gardens twice a day, morning and night.
In spite of the heat, the friendly smell of cucumbers hovers over the
gardens.

Pyotr and Nastya have meadowland at the same spot, about ten miles
from the village. It's hard to run back and forth all the time, and for that
reason they go and stay for a week at a stretch in order to start a little
earlier and end a little later each day. Tanya is left to take care of the two
families, with their kids and household chores, all by herself. Vasily
wouldn't have to go anywhere either, but he's gotten used to these

expeditions by now and feels obliged to help his son and daughter. This year is the first time that Vaska, Pyotr's nine-year-old son, has tagged along with them to the hay meadows.

It is good haying weather. The hay dries out quickly in the heat, but it's hard to mow. The grass has been standing too long and is dry clear down to the roots so that the only way to get anywhere is to keep whetting the scythes. Vasily mows with a swath that is wide but not very long. He stops often and smokes, wiping the sweat from his forehead and from the back of his head with his shirtsleeve.

"Vaska!" he shouts. "Where's the canteen?"

Vaska brings the water on the double, and Vasily drinks greedily, then cranes his neck and squints at the sun. The sun, like a ball, seems to have rolled into a pit that it can't roll out of for anything—now it's going to scorch them nonstop.

"Ya wish some lousy little cloud would cover it up," Vasily mutters and gets back to his scythe again.

Pyotr is mowing over to the side. He's wearing a T-shirt and has a handkerchief tied around his head. By now his scythe is squeaking with dullness as it plunges into the grass. Pyotr lifts it up, dips a whetstone into some water, and begins running it rapidly along the blade. Then he looks back at Vasilisa—she has been sitting motionless on a log for quite some time now.

"Mother," he yells. "You should go into the hut! Let the heat die down and then mow a little."

Vasilisa does not reply.

"Mama," yells Nastya after hearing Pyotr. "Go put dinner on. We're all coming now."

Vasilisa gets up and goes over to Pyotr.

"I got no strength," she tells him mournfully and sighs. "I'm worn out. Thought I'd help, but I reckon I can't."

"What's the matter, Mother?" asks Pyotr.

"I'll perk up. Don't give it a thought. I'll go lay down a bit and perk up, and tomorrow I'll be myself. It's 'cause I'm rusty. Haven't hayed in a whole year."

She walks off toward the hut all stooped over, and the three of them—Vasily, Nastya, and Pyotr—follow her with their eyes.

"Let's take a smoke break!" Vasily shouts to Pyotr.

Pyotr goes over to him and, gripping the canteen, takes a long drink. Then he blows away the drops of sweat clinging to his forehead and sits down.

"What's with your mother?" asks Vasily.

"She's old," replies Pyotr in his usual voice. "How old is she?"

"She's two years younger than me."

"She's old," Pyotr says again.

They sit around the campfire late into the evening, drinking tea after supper. Sometimes the fire rises up, and weariness is clearly visible on each of them, like a piece of clothing, and then the fire dies down again. In the darkness behind the hut, a dog is loudly licking out a tin can. Night falls on the trees and the mowed hay, and only on the fire does it hesitate to fall, afraid of getting burned. The fire is stirred by this and keeps leaping up.

They do not go to sleep for a long time. The haying has begun, the first day went like it should, and all this is alive in them, in feelings of closeness that haven't subsided yet.

"Time to turn in," Vasily says at last. "We did nine haystacks in one day, and that's pretty good."

"No, more," Nastya quickly corrects him. She always speaks quickly. "I put up five stacks in no time all by myself."

"More would've been better," Pyotr replies.

"Got to speed it up tomorrow." Vasily gets to his feet. "Bad weather's coming."

"What's he mean, bad weather?" Vasilisa asks suspiciously and looks at Pyotr.

"The dog was eating grass," Vasily tells Pyotr. "It's a sure sign."

Pyotr remains silent.

◢ Vasily and Pyotr got married the same year, even the same month. Pyotr, who was barely twenty then, brought home Tanya, the blacksmith's daughter, who lived at the lower end of the village. Vasily brought a stranger to his shed, not a country girl at all but a woman who had accidentally wandered into the village one day and had lingered on, going from cottage to cottage making jumpers and dresses for the women. She was quite handy at this and did not charge much for her sewing, and she kept getting orders one after another. They said that the newcomer was from the Ukraine and had come to look for her son, who had vanished during the war, but she didn't have enough money for the return trip and had decided to earn some on her own.

Nobody knew where or how she and Vasily had reached an understanding. They had already celebrated Pyotr's wedding, at which Nastya sang and danced more than anybody else, the October holidays had come and gone, and the first big snow had fallen—it came late that autumn. Just before this, when he was getting ready to go hunting, Vasily had suddenly halted his preparations and called Pyotr over.

"You ever seen this new woman?" he asked his son, not looking at him.

"The one that makes clothes?"

"Uh-huh."

"Sure, I seen her. She goes all over the village."

"I want to bring her home with me," Vasily said. Then he turned to Pyotr.

"You can't be serious, Father!" Pyotr said in amazement, unable to restrain himself.

"What of it? Some reason I can't?"

"Well, why not?" Pyotr began to mutter, not knowing what to say. "Why, sure. You're not old yet. Who says you can't?"

"It's not a matter of being old or not," Vasily corrected him sadly. "I'm sick of doing all the wash for myself, cooking kasha for myself. I live like a convict. Need a woman around the house—that's what I'm talking about."

They were silent for a while.

"Come by tomorrow just before dark. We'll split a bottle of booze three ways—that's how we'll celebrate the wedding. I'll have Nastya fix some food."

At home Vasilisa was toiling in the kitchen.

"Mother!" Pyotr yelled excitedly as he went inside. "Father's getting married."

"Oh," replied Vasilisa impassively.

"I'm telling the truth. He's bringing her home tomorrow."

"Let'm get married a thousand times. I don't have nothing to do with him."

"You're probably hurt, aren't you?"

"What's all this nonsense, you blabbermouth?" Vasilisa lit into him. "Sure, I'm hurt. I'm all worn out from hurting—it couldn't get no worse! She's nuts if she takes up with him. A good woman wouldn't."

Vasily's new wife was named Alexandra, and she wasn't much older than Anna, his oldest daughter. Vasilisa saw her for the first time from the window one morning, when Alexandra, lame in one leg, was walking across the yard to the outhouse.

"So she's a cripple," Vasilisa rejoiced. "I said a good woman wouldn't take up with him, and that's just what happened. They'll make a fine pair. Birds of a feather flock together."

Alexandra stayed out of sight at first, biding her time in the shed. Vasily made the tea himself and went to the store by himself, but he, too, tried not to go outside any more than was necessary. To the villagers his marriage was a scoop of honey poured onto an anthill. They discussed it and argued about it from every possible angle, and it became the most important event after the war, a good deal more important than any death that had occurred in recent years. The women suddenly started running

out of salt and bread, their washboards and irons disappeared somewhere, and they went to Vasilisa for all these things, striking up a conversation about the newlyweds—it was implied, of course, that they
were asking about Pyotr and Tanya. And only Granny Avdotya, who
was hard of hearing even back then, did not feel obliged to play games.

"They say you got yourself a sister, Vasilisa!" she shouted, making
herself comfortable on a bench.

"You got nothing to do, old woman, so you go around rinsing your
mouth with gossip," replied Vasilisa angrily.

"Don't it bother you a lot?"

"I couldn't care less. It's not me that has to wash their underwear."

Granny Avdotya threw a searching look around the cottage and
shouted again.

"Don't she never drop in?"

"Just let her drop in—I'll scratch her eyes out."

"That's right, scratch 'em out," Granny Avdotya agreed. "Give her
free rein and she'll drive you out of the cottage. You keep your eye on
her, Vasilisa."

They encountered each other shortly after that—it was impossible to
live on the same premises and not run into each other at all. Leaving the
shed one day, Alexandra suddenly saw Vasilisa right in front of her and
stopped hesitantly, not knowing how to react. Vasilisa looked her over
with interest and waited.

"Hello." Completely at a loss, Alexandra greeted her in a barely
audible voice.

"So that's how it is—'h'llo,' is it?" Vasilisa was amazed and angry.
"And couldn't I offer you some tea? Keep on limping wherever you were
limping to, you cripple. I'm not made of sugar. I'm not gonna melt at
your 'h'llo.' How d'ya like that, h'llo? Such good manners!"

She could not calm down for a long time, and she growled at Pyotr,
shouted at Nastya through the wall, and banged dishes around, filling
the whole house with the clatter. She felt she'd been insulted but had
not managed to give a proper reply, and she kept repeating all kinds of
variants of the ill-fated "hello" uttered by Alexandra, as if it hadn't
stopped stinging.

Nastya made friends with Alexandra and in just a month was calling her "Shura." And then a sewing machine began rattling away at
Nastya's—it was Alexandra making little shirts and pants for the kids,
and they, the little fools, went running to Vasilisa to show off their new
clothes. After looking in once when she heard the clack of the sewing
machine, Tanya also became a constant visitor in Nastya's part of the cottage—she, too, cut and sewed and then appeared in a new housecoat
and a new skirt. Vasilisa became gloomy and remained silent. Through

the wall she could hear them talking and laughing on the other side of the cottage. Vasilisa felt that nobody noticed her anymore, nobody took her into account. They were simply putting up with her, as if to say, "You're alive, so just go on and live."

"Do you call her 'Mother' yet?" she asked Nastya in an injured tone.

"Mama, don't try to butt in where you shouldn't," Nastya said angrily.

"Give her my name if you want. I'm like to die soon, but she whinnies like a filly—she's young."

"You've lived a whole lifetime, Mother, but you got no sense," said Pyotr, standing up for Alexandra. "You go around ranting and raving, but for what? You yourself don't even know. What's she ever done to you?"

Vasilisa fell silent and retreated into herself.

One day after New Year's, when Vasilisa had gone to visit somebody, Alexandra finally dared to enter the cottage. She would never have darkened the doorstep on her own, but Tanya had invited her in to help figure out a pattern. They got to talking, and then Alexandra looked out the window and gasped—Vasilisa was shutting the gate behind her. Alexandra rushed to the door, but couldn't slip past Vasilisa without being noticed.

"Wha-at's this now?!" Vasilisa shouted when she caught sight of her. "Ah, it's you, the enemy! So you wanted to go inside the cottage. I'll show you the way right now, I'll—"

"Tanya asked me in," Alexandra tried to justify herself.

"The shed's too small for her!" thundered Vasilisa, swiftly scanning the yard as if searching for a stick. "Nastya's side is too small for her— she wanted to get in here! I'll make you clear out!"

"Don't you dare!" Alexandra tried to defend herself.

"Oh, I dare, all right! I'm gonna break your other leg!"

"You're in a real rage, aren't you?" Alexandra shouted, suddenly taking the offensive. "You want to outlive me? It'll never happen! He still won't live with you." Pushing off with one leg, she advanced toward Vasilisa, on the attack. "He's mine! He doesn't need you! Not you, not you!"

"What's this?!" Taken aback, Vasilisa bellowed, "Git, you alley cat!" She yelled, "Git, you alley cat!" one more time and went into the house without turning around.

"That lame-leg's not to set foot in here no more!" Vasilisa scolded Tanya sternly. "Not so long as I'm the woman of this house and not her. My blood's gone bad even without her. My life sure hasn't been no picnic. Once I die, maybe you'll all remember me in your prayers."

She took off her scarf, which she rarely did, and began combing her gray hair. Frightened, Tanya sought refuge on the bed and kept quiet.

"Wish I had some kvass to drink now," Vasilisa said to Tanya unexpectedly.

"Is there any kvass?" asked Tanya joyfully. "I'd've gotten—"

"No, there's not," Vasilisa sighed.

After a while Vasilisa seemed to get used to Alexandra. She didn't growl anymore, and she didn't rant and rave. Instead, she would look away when she met her and pass by in silence. Vasilisa didn't bring up what had happened—either she felt guilty or she simply didn't want to stir up painful feelings. She became silent and pensive; after finishing her housework, she would go off to have tea with the old women in the evenings and would come back only at bedtime.

"You haven't gotten sick on us, have you, Mother?" asked Pyotr.

"You think I got time to be sick?" she replied coldly and left.

It later came out that Vasilisa had written a letter to her middle son, who lived in a logging community about thirty kilometers from the village, asking him to take her in. Her son had joyfully agreed and had even made plans to go get her before she let him know through people traveling in that direction that there was no hurry. She couldn't quite make up her mind to move to a new place.

"The grass is always greener on the other side," she said to Tanya, sighing. "Why should I head out for some other place now when I'm gonna die pretty soon anyway?"

Vasilisa had grown attached to Tanya recently. Feeling sorry for her, she tried not to rattle the dishes in the morning and would not let her do any heavy work. Tanya was sick a lot, and when she got sick, her smile was sad and guilty.

"Go ahead and be sick," Vasilisa comforted her. "Later on you'll bring a bunch of kids into the world, and then you won't have time to be sick. Life is long. Your life won't be no picnic either. Your husband isn't ex- actly a gem."

Then she went to Nastya and said, "Nastka, why don't you run out to the shed and talk to those folks? They've probably got some raspberries. Tanya ought to have raspberries to put in her tea. Tell that Alexandra of yours that they're for Tanya."

Winter came and went. In March the melting snow ran downhill in rivulets and roosters began to sing in people's yards. To get Nastya's kids into the house you had to use either honey biscuits or a strap. They would run out and leave the door open, and anybody who felt like it could walk right in and clean them out. While their mother was at work, Vasilisa kept track of them as best she could—but you couldn't keep an eye on everything, could you?

One day Vasilisa went to see if anyone was home at Nastya's. Open- ing the unlocked door, she suddenly froze. Somebody in the room was crying. Taking careful steps, Vasilisa glanced furtively into the room—on the bed, her head buried in a pillow, lay Alexandra, sobbing.

"So that's it." Vasilisa was astonished. "She's crying."

She waited, but Alexandra still did not calm down. Vasilisa thought for a moment and then walked up to the bed.

"You can't drown your sorrow with tears," said Vasilisa softly, just to make her presence known.

Alexandra jumped with fright and sat up on the edge of the bed.

"Or maybe there's no sorrow at all," Vasilisa continued. "Women's eyes were put on top of a wet spot, just like a hen's."

Alexandra, still sobbing, continued to look at her with fright.

"Come on, dear lady, let's go to my house," Vasilisa suggested suddenly. "I'll get the samovar going and we'll have some tea."

Alexandra began to shake her head, declining.

"Come on, come on. Don't get your hackles up," Vasilisa said firmly. "I don't mean you no harm, and you don't mean me none. Me and you got nothing to fight over."

She led her home and had her sit down at the table. Alexandra alternately sobbed and hiccuped.

"I can't stand it when women cry," Vasilisa explained, addressing Tanya, who was lying in bed, astonished. "For me it's a sharp knife through the heart. Life's like a five-kopeck coin—on one side it's heads, on the other it's tails. Everybody wants heads, but they don't realize that with either the one side or the other, it's still worth five kopecks. Ah, dear ladies!" She sighed. "If we're going to cry a lot, it'll get damp, and the damp'll make everything moldy. Who ever told you that when things get bad you got to cry?"

She went off into the kitchen and began banging around with the samovar.

"Well?" she asked Alexandra when she returned, and she pointed in the direction of the shed. "Is it him or what?"

"No." Alexandra shook her head. "It's on account of my boy, my son."

She looked at Vasilisa and remained silent.

"Tell me about it," said Vasilisa. "You'll feel better."

"No, I won't. I'll wait for the tea, to wash it down. I can't like this."

Alexandra was silent for a while, but it was more than she could bear, and she began telling her story almost immediately.

"He was four years old, still really little. They took me off to be a defense worker, while he stayed with my mama. They were evacuated without me. I couldn't get back into the city for a long time, and when I got there, they were gone."

She let out another sob.

"Tea's coming right up," Vasilisa reminded her.

"Mama was wounded along the way, so they took her off the train, but it carried him farther on. They said it was to your region."

"Tea's coming right up," Vasilisa said again.

"Now I'm having dreams about him. When he turned ten, I dreamed about a ten-year-old, and when he turned fifteen, he was that old in my dreams, too. But now he's all grown up. He comes last night and says, 'Mama, give me a mother's blessing. I want to get married.'"

"And what'd you say?" asked Vasilisa, leaning forward with her whole body.

"And I tell him, 'Wait a bit, Son. When I find you, then you can get married.' 'But are you going to find me soon?' he asks."

"Oh, dear!" exclaimed Vasilisa.

"'Yes, soon,' I say. 'Very soon, Son.' Then he walks away from me. 'Hey!' he shouts. 'Come and look for me, Mama.'"

Not moving a muscle, Vasilisa waited for her to continue. Alexandra was silent.

"He just went away?"

"Yes."

"And didn't say where to look?"

"No."

"Should've asked. Should've found out."

Alexandra shrugged her shoulders helplessly.

They drank tea and talked, and then they kept on talking even after the tea was gone. And a few days later Alexandra stopped by the house early one morning to say good-bye to Vasilisa.

"I'm ready to go," she said sadly. "I'm moving on."

"Go with God," Vasilisa blessed her. "Go, Alexandra, go. The earth belongs to all of us, so be on your way. "I'll pray for you."

She went out to see her off beyond the gate and followed her with her eyes for a long time, as she once did during the war when she was seeing off her children.

That morning Vasily came to sit by the samovar for the first time. Vasilisa poured him a glass of tea and put it in the middle of the table.

Vasily has been complaining more and more often lately about his lower back. He sits on the bed and, rocking back and forth, tries to straighten out his spine. He frowns and groans, and beads of sweat glisten on his exhausted face, which is covered with a reddish stubble.

"Ow," he moans. "It was just waiting to get me, the damned thing, just lying in wait, the Evil Spirit! Wish it'd let up for a minute."

Growing weak, Vasily lies down and closes his eyes. He cannot lie flat comfortably either and rises part way up again.

"Vaska!" he shouts through the open door.

Nobody answers him.

"Vaska!"

Vaska is not around.

Pyotr comes to see Vasily after work.

"You tell Vaska he's supposed to look in on me," says Vasily. "Otherwise I'm alone the whole day. I'll die and nobody'll close my eyes."

"How're you doing?" asks Pyotr.

"What do you mean how'm I doing? You can see for yourself. My whole back is giving out. Makes you want to holler for help."

"You need a doctor."

"Doctors, doctors," Vasily flares up. "A doc's assistant come by yesterday, but what's the use? I tell her my lower back hurts, and she gives me this blank look. Till I come along, she didn't even know people have lower backs."

"They got a different name for it."

"They call the runs something else, too, but they're still supposed to cure them. That's what they went to school for."

"What'd she say?"

"Nothing. She thumped on me for a while and left, like she's off on some excursion. 'I'll come again tomorrow,' she says, and nothing changes."

He leans back against the wall and moans. A minute later he straightens up again.

"Run to the store, would you?" Vasily asks him. "Makes me feel better. If this would ease up for even a little bit, I could get my bearings. There's money above the door. And you come and have a drink with me to unwind."

Pyotr gets up, finds the money in silence, and leaves.

The next day it's Vaska who runs to the store for vodka.

"I got some candy with the change," he brags to Vasilisa.

"Great medicine they've come up with," says Vasilisa sarcastically, with pleasure. "Down a glass of booze, grunt, and whatever ails you goes away, avoiding you like the plague."

After the vodka Vasily really does relax and fall asleep. But then the pain gets even stronger, as if it is furious at being forced to retreat, and rages with new strength.

At long last the woman doctor comes again and says that they need to take Vasily to the county seat for X rays. Vasily silently gives his consent; he is tired. He wants to have a drink as soon as possible and go to sleep, and then they can take him all the way to Moscow if they want. He'll put up with all of it and do everything just the way they tell him to. He's lived a pretty long life, and somebody, evidently, can't be born while he's still here, or it's simply that his turn has come and now he's holding things up.

The doctor leaves, and Vasily quickly pours himself a full glass and half a glass for Pyotr. They drink, and in a minute Vasily livens up.

"Tell me," he asks, "Why is it that people are born and die most often at night?"

"I don't know." Pyotr shrugs his shoulders.

"There, that's just it—nobody knows. Why does a person come into the big wide world at night and go out at night? That's not right. I want to die during the day. People are talking, chickens are flapping their wings, dogs are barking. It's scary at night—everybody's asleep. This is when a baby screams—it's just come out of its mother. Some place else an old man screams—life is going out of him. But the people in between are asleep. That's what's so scary, that they're asleep. They wake up, but the nomads have already come and gone. People do their work, or don't do it, night comes again, they sleep again, and again everything is set in motion. O-ho-ho! Nobody'll help you at night, nobody'll say, 'Go ahead and die, Vasily. Don't be afraid. You've done everything you could, and what you didn't do, somebody else will.' You got to comfort a person, and then he's not scared to lie down in a coffin."

"What's this all about, Father?" asks Pyotr, frightened. "How come you're talking nonsense?"

"Nonsense, you say? To me it's scary. Now you'll get up and leave, and I'll be alone. I got used to being alone—I mean, to living alone. To die alone is scary. I'm not used to it."

He reaches for the bottle.

"Let's pour the rest, and I'll lie down."

Pyotr goes home and tells Vasilisa, "Father's in bad shape."

Vasilisa does not reply.

It's day again. The shed door is opened once more.

"Vaska!" shouts Vasily.

Vaska is not around.

Holding the ends of her scarf in her hands, Vasilisa cautiously glances through the door.

"Vaska's not here. Don't waste your breath for nothing," she says.

Vasily half rises and looks at her.

"Is that you, Vasilisa?" he asks in a weak voice. "Where's Vaska?"

"He's run off somewhere."

"Come in, Vasilisa. Nothing to stop you now, is there?"

Vasilisa steps through the doorway and stops.

"Come here, Vasilisa."

"You taken sick or something?" Vasilisa asks from the doorway.

"I got a feeling my death is not far off. Come here and we'll say good-bye."

She cautiously approaches and sits down on the edge of the bed.

"We had a pretty bad life together, Vasilisa," whispers Vasily. "I'm the one to blame for everything."

"It wasn't bad at all." Vasilisa shakes her head. "The children grew up, and now they got jobs."

"It was bad, Vasilisa. In the face of death I'm ashamed."

Vasilisa brings the ends of her scarf to her lips and leans over Vasily.

"Where'd you get that idea, Vasily?" she whispers. "Where'd you ever get that idea?"

"Your tears are falling on me," Vasily whispers joyfully. "There's another one."

He closes his eyes and smiles.

"Where'd you get that idea, Vasily? Good Lord, what a sin!"

She shakes him by the shoulders, and he opens his eyes and says, "Let's say good-bye, Vasilisa."

He offers his hand to her, she squeezes it, and, sobbing, she stands up.

"Now go," he says. "I feel better now."

She takes one step, and a second one, and then turns around. Vasily is smiling. She sobs and goes out.

He's smiling, just lying there and smiling.

The day is still, like just before a rainstorm. On a day like this it's nice to drink buttermilk—not too cold and not too warm—and look out the window to see what's going on outside.

1966

FRENCH LESSONS

Preface: "Lessons in Kindness"

This story, when it first appeared in book form, helped me locate my former teacher, Lidia Mikhaylovna. She had bought my book, recognized me as the author and herself as the heroine of the tale, and then written me a letter.

Surprisingly, it turns out that Lidia Mikhaylovna cannot recall having sent me a box of pasta in somewhat the same manner as in the story. I have a clear recollection and couldn't possibly be wrong about this—it really happened. At first I was taken aback—how could she fail to remember?! How could anyone forget such a thing?! But after giving it some thought, I realized that there is actually nothing surprising about this at all. The person who does a truly good deed does not remember it as long as does the person for whom it is done. And this is how it ought to be. A truly good deed, by definition, is not done with the expectation of instant return ("I scratched your back, now you scratch mine!"). On the contrary, it is altruistic and confident of its own quiet but wonder-working power. And if, after many years, a person's past good deed comes back to him from a different quarter, this means it has made the rounds of that many more people and the circle of its effect has grown that much wider.

As you have undoubtedly guessed, this story is largely autobiographical, that is, the author describes events from his own life. Why does he do this? Certainly not because he lacks imagination, as it might appear, and not because, taking advantage of his status as a writer, he arrogantly insists on portraying everything that happens to him. There is such a thing as a person's spiritual memory, his spiritual experience, which must be present in each of us, regardless of our age. These are the main things, of a seemingly higher realm, that give us moral momentum, that we derive from the events of our lives, and that hold interest not only for ourselves alone. When this occurs and when the moral residue of external events seems important to us, we naturally want to share it with others.

And so it happened that after more than twenty years had elapsed, I sat down at my desk and began to recall what I experienced as a fifth-grader, as a young kid from a remote Siberian village. More precisely, I began to write down things that I had never forgotten and that had persistently begged to be told. I have written this story in the hope that the lessons I once learned will be taken to heart by youngsters and grown-ups alike.

Dedicated to
Anastasia Prokopievna Kopylova

Isn't it odd? Why do we always feel just as guilty when we think of our teachers as when we think of our parents? And not because of anything that happened at school—no, not at all. It's because of what became of us later.

In 1948 I entered fifth grade. To be more exact, I went away to school. Since our village only had a four-year elementary school, I had to pack up and leave home to continue my education in the nearest town, which was over fifty kilometers away. My mother went there the week before and arranged for me to room with a woman friend of hers. And on the last day of August, Uncle Vanya, whose job was to drive our kolkhoz's only pickup truck, dropped me off on Podkamennaya Street, where I would be staying. He helped me carry my bedroll into the house, gave me an encouraging farewell pat on the shoulder, and took off. And so, at the age of eleven, I began life on my own.

Famine still held us in its grip that year, and my mother had three kids to feed, with me being the oldest. In the spring, when we were especially hungry, I had swallowed some potato sprouts and grains of oats and rye, and I had made my sister swallow them, too, in hopes of getting them to take root in our stomachs—then we wouldn't have to think about food all the time. We faithfully poured pure water from the Angara River on those seeds all summer, but for some reason there was nothing to harvest, or there was so little that we couldn't detect it. Nevertheless, I don't think this was a totally useless venture, and some day it may even come in handy for the human race. Through inexperience we simply hadn't done it right.

It's hard to say just how Mother got up the courage to ship me off to town ("town" is what we called the county seat). Our father wasn't with us, we were quite poor, and she evidently figured that things couldn't possibly get any worse. I enjoyed going to school, did well in my studies, and was regarded in the village as a scholar. The old women had me write letters for them and read them the replies. I'd gone through all the books we had in our meager village library, and I would spend evenings reciting all manner of stories from them to the other kids—not only retelling them but also adding things on my own. But I was especially trusted when it came to the lottery. During the war, people had bought a lot of bonds, which doubled as lottery tickets. Columns of winning numbers were often printed, and then people would bring their bonds to me. They thought I had an eagle eye. Our village did have some winnings, mostly small ones, but in those years the collective farmers were thankful for each and every kopeck, and occasionally, with my assistance, they were blessed with completely unexpected good fortune. Their joy would automatically spill over onto me, too. They singled me out from the other village kids and even fed me. One time, after winning four hundred rubles, a fairly tightfisted, stingy old man named Uncle Ilya excitedly scraped together a bucket of potatoes for me, which in the springtime was quite a treasure.

And just because I had a knack for lottery numbers they used to say to my mother, "Your boy's got a good head on his shoulders. You oughta make sure he learns a thing or two. Schooling won't be lost on him."

So Mother, in spite of all our hardships, got me ready to leave, even though not a single kid from our village had ever gone to school in town before. I was the first. And I didn't fully realize what lay in store for me, what trials awaited me, poor fellow, in my new place of residence.

My schoolwork went well there, too. What else could I do? That's why I'd gone. I had no other business there, and I still hadn't learned to make light of the responsibilities that had been placed on me. I would not have dared to show up at school if even a single homework assignment hadn't been done, and so I got A's in all subjects, except French.

My problem with French was pronunciation. I had no trouble memorizing words and common expressions, I was quick at translation, and I coped splendidly with the intricacies of spelling, but pronunciation completely gave away my Angara origins, where down to the present generation no one has ever spoken foreign words, if they even suspect that such things exist. I spewed out French like a series of village tongue twisters, swallowing half the sounds, the nonessential ones, and blurting out the other half in short, barking bursts. Lidia Mikhaylovna, the French teacher, would frown helplessly when listening to me and close her eyes. She'd never heard anything like that, of course. Time and time again she would demonstrate how to pronounce the nasals and the vowel clusters. She'd ask me to repeat them—and I would panic. My tongue would stiffen in my mouth and refuse to budge. It was all to no avail. But the worst part began only when school was over. At school I was unwillingly distracted, under constant pressure to do things, and pestered by the other kids—I had to run around and play with them whether I wanted to or not. And in class I had to work. But whenever I was alone, homesickness immediately overwhelmed me—I missed the village, I missed my home. Before that I had never spent a single day away from my family and naturally I wasn't ready to live among total strangers. I felt so bad, so bitter and frustrated—it was worse than any illness. I had only one wish, one dream—to go home, just to go home. I lost a lot of weight, and when Mother came for a visit at the end of September, she became alarmed. While she was there I braced myself and didn't complain or cry, but when she was about to leave, I lost control and ran bawling after the truck. From inside the cab, Mother motioned me to go back and not disgrace both myself and her—this I couldn't comprehend at all. Then she changed her mind and had the driver stop.

"Get your stuff," she demanded when I ran up to the truck. "That's enough education for you. We're going home."

I came to my senses and ran back.

But it wasn't just homesickness that made me lose weight. Besides that, I still never got enough to eat. In the autumn, when Uncle Vanya was hauling grain in the pickup to the storage elevators not far from town, they would send me food quite often, about once a week. But the trouble was that I needed more. They had nothing to send except bread and potatoes. On rare occasions Mother would fill a jar with cottage cheese that she'd gotten by trading something, since she didn't have a cow of her own. Whenever they brought me food it seemed like a lot, but two days later I'd look, and it would all be gone. Very quickly I began to notice that at least half my bread was disappearing in a most mysterious manner. I checked—and sure enough, now you see it, now you don't. The same thing was happening to my potatoes. Who was stealing my food? Was it Aunt Nadya, that scolding, worn-out woman muddling along by herself with three kids? Was it one of her older girls, or maybe the boy, Fedka, her youngest? I didn't know who it was. I was afraid even to think about it, much less keep watch. It simply pained me because Mother was taking food from the family, from my little sister and brother, for my sake, and that food was somehow getting lost in the shuffle. But I forced myself to accept that, too, with humble resignation. Mother's life would not have been any easier if she had learned the truth.

Famine in town was not at all like famine in the countryside. There you could always find something to nibble at any time of year, especially in the autumn, when there'd be things to gather, dig up, and pick up from the ground. There were fish in the Angara and game birds in the forest. In town I felt surrounded by a complete void: strangers, strangers' gardens, strangers' land. Ten rows of small fishnets lay across a little stream. One Sunday I sat on the bank all day with a fishing pole and caught three tiny teaspoon-sized gudgeons—that sort of catch wouldn't fatten you up either. I didn't go there anymore—why waste the time! In the evenings I would stand around at the market near the tea room memorizing how much everything cost, practically choke on my own saliva, and go back empty-handed. There was always a hot teakettle on Aunt Nadya's stove; after warming up my stomach by slurping down some plain boiled water, I would go to bed. The next morning I'd be off to school again. That is how I held out until the joyous moment when the pickup arrived at the gate and Uncle Vanya knocked on the door. Half-starving and knowing that my victuals wouldn't last very long anyway no matter how I tried to ration them, I would eat my fill, stuffing my belly to the bursting point, and then, a day or two later, I'd "put my teeth on the shelf" again.

One day in September Fedka asked, "You aren't scared to play '*chika*,' are you?"

"What's '*chika*'?" I asked, not knowing what he meant.

"It's a game. You play for money. If you've got some, let's go play."

"I don't have any."

"I don't either. Let's go watch anyway. You'll see what a great game it is."

Fedka led me off beyond the gardens. We walked along the edge of a long, hunchbacked hill that was completely covered by tangled black nettles with dangling clusters of poisonous seeds. We made our way across an old dump, leaping from one trash pile to another, and down below, in a small, level empty clearing, we saw some boys. As we approached, the boys pricked up their ears. They were all about the same age I was, except for one—a strapping, muscular guy with a long tuft of red hair over his forehead whose strength and power over the others were obvious. I recognized him as a seventh-grader.

"What did you bring him for?" he asked Fedka with irritation.

"He's one of us, Vadik, one of us," Fedka tried to explain. "He lives at our house."

"You gonna play?" Vadik asked me.

"Don't have any money."

"Just make sure you don't squeal on us."

"What do you mean!" I was insulted.

They didn't pay any attention to me after that, and I stepped out of the way and began watching the game. Not everyone was playing— sometimes six played, sometimes seven, while the others only watched, rooting mainly for Vadik. He was the boss there, that I realized right away.

It took no time at all to figure out how the game was played. Each player put ten kopecks into the kitty, the pile of coins was placed tails up in the playing area—marked off by a thick line about two meters from the pot—and they'd throw a round stone called a puck from a boulder that had sunk into the ground and served as a support for the front foot. You had to throw it in such a way that it skipped as close as possible to the line without going over it—then you earned the right to hit the pot and scatter the coins first. After that you tossed the puck at the pot, trying to flip the coins so they'd land heads up. If you flipped one over, it was yours to keep, and you could throw again. If you failed, you gave the puck to the next player. But the most important thing was to cover some of the coins with the puck. If even one of them lay under the puck heads up, the whole pot went into your pocket with no argument, and the game started all over again.

Vadik was crafty. He would go up to the boulder after everyone else, when the whole pecking order was spread out before his eyes and he could see where to throw the puck to get first crack at the pot. The money usually went to the first throwers; seldom was there any left for the last ones. No doubt everyone realized what Vadik was up to, but no one dared say anything. To be sure, he was a good player in his own right. Approaching the rock, he would hunker down slightly and, narrowing his eyes, take careful aim at the target, then slowly and smoothly straighten up—the puck would slide out of his hand and fly exactly where he had aimed. With a quick movement of his head he would throw back his tousled hair, casually spit to one side, showing that he'd done a good job, and then saunter toward the money at a deliberately slow pace. If the money was in a pile, he'd strike it with a sharp, ringing bang, while individual coins he would nudge gently, bouncing the puck so that the coin would not be hit directly and fly into the air but would rise just enough to flip over to the other side. No one else could do this. The other boys threw haphazardly and then got out more coins, and the ones who had no more to get out joined the spectators.

It seemed to me that I would be able to play this game if only I had some money. In the village we had always played knucklebones, and you need a keen eye for that, too. Besides, I loved to dream up amusements for myself that required good aim. I would gather up a handful of stones, find a difficult target, and keep throwing at it until I achieved perfect results—ten out of ten. I could throw both overhand and underhand, dropping the stone on the target from above. So I had a knack for this sort of thing. What I didn't have was money.

Because our family seldom had any money, Mother sent me bread; otherwise I would have bought my bread there in town. And where could they have gotten money on the kolkhoz when farmers didn't receive salaries? Nevertheless, two or three times Mother had enclosed a five-ruble bill in her letters—for milk. In today's terms that would be fifty kopecks, which didn't make me rich, but it was money all the same and just enough to buy five half-liter containers of milk at the market for a ruble apiece. I'd been ordered to drink milk to avoid anemia, since I was having frequent dizzy spells for no reason.

When I received a five-ruble bill for the third time, however, I didn't go buy milk but got change for it and headed off beyond the dump. You couldn't deny that the boys had used their heads in choosing that spot. The clearing was surrounded by hills and completely out of sight. In town, where the boys could be observed, adults would get after them for playing such games and threaten them with the school principal or the police. There no one interfered with them. And it wasn't far away—you could run to the clearing in ten minutes.

The first time I played, I threw away ninety kopecks—the second time, sixty. I was sorry to lose the money, of course, but I felt that I was acquiring the rudiments of the game and that my hand was gradually getting used to the puck and learning how to put just the right amount of force into each throw to make the puck go where I wanted it to. My eyes were also learning to know in advance where the puck would land and how much farther it would slide along the ground. In the evening, after the other boys had all gone home, I would return, get the puck out from under the rock where Vadik had hidden it, dig the change out of my pocket, and practice throwing until it got dark. I reached the point where three or four out of every ten throws would land squarely on the money.

And finally the day arrived when I ended up a winner.

Autumn that year was warm and dry. Even as late as October you could still be outdoors without a jacket. Rain fell rarely and seemed accidental, as though driven in by a weak passing breeze from bad weather somewhere else. The sky was a summer blue, but it seemed to have shrunk, and the sun set early. When there were no clouds, the air hovered over the hills in a haze, carrying the slightly bitter, intoxicating smell of dry wormwood; distant voices could be heard clearly, along with the cries of birds heading south. The grass in our clearing, though yellowed and withered, still remained alive and soft, an ideal playground for the boys who were sitting out the game, or, to be more exact, who had already lost.

Now I ran over there every day after school. The other boys kept changing, new ones appeared, and only Vadik never missed a game. Play couldn't even begin without him. Trailing Vadik like a shadow was a stocky kid with a big shaved head whose nickname was "Birdy." I had never seen Birdy in school before, but, getting ahead of myself, I'll say that at the beginning of the third quarter he suddenly descended on our class like a bolt out of the blue. It turned out that he had to repeat fifth grade and he'd come up with some excuse for staying home until January. Birdy normally won, too, although not quite as often as Vadik, yet he never came out behind. No doubt he didn't lose anything because he was in cahoots with Vadik, and Vadik gave him a little help.

Sometimes Tishkin, another boy from our grade, would join us in the clearing. Tishkin was a nervous kid with blinking little eyes who loved to raise his hand in class. His hand would shoot up whether he knew the answer or not. When the teachers called on him, he was silent.

"Why did you raise your hand?" they'd ask Tishkin.

He would blink his little eyes. "I had the answer, but I forgot it while I was standing up."

Tishkin and I weren't friends. My shyness, general silence, excessive rural reticence, and, most of all, uncontrollable homesickness left me with no desire whatsoever to make friends; at that time I hadn't gotten close to any of the other boys yet. They weren't drawn to me either, and I kept to myself, not able to understand my loneliness or to separate it from my wretched situation as a whole—I was alone because I was there instead of at home in the village, where I had lots of friends.

Tishkin didn't seem to notice me at all when we were in the clearing. After quickly losing his money, he would disappear and not come back to the game for a long time.

And I was winning. I started to win consistently, every day. I had my own system—you didn't necessarily have to shoot the puck across the playing surface to earn the right to throw first. That wasn't so simple when there were a lot of players, because the closer you landed to the line, the greater the danger of going over it and ending up last. You were better off covering the coins when you threw. And that is what I did. It was risky, of course, but with my skill it was worth the risk. I could lose three or four times in a row, but by winning the pot on the fifth time around, I would recoup my losses threefold. Then I would lose some and win some more back again. I rarely got the chance to knock over the coins with the puck, but when I did, I used my own method for that, too. While Vadik would bounce them back in his direction, I, on the contrary, would nudge them farther away. It was unusual, but that way the puck would hold a coin in place without letting it spin and then flip it over as it slid away.

Now I had money. I didn't let myself get too involved in the game or hang around the clearing until evening. I needed only one ruble, just one ruble a day. Once I got it, I'd run off to the market and buy a container of milk (the women there would grumble when they saw my bent, battered, worn-out coins, but they would pour milk for me anyway). Then I'd eat dinner and sit down to do my homework. I still never ate enough to get full, but the very thought that I was drinking milk gave me strength and tamed my hunger. And now my dizzy spells seemed to occur far less often.

At first Vadik reacted calmly to my winnings. He himself never lost, and my take was probably not coming out of his pocket. He even praised me on occasion by advising the other boys to learn from me: "That's the way to throw, you duffers." Vadik, however, soon noticed that I was leaving the game too quickly, and one day he stopped me.

"What are you doing? Going to grab the pot and run? What a sneak you are! Keep on playing."

"I've got homework to do, Vadik," I pleaded.

"If you've got homework, you shouldn't even come here."

Then Birdy chimed in. "Who says you can do that when you're playing for money? In case you don't know, they beat guys up for that. Got it?"

After that, Vadik never let me throw ahead of him, and he always sent me up to the rock last. He had a good throw, and quite often I reached into my pocket for another coin without even touching the puck. But my throw was better, and if I got the chance to throw, the puck would fly straight to the money like a magnet. Even I was amazed at my own accuracy. I should have thought to hold back a little, to play less conspicuously, but I naively kept on bombing away at the pot without relenting. How could I have known that no one has ever been forgiven for striving to get ahead of the pack? Don't expect any mercy then. Don't expect anyone to intercede for you, because others think you're an upstart, and the one who follows in your wake will hate you the most. This is the lesson I had to learn the hard way that autumn.

I had just landed on the money again and was about to gather it up when I noticed that Vadik was standing on one of the widely scattered coins. All the others lay tails up. In such instances you usually yelled "Pile 'em!" when you threw so that in case there wasn't a single coin heads up, the money would be gathered into one pile for another try. But I, as always, had hoped for good luck and hadn't yelled anything.

"Don't pile 'em!" Vadik decreed.

I walked up to him and tried to move his foot off the coin, but he shoved me away, quickly snatched it off the ground, and showed me tails. I'd had time to notice that the coin was heads—otherwise he wouldn't have bothered to cover it up.

"You turned it over," I said. "It was heads. I saw it."

He shoved his fist under my nose.

"Did you ever see this before? Take a whiff. What does it smell like?"

I had to give in. It was foolish to try to stand my ground. If a fight were to break out, not a soul would take my side, not even Tishkin, who was fidgeting nearby.

Vadik's sinister, narrowed eyes were staring straight at me. I crouched down, calmly hit the nearest coin, flipped it over, and nudged another one. "By hook or by crook," I decided, "I'll still win all of them right now." Once again I aimed the puck for a throw but never got it off. Suddenly someone jabbed me with a knee from behind and I clumsily keeled over onto the ground headfirst. All around me kids burst out laughing.

Birdy stood behind me, smiling expectantly. I was stunned. "Why'd you do that?!"

"Who said I did it?" he countered. "Where'd you dream that up?"

"Give it here!" Vadik said, reaching out for the puck, but I didn't hand it over. My fear was drowned out by a feeling of humiliation. Nothing on earth could have frightened me then. But why? Why were they treating me this way? What had I done to them?

"Give it here!" Vadik demanded.

"You turned the coin over!" I shouted at him. "I saw you turn it over. I saw you."

"Just say that one more time," he said while advancing toward me.

"You turned it over," I said softly, knowing full well what would happen next.

The first guy to hit me, again from behind, was Birdy. He sent me flying toward Vadik, who quickly and deftly butted his head into my face without even aiming, and I fell down with a bloody nose. No sooner had I jumped to my feet than Birdy threw himself at me again. I still could have broken loose and run, but for some reason I never gave that a thought. I was spinning between Vadik and Birdy, hardly defending myself at all, pressing a hand over my nose to try to stop the bleeding, and in despair I stubbornly kept yelling one and the same thing, which only increased their fury. "You turned it over! You turned it over! You turned it over!"

They took turns punching me, first one, then the other, then one, then the other. A third guy, small and nasty, kicked me in the legs, which were almost completely covered with bruises afterward. I just tried to stay on my feet, not to fall down no matter what, which even at that point I would have considered a disgrace. But finally they tumbled me to the ground and stopped.

"Get out of here while you're still alive!" commanded Vadik. "Get a move on!"

I got up and, sobbing and sniffling through my battered nose, dragged myself up the hill.

"Just try squealing to anybody—we'll kill you!" Vadik promised as I walked away.

I did not respond. Everything inside me had somehow closed up and hardened in humiliation, and I no longer had the strength to call up a single word.

Only when I reached the top of the hill did I let go and, like someone deranged, shout as loudly as I could, so that the whole town probably heard, "You turned it o-o-ver!"

Birdy started to chase after me, but quickly went back. Vadik evidently decided that I'd had enough and stopped him. I stood there sobbing for about five minutes and looked down at the clearing where the game had resumed, then descended the other side of the hill to the gully covered with black nettles. I fell down on the rough, dry grass, and, no longer able to hold back, I began to sob bitterly and violently.

That day there was not and could not have been anyone in the whole wide world more unhappy than I.

The next morning I looked at myself in the mirror with horror. My nose was swollen and puffed up, I had a shiner under my left eye, and just below that a fat, bloody cut wound across my cheek. How I could go to school in that condition was beyond my imagination, but I had to go anyway. I couldn't bring myself to skip classes for any reason whatsoever. Let's face it, some people are endowed by nature with noses prettier than mine, and if it weren't in its usual place, you'd never guess it was a nose at all, but there was no justification for the shiner and the cut. They quite obviously stood out through no choice of my own.

Covering my eye with one hand, I darted into the classroom, took my seat, and put my head down on the desk. As if to spite me, our first lesson was French. Lidia Mikhaylovna, in her role as class supervisor, took greater interest in us than did the other teachers, and it was difficult to conceal anything from her. She would enter the room and greet us, but before seating the class, she had the habit of carefully examining almost every one of us and making suggestions that seemed humorous but that we were obliged to follow. And of course she immediately spotted the marks on my face despite my best attempts to hide them. I realized this because the other kids started to turn around and stare at me.

"Well, well," said Lidia Mikhaylovna as she opened her record book. "Today we have some of the wounded among us."

The class burst out laughing, and Lidia Mikhaylovna lifted her eyes in my direction again. They squinted and seemed to look past you, but by then we had already learned to recognize what they were looking at.

"So what happened?" she asked.

"I fell," I blurted out. For some reason I hadn't thought up an even minimally decent explanation ahead of time.

"Oh, that's too bad. Did you fall yesterday or today?"

"Today. No, I mean last night, when it was dark."

"Fell, ha!" shouted Tishkin, choking with glee. "It was Vadik from seventh grade who let him have it. They were playing for money, and he started arguing and got what he deserved. I saw it. And he says he fell."

I was stunned by such treachery. Was he doing this intentionally, or didn't he understand anything at all? Playing for money could get you kicked out of school in a big hurry. Now he'd done it! My head began to spin and ache from fear. I'm sunk, now I'm sunk. Thanks, Tishkin. That's Tishkin for you. You really did me a favor. You cleared it all up, that's for sure.

"Tishkin, there's something else I wanted to ask you about," said Lidia Mikhaylovna, expressing no surprise and maintaining her calm, slightly indifferent tone as she interrupted him. "Go to the board, now that you're all warmed up, and get ready to recite." She waited until the distressed and suddenly unhappy Tishkin had made his way to the board and then said to me briefly, "I'd like you to stay after school."

What I feared most of all was that Lidia Mikhaylovna would drag me off to the principal's office. That meant that besides having a talk with me today, tomorrow they'd march me out in front of the school lineup and force me to explain what made me engage in this filthy business. That's how the principal, Vasily Andreevich, would question the offender no matter what he'd done wrong—broken a window, gotten into a fight, or been caught smoking in the lavatory. "What made you engage in this filthy business?" He would pace back and forth in front of the lineup with his hands behind his back, thrusting his shoulders forward in time with his long strides so that his dark, bulging, tightly buttoned field jacket seemed to move by itself a little ahead of him, and he would goad the kid, "Come on, let's have an answer. We're waiting. Look—the whole school is waiting to hear what you have to say." The pupil would begin to mumble something in his own defense, but the principal would cut him off. "Answer my question, answer my question. How did I put the question?"

"What made me do it?"

"Exactly what made you do it? We're listening."

The matter usually ended with tears, and only after that would the principal calm down, and then we would go off to our classes. This was harder on the kids in the upper grades, who didn't want to cry but still couldn't answer Vasily Andreevich's question. Once our first-hour classes started ten minutes late because all that time the principal was questioning one ninth-grader. But when he failed to get anything intelligible out of him, he led the boy away to his office.

And I wondered what I would say. Better they expel me immediately. No sooner had this thought flashed through my mind than I realized that I would then be able to go home. But I instantly got scared, as though I'd been burned. No, I certainly couldn't go home in such disgrace. It would be different if I quit school on my own . . . But even then people could say that since I hadn't passed this voluntary test, I wasn't dependable, and everyone would begin to avoid me completely. No, anything but that. I'd better endure this place a while longer, I'd better get used to it, I couldn't go home this way.

Scared stiff, I waited for Lidia Mikhaylovna in the hallway after school. She came out of the teachers' lounge and, with a nod, led me into the classroom. She sat down at her desk as always, and I started to settle into a desk in the third row some distance away, but Lidia Mikhaylovna motioned me to the first desk right in front of her.

"Is it true that you play for money?" she began at once.

She spoke too loudly. It seemed to me that in school one should talk about such things only in a whisper, and I became even more frightened. But there was no point in trying to hide anything. Tishkin had managed to betray me lock, stock, and barrel.

"Yes, it's true," I muttered.

"Well, then, how do you come out? Do you win or lose?"

I stopped short, not knowing which was better.

"Let's tell it like it is. You probably lose, right?"

"I . . . I win."

"Well, that's something. At least you win. And what do you do with the money?"

When I started school there it took me a long time to get used to Lidia Mikhaylovna's voice. It confused me. In our village people spoke by drawing their voices up from deep down inside, and for that reason you could hear them loud and clear, but Lidia Mikhaylovna's voice was somehow shallow and soft so that you had to listen to it carefully. This certainly didn't come from feebleness—sometimes she could speak up even to my satisfaction—but rather it seemed to come from reticence and unnecessary economizing. I was ready to blame it all on French. Back when she was a student and still adjusting to a foreign tongue, her fettered voice had naturally shrunk and grown weak, like a caged bird's. Just see if it might ever open up and get strong again. At that moment, for instance, Lidia Mikhaylovna was questioning me as though she were currently preoccupied with something else, something more important, but there was still no way to avoid answering her questions.

"Well, so what do you do with the money you win? Buy candy? Or books? Or are you saving it up for something? You must have a lot by now, don't you?"

"No, not much. I only win a ruble at a time."

"And then you stop playing?"

"Yes."

"Just a ruble? Why only a ruble? What do you do with it?"

"I buy milk."

"Milk?"

Seated before me, she was thoroughly tidy, intelligent, and beautiful, beautiful in both her attire and in her feminine youthfulness, of which I was vaguely aware. I smelled the fragrance of perfume, which I took to be her very breath. And besides, she taught not just some ordinary subject like arithmetic or history but the mysterious French language, which also gave off a special fairy-tale aura that not everyone could grasp—like me, for instance. Not daring to look her straight in the eye, I didn't dare deceive her either. And why, after all, should I have tried to fool her?

She paused, scrutinizing me, and I had a gut feeling that under the gaze of her squinting, penetrating eyes all my absurdities and misfortunes rose up and overflowed with all their repulsive might. I was, of course, a sight to behold. Squirming behind the desk in front of her was a skinny, uncivilized kid with a battered face, unkempt and lonely without his mother, wearing a faded old jacket with drooping shoulders that fit across the chest but left his arms hanging way out. There were traces of yesterday's fight on his easily stained, light-green pants, which had been shortened from his father's riding breeches and were now tucked into his shoes. Even before that I had noticed how quizzically Lidia Mikhaylovna would look at my footwear. I was the only kid in our whole grade who went around in such clodhoppers. Finally the next autumn, when I categorically refused to go back to school in them, Mother sold her sewing machine, the only valuable thing we had, and bought me some canvas boots.

"And yet you shouldn't play for money," Lidia Mikhaylovna said earnestly. "You should get along without that somehow. Can you?"

Still not quite believing that I had escaped punishment, I found it easy to promise.

"Yes, I can."

I spoke sincerely, but what can you do when your sincerity slips out of its moorings?

I should say in my own defense that those were very bad days for me. Because of the dry autumn, our kolkhoz had delivered its quota of grain early, and Uncle Vanya didn't come to town anymore. I knew that at home Mother was beside herself worrying about me, and that didn't make my life any easier. The sack of potatoes that Uncle Vanya had brought on his last trip had vanished as quickly as if they'd been fed to livestock, no less. It's a good thing that I had suddenly come to my senses and had thought to hide some in the abandoned shed in the back yard, because now this cache alone was keeping me alive. I would slip into the shed after school, sneaking up to it like a thief, stuff several potatoes into my pockets, and run to the end of the street and off into the hills to build a fire somewhere in a handy hidden gully. I was hungry all the time. I could feel convulsive waves rolling through my stomach even in my sleep.

In hopes of running across a new gang of players, I cautiously began to search the neighboring streets. I wandered through vacant lots and followed the kids who were drawn into the hills. But all to no avail. The season was over, and cold October winds were blowing. And only the kids in our clearing continued to gather as before. I hung around nearby and saw the puck sparkling in the sunlight, Vadik waving his arms and giving orders, and other familiar figures bending over the pot.

Finally I couldn't stand it any longer and went down to join them.I knew that I was headed for humiliation, but it was no less humiliating to accept once and for all that they had beaten me up and banished me. I was itching to see how Vadik and Birdy would react to my return and how I would handle myself. But most of all I was driven by hunger. I needed that ruble—no longer for milk but for bread. I didn't have any other way to get it.

When I approached, the game came to a stop, and all the players fixed their eyes on me. Birdy was wearing a cap with the earflaps up—it sat there casually and tauntingly, like everything else he had on—and a short-sleeved checked shirt that wasn't tucked in. Vadik was showing off in a handsome, thick zippered jacket. A bunch of quilted jackets and boys' winter coats lay nearby, thrown into one heap where a little kid of five or six sat huddled in the wind.

Birdy greeted me first. "What did you come for? Need another beating?"

"I came to play," I replied as calmly as possible while keeping an eye on Vadik.

"Who said anybody here'll play with you?" Birdy let out a curse.

"Nobody."

"What do you think, Vadik? Should we beat him up right away or wait awhile?"

"How come you're giving this guy a hard time, Birdy?" asked Vadik, narrowing his eyes at me. "You heard him. The guy came to play. Maybe he wants to win ten rubles off each of us."

"You don't even have ten rubles each," I said, just so they wouldn't think I was a coward.

"We got more than you ever dreamed of. Put your money where your mouth is, or else Birdy might really get mad. He's got a pretty hot temper."

"Should I give it to him now, Vadik?"

"Forget it. Let him play." Vadik winked at the other kids. "He plays great. We can't hold a candle to him."

This time I was a little smarter and understood what Vadik's kindness was all about. He'd evidently gotten fed up with the same dull, monotonous play, and that was why—in order to titillate his nerves and savor the taste of a real game—he decided to count me in. But as soon as I wounded his ego, they'd make me pay for it again. He'd find some reason to pick on me, and Birdy was always at his side.

I decided to play cautiously and not go for the pot. I rolled the puck just like everybody else so as not to stand out from the crowd, fearing I'd accidentally land on the money, and then I gently nudged the coins and looked back to make sure that Birdy hadn't come up from behind. For the first few days I didn't even dream of getting a ruble. Twenty or thirty kopecks, the price of a hunk of bread—that was enough. I'd take it.

But what had to happen sooner or later naturally happened. On the fourth day, when I'd won a ruble and was ready to leave, they beat me up again. To be sure, it didn't turn out too badly this time, but one trace remained—a big fat lip. In school I had to keep sucking it in. But no matter how hard I tried to conceal it, no matter how much I sucked it in, Lidia Mikhaylovna spotted it. She deliberately called me up to the board and made me read a passage of French. I couldn't have pronounced it correctly with ten healthy lips, much less with only one.

"Enough, please, enough!" Lidia Mikhaylovna looked frightened and began waving both hands to ward me off as though I were the Evil Spirit. "Just what is this, anyway?! I see that I'll have to work independently with you. I have no choice."

And so began a period of awkward and agonizing days. First thing each morning, I would fearfully begin to anticipate that moment when I'd be forced to stay alone after school with Lidia Mikhaylovna and, twisting my tongue, repeat words that didn't yield to pronunciation, that were thought up just for punishment. Why else, pray tell, if not for the sake of mockery would anyone combine three vowels into one thick, elongated sound—for instance, the *o* in the word *beaucoup* (meaning "much")—it's enough to make you choke. Why force certain humming sounds through the nose when for eons it has served quite a different human need? What's the purpose? This lies beyond the bounds of reason. I would be drenched in sweat, red in the face, and gasping for breath while Lidia Mikhaylovna mercilessly and ceaselessly forced me to get callouses on my poor tongue. And why only me? There were all kinds of kids at school who spoke French no better than I did, but they were free to play and to do what they wanted while I was condemned to take the rap alone for all of them.

As it turned out, the worst was yet to come. Lidia Mikhaylovna suddenly decided that we didn't have enough time between the first and second shifts at school, and she told me to come to her apartment in the evenings. She lived right next door to the school, in the teachers' quarters. In the other, larger part of Lidia Mikhaylovna's building lived the principal himself.

Just getting there was pure torture. Already shy and reserved by nature and easily flustered over any trifle, I was literally petrified the first time I showed up at my teacher's clean, tidy apartment, afraid even to breathe. She had to tell me to take off my coat, to go into the living room, to sit down—she had to move me around like an object and practically force the words out of me. That did nothing to facilitate my progress in French. But strangely enough, we devoted even less time to the lessons there than we did at school, where the second shift supposedly interfered. Moreover, as Lidia Mikhaylovna attended to something in the apartment, she asked me personal questions or talked about herself. I suspect that she deliberately made up one story for my benefit, saying she'd majored in French only because that language had been hard for her in school and she had decided to prove to herself that she could become just as proficient as anyone else.

Seeking refuge in a corner, I kept listening for permission to go home, hoping I wouldn't have to wait long. There were lots of books in her living room. On the end table near the window stood a large, beautiful combination radio and record player—a marvelous rarity for those times and something entirely new to me. Lidia Mikhaylovna put on records, and a smooth male voice was once again teaching French. One way or another the language had me trapped. Lidia Mikhaylovna moved around the room in a simple housedress and soft felt slippers, making me shiver and shake whenever she came close to me. I just couldn't believe that I was sitting in her home. Everything there was too unusual and unexpected for me, including the very air, which was saturated with the delicate and unfamiliar smells of a life unlike the one I knew. I couldn't help but get the feeling that I was peering at that other life from the sidelines, and I felt so awkward and ashamed of myself that I hunched down even deeper into my pitiful little jacket.

Lidia Mikhaylovna was probably about twenty-five at the time. I remember her face well, with its regular and thus not terribly animated features and slightly crossed eyes, a condition she tried to conceal by squinting. I recall her tight-lipped smile that rarely widened into a grin and her coal-black hair cut short. But despite her appearance, her face displayed none of the harshness that I later noticed becomes almost a trademark with teachers as the years pass, even with those who are the kindest and gentlest by nature. But there was a cautious bewilderment mixed with a little cunning that fit her perfectly and seemed to say, "I wonder how I ended up in this place and what I'm doing here?" I now think that she must have been married at one time before I knew her. Her voice, her step—delicate but confident and relaxed—her entire manner exuded boldness and experience. And besides, I've always held the view that girls who study French or Spanish become women sooner than their classmates who study Russian, let's say, or German.

Now I'm ashamed to recall how frightened and distressed I became when Lidia Mikhaylovna, after finishing our lesson, would invite me to have supper with her. Even when I was aching with hunger, my appetite would disappear with the speed of a bullet. Sit down at the same table with Lidia Mikhaylovna! No, no! I'd rather learn the entire French language by heart by tomorrow than come back here ever again. Even a morsel of bread would undoubtedly have gotten stuck in my throat. Apparently I'd never suspected that even Lidia Mikhaylovna ate the most ordinary food just like all of us and not some kind of manna from heaven—that's how extraordinary a person she seemed to me, how unlike all the rest.

I would jump up and, mumbling that I was full, that I didn't want anything to eat, I would back toward the door, sticking close to the wall. Lidia Mikhaylovna would look at me with astonishment and hurt feelings, but no power on earth could have stopped me. I would run out of there. This scene was repeated several times, and then Lidia Mikhaylovna, totally exasperated, stopped inviting me to her table. I breathed more freely.

One day at school I was told that a man had delivered a package for me and that it was downstairs in the cloakroom. That must have been Uncle Vanya, the truck driver from our kolkhoz—what other man could it be?! The house where I lived had probably been locked, and Uncle Vanya couldn't wait around till I got home from school—that's why he'd left it in the cloakroom. I could hardly wait until the end of classes and then I raced downstairs. Auntie Vera, the school janitor, showed me the corner where they'd put the white plywood box, the kind they package things in for mailing. I was surprised. Why in a box? Mother usually sent food in an ordinary sack. Maybe it wasn't meant for me at all? No, my last name and grade were spelled out on the lid. Evidently Uncle Vanya had written them there when he got to the school, so there wouldn't be any mix-up. How had Mother ever thought of sealing up food in a box?! Look how smart she'd gotten!

I couldn't carry the package home without first finding out what was inside—I was too impatient. Clearly it was not potatoes. The container was probably too small for bread and not the right shape either. Besides that, they'd just sent me bread recently, and I still had some left. Then what was in it? Right then and there, at school, I ducked under the stairs where I remembered seeing an axe, and, after finding it, I pried off the lid. It was dark under the stairs, so I crawled back out and, looking around like a thief, set the box on the nearest window ledge.

I peered into the box and was dumbfounded. On top, neatly covered with a big sheet of white paper, lay pasta. Fantastic! The long yellow tubes, arranged side by side in even rows, sparkled in the light—a treasure more sumptuous than anything I could imagine. Now I knew why Mother had used a box—so that the pasta wouldn't break or shatter, so it would reach me safe and sound. I carefully took out one tube, inspected it, blew into it, and unable to hold back any longer, began to chomp on it voraciously. Then I grabbed a second one the same way, and a third, thinking about where I might hide the box so that my pasta wouldn't get eaten by the altogether too gluttonous mice in my landlady's cupboard. That's not why Mother had bought it, why she'd spent her last savings. No, I wouldn't be that careless with pasta. This wasn't just any old sack of potatoes.

Then suddenly I came to my senses. Pasta . . . Really now, where could Mother have gotten pasta? In all my life I'd never seen any in our village. You couldn't buy it there for all the money in the world. So what was going on here? I hastily dug through the pasta in hope and despair and found several big lumps of sugar and two bars of hematogen* at the bottom of the box. The hematogen confirmed that it wasn't Mother who'd sent the package. In that case, who was it? Who? I looked at the lid again. Sure enough, my grade, my last name—it was for me. Interesting, very interesting.

I tapped the nails back into the lid and, leaving the box on the window ledge, went up to the second floor and knocked on the door of the teachers' lounge. Lidia Mikhaylovna had already left. Never mind, we'll find her, we know where she lives, we've been there before. So this is what she's up to: if you won't sit down at my table, you'll get food delivered to your home. So that's how it is. But it won't work. It couldn't be anyone else. It definitely wasn't Mother. She wouldn't have forgotten to enclose a note, and she would have told me where she'd gotten it, in what mines she'd dug up such a treasure.

When I squeezed sideways through her door with the package, Lidia Mikhaylovna pretended not to understand. She looked at the box that I set down on the floor in front of her and asked in surprise, "What's this? What on earth did you bring me? And for what reason?"

"You're the one who did this," I said in a shaky, stuttering voice.

"What have I done? What are you talking about?"

"You sent this package to the school. I just know it was you."

I noticed that Lidia Mikhaylovna was blushing and looked embarrassed.

That was apparently the only time I had not been afraid to look her straight in the eye. I couldn't have cared less whether she was my teacher or a distant aunt. Now I was the one asking the questions, not her, and I was asking them not in French but in Russian, where I didn't have to worry about any articles. And she had to answer.

"Why have you decided it was me?"

"Because we don't have pasta in our village. And we don't have hematogen either."

"How can that be? You never have them?" Her astonishment was so genuine that she gave herself away completely.

"Never. You should have known that."

Lidia Mikhaylovna suddenly burst out laughing and tried to hug me, but I moved away from her.

"You're right. I really should have known. How could I have made such a mistake?!" She paused for a moment, deep in thought. "But hon-

---

*Hematogen—a remedy for anemia consisting of hemoglobin in a base of glycerine and wine.

estly, I could hardly have guessed! I'm a city girl, after all. You say you never have these things? What do you have, then?"

"We have peas. We have radishes."

"Peas . . . radishes . . . Along the Kuban River we have apples. My, how many apples there are right now! I wanted to go back to the Kuban recently, but for some reason I came here instead." Lidia Mikhaylovna sighed and glanced at me out of the corner of her eye. "Don't be angry with me. I wanted to do what was best for you. Who would have thought that I'd slip up on pasta? Never mind, I'll know better next time. But here, you take this pasta—"

"I won't take it," I interrupted.

"But why do you say that? I know you're hungry. And I live by myself. I've got lots of money. I can buy whatever I want, but living alone, you know . . . And I don't even eat very much because I'm afraid of putting on weight."

"I'm not hungry at all."

"Please don't argue with me. I know. I spoke with your landlady. What's so bad about taking this pasta now and making yourself a good dinner tonight? Why can't I help you—just once in my life? I promise not to force any more packages on you. But please take this one, for my sake. You have to eat your fill in order to study. We have a lot of well-fed goof-offs at school who can't figure out anything and undoubtedly never will, but you're an able kid. You shouldn't quit school."

Her voice was beginning to break down my resistance. I was afraid she would convince me, and, angry with myself for recognizing the validity of Lidia Mikhaylovna's arguments and for planning to reject them anyway, I shook my head, mumbled something, and ran out the door.

Our lessons didn't end with that. I continued to visit Lidia Mikhaylovna. But now she really took me in tow. She'd evidently decided, Well then, if it's just French, then let it be French. It's true that some good was coming of this. Gradually I began to enunciate French words tolerably, and they no longer broke off and fell at my feet like heavy cobblestones but tried to take wing with a lilt.

"That's good," said Lidia Mikhaylovna encouragingly. "You still won't get an A this quarter, but next quarter you will for sure."

We didn't bring up the subject of the package, but I was on my guard just in case. Lidia Mikhaylovna was capable of coming up with almost anything. I knew from my own experience that when something isn't working out, you'll do everything to make sure it does; you won't back off that easily. I had the feeling that Lidia Mikhaylovna was always sizing me up expectantly, chuckling over my primitiveness all the while. I would get angry, but my anger, however strange this may seem, helped me behave more confidently. I was no longer the meek, helpless kid who'd been scared to set foot in there. Little by little I was getting used to Lidia Mikhaylovna and her apartment. I was still bashful, of course, taking refuge in a corner, covering up my clodhoppers under the table, but my former constraint and sullenness were receding, and now I had the courage to ask Lidia Mikhaylovna questions and even to get into arguments with her.

She made one more attempt to seat me at her supper table. But in this matter I was unbending. I had enough stubbornness for ten people.

We probably could have curtailed those review sessions at her home. I had grasped the essentials, my tongue had loosened up and begun to move, and the rest would have come with time during our regular classes. Years and years lay ahead. What would I do later if I were to learn it all from beginning to end in one fell swoop? But somehow I couldn't say this to Lidia Mikhaylovna, and she evidently didn't feel that we'd achieved our goal at all, so I kept my nose to the French grindstone. But was it really such a grind? Somehow, without ever expecting to and without noticing, I'd automatically developed a taste for the language, and in my spare time I'd look things up in my little dictionary without any prodding and glance ahead at more advanced passages in the textbook. Punishment was turning into pleasure. I was still spurred on by pride. Where I had failed I would succeed and succeed just as well as the very best of them. I was cut from the same cloth, wasn't I? If I had no longer been required to go to Lidia Mikhaylovna's, I would have managed all by myself.

One day, about two weeks after the incident with the package, Lidia Mikhaylovna asked with a smile, "Well, have you given up playing for money? Or do you still get together in some out-of-the-way spot and play now and then?"

"How could we play now?!" I asked with surprise, glancing out the window at the snow.

"And what kind of game was it? How is it played?"

"What do you care?" My guard went up.

"I'm just curious. When I was a kid we sometimes played a game like that, too. I'd simply like to know whether yours is the same game or not. Come on, tell me about it. Don't be afraid."

I told her all about it, leaving out, of course, the parts about Vadik, Birdy, and the little tricks I used in the game.

"No," said Lidia Mikhaylovna, shaking her head. "We played 'hit the wall.' Do you know what that is?"

"No."

"Here, watch." She sprang up gracefully from the table she'd been sitting at, found a couple of coins in her purse, and moved a chair away

from the wall. "Come here and watch. First I bounce a coin off the wall."
Lidia Mikhaylovna tossed it gently, and the coin, hitting the wall with a
ping, rebounded in an arc and fell to the floor. "Now"—Lidia Mikhaylovna put the other coin in my hand—"it's your turn to throw, but keep
this in mind: you have to toss it so that your coin will land as close as
possible to mine. So that you can measure the distance by reaching with
the thumb and little finger of one hand. Another name for the game is
'measures.' If you can reach, that means you win. Go ahead and throw."

I threw, and my coin, landing on its edge, rolled off into a corner.

"Oh, no," said Lidia Mikhaylovna, dismissing my toss with a wave of
her hand. "Too far. This time you start. Don't forget—if my coin touches
yours even slightly, even on the edge, then I win double. Have you
got it?"

"What's so hard about that?"

"Shall we play?"

I couldn't believe my ears. "How can I ever play with you?"

"And why not?"

"Because you're a teacher!"

"What's that got to do with it? Teachers are people, too, aren't they?
Sometimes I get tired of being only a teacher—teach, teach, teach all day
long, constantly reminding myself that I mustn't do this, I mustn't do
that." Lidia Mikhaylovna narrowed her eyes even more than usual and
looked out the window, lost in her own thoughts. "Occasionally it helps
to forget that you're a teacher. If you don't, you become such an ogre,
such a bogeyman, that real people get bored with you. Maybe the most
important thing for a teacher is not to take yourself too seriously, to realize that there's actually very little you can teach." She pulled herself together and immediately became more cheerful. "At your age I was a
pretty naughty little girl. My parents had their hands full with me. Even
now I still often get the urge to skip and jump and race off somewhere,
to do something that's not in the curriculum and not scheduled, just because I want to. Once in a while I skip and jump right here. A person
gets old not when he reaches old age but when he stops being a child.
I'd have a good time jumping every day if Vasily Andreevich didn't live
next door. He's a very strict person. Under no circumstances should he
find out that we're playing 'measures.'"

"But we're not even playing 'measures.' You only showed me how."

"We could play just for fun, as they say. But all the same, don't you
tell on me."

Good Lord, what was the world coming to! Not long ago I had been
scared to death that Lidia Mikhaylovna would drag me off to the principal's office because I was playing for money, and now she was asking
me not to squeal on her. Doomsday had arrived—that's what it was. I
looked around, afraid of who knows what, my eyes blinking nervously.

"Well, what do you say? Shall we try it? If you don't like it, we'll quit."

"Okay," I agreed reluctantly.

"You start."

We grabbed our coins. I could see that Lidia Mikhaylovna had actually played before, while I was just starting to size up the game. I still hadn't figured out for myself how to bounce a coin off the wall—on its edge or flat—or how high or how hard to throw it. I was throwing blindly. If we'd been keeping score for the first few minutes, I would have lost quite a bit, although there was nothing tricky about that game called "measures." Understandably, what held me back and upset me most of all, what kept me from learning the game, was playing it with Lidia Mikhaylovna. Such a thing couldn't have happened even in my worst thoughts or wildest dreams. It took a good deal of time and effort to collect my wits, but when I did and gradually began to focus on the game, Lidia Mikhaylovna suddenly stopped it.

"No, this isn't very interesting," she said, straightening up and brushing back the hair that had fallen into her eyes. "If we're going to play, let's play for real, otherwise we're like a couple of three-year-olds."

"But that means playing for money," I reminded her shyly.

"Of course. And what do we have in our hands? There's nothing quite like playing for money. This makes it both good and bad at the same time. Even if we agree on very small stakes, it will make it interesting."

I was speechless, not knowing what to do or how to react.

"You're not scared, are you?" asked Lidia Mikhaylovna, egging me on.

"What do you mean?! I'm not scared of anything."

I had a little change with me. I gave Lidia Mikhaylovna her coin back and reached into my pocket for one of my own. Okay, Lidia Mikhaylovna, let's play for real if that's what you want. What's it to me—I'm not the one who started this. Vadik didn't pay any attention to me at first either, but then he woke up and came after me with his fists. I learned that game, and I'll learn this one, too. It isn't French, and I'll even have French under my belt pretty soon.

I had to accept one condition. Since Lidia Mikhaylovna had larger hands and longer fingers, she would measure with her thumb and middle finger while I would measure with my thumb and little finger, the way you were supposed to. That was only fair, and I agreed to it.

The game began again. We moved from the living room to the entryway, where we had a little more space and could throw against the smooth, wooden room divider. We threw, got down on our knees, crawled around on the floor, bumping into each other, stretched out our fingers, measuring between the coins, then got to our feet again, and Lidia Mikhaylovna kept score. She made a lot of racket during the game. She'd let out a shout, clap her hands, and tease me all the time—in other words, she behaved like a typical little girl instead of a teacher, and sometimes I even got the urge to yell at her. But she still won, and I lost. Before I knew it, I'd blown eighty kopecks. I had a lot of trouble cutting my debt down to thirty, but then Lidia Mikhaylovna, shooting from a long way out, landed her coin on mine, and the score quickly jumped to minus fifty. I began to get worried. We had agreed to settle up at the end of the game, but if things went on this way, I would soon be out of money. I had just a little over a ruble. And so I couldn't lose more than a ruble—otherwise I'd be disgraced, disgraced and ashamed for the rest of my life.

And then I happened to notice that Lidia Mikhaylovna wasn't even trying to beat me at all. When measuring, she would bend her fingers instead of extending them to their full length—once, when she supposedly couldn't reach a coin, I reached it without any effort. That hurt my feelings, and I stood up.

"None of that," I announced. "I won't play that way. Why are you trying to let me win? That's dishonest."

"But I really can't reach them," she said, denying the accusation. "My fingers are kind of stiff."

"Yes, you can."

"All right, all right, I'll try harder."

I don't know how it is in mathematics, but in life the best proof for something lies in its opposite. The next day when I saw Lidia Mikhaylovna slyly move a coin toward her finger in order to reach it, I was dumbfounded. Glancing at me and somehow not noticing that I could see right through her obvious cheating, she continued to move the coin as though nothing were wrong.

"What are you doing?" I asked indignantly.

"Who, me? What does it look like I'm doing?"

"Why did you move the coin?"

"But I didn't. It was right here to start with," Lidia Mikhaylovna said with utter unscrupulousness and even a kind of glee, sticking to her guns just the way Vadik or Birdy would have.

That's terrific! And she calls herself a teacher! I'd seen with my own eyes from twenty centimeters away how she nudged the coin, and she tries to tell me she didn't touch it, and laughs at me to boot. Does she think I'm blind, or what? Or some little kid? And she calls herself a French teacher. In an instant I completely forgot that just the day before Lidia Mikhaylovna had been trying to let me win, and now I watched her like a hawk to make sure she didn't cheat in her own favor. What do you know about that! And she calls herself Lidia Mikhaylovna.

That day we worked on French for about fifteen or twenty minutes, and even less on the following days. We had found another common interest. Lidia Mikhaylovna would have me read a passage aloud, make corrections, and listen to me again. Then, without wasting time, we'd switch to the game. After two insignificant losses I began to win. I quickly got the hang of "measures," I fathomed all its secrets, I knew how and where to throw and what tricks to use so that Lidia Mikhaylovna wouldn't be able to reach my coin.

And once again I had money. Once again I was running to the market and buying milk—now in round, frozen chunks. I would carefully shave the layer of cream off the top, stuff the crumbling, frozen slices into my mouth, and, savoring their nourishing sweetness throughout my whole body, close my eyes with satisfaction. Then I'd turn the chunk over and use the knife to tap the slightly sweet milk solids loose. I'd let the rest melt and then drink it while eating a piece of bread.

That wasn't bad, you could stay alive that way, and in the near future, as soon as the wounds of war had healed, we were promised happier times.

Of course, I felt uncomfortable taking Lidia Mikhaylovna's money, but I consoled myself each time with the knowledge that those were honest winnings. I never asked if we could play. Lidia Mikhaylovna suggested it herself. I didn't dare refuse. The game seemed to give her a lot of pleasure—she'd become cheerful, and she'd laugh and pick on me.

If only we'd known how all this would end . . .

Kneeling across from each other, we'd gotten into an argument about the score. Just before that, as I recall, we'd been arguing about something else.

"You don't understand, you scatterbrain," contended Lidia Mikhaylovna, waving her arms as she crawled toward me. "Why would I try to cheat? I'm keeping score, not you. I know better. I lost three times in a row, and before that you won at '*chika*.'"

"'*Chika*' doesn't count."

"Why doesn't it count?"

"You won at '*chika*,' too."

We were shouting and interrupting each other when we heard a surprised, you might even say astonished, but gruff and trembling voice.

"Lidia Mikhaylovna!"

We froze. Vasily Andreevich was standing in the doorway.

"Lidia Mikhaylovna, what's the matter with you? What's going on here?"

Lidia Mikhaylovna, beet red and all disheveled, got up from her knees very, very slowly, and, smoothing her hair, she said, "Vasily Andreevich, I would have expected you to knock before coming in."

"I did knock. No one answered. What's going on here? Please explain this. As your principal I have a right to know . . ."

"We're playing 'hit the wall,'" Lidia Mikhaylovna calmly replied.

"You're playing for money with this . . .?" Vasily Andreevich gave me a poke with his finger, and I, terrified, crawled around the room divider to go hide in the living room. "You're playing with a pupil?! Did I understand you correctly?"

"That's right."

"Don't tell me . . ." The principal was choking and gasping for air. "I'm not even sure what to call your action here. This is a crime. It's perversion. Corruption of a minor. And . . . and . . . so on . . . I've worked in schools for twenty years, I've seen all sorts of things, but this—"

And he threw up his hands.

Lidia Mikhaylovna left three days later. On the eve of her departure, she met me after school and walked me home.

"I'm going back to my Kuban," she told me as we said good-bye. "And I want you to continue your studies without worrying. No one is going to lay a finger on you for this foolish incident. It's all my fault. So go on with your studies." She patted me on the head and walked away.

And I never saw her again.

In the middle of the winter, after our January break, I received a package in the mail at school. When I opened it, after getting the axe out from under the stairs again, I found sticks of pasta lying in neat, tightly packed rows. And underneath, wrapped in thick cotton wool, I found three red apples.

Until then I'd only seen pictures of apples, but I guessed that's what they were.

1973

LIVE AND LOVE

To someone who doesn't have it, independence seems so fascinating and attractive that he would give up anything for it. Sanya was literally stunned by this word when he took a close look at it. He didn't have a good grasp of it, and he didn't ponder it, for there was nothing special to ponder. He simply took a close look and saw what it was. *Independence*—to stand on your own two feet in life, without any prompting or support—that's what it meant. Sometimes in order to make an important decision, only one little thing will be missing, and that's what happened this time, too. As soon as Sanya saw what independence was, he would have liked to stand in his very own place, one that belonged to him alone, where he would become independent, to stand with such certainty and ease that there could be no doubt about its being his place, and he made up his mind: that was it, enough. Enough running around when ordered, acting when prompted, believing in fairy tales . . . A person could be fifteen years old, but to Papa and Mama he was still a baby, and this would never end if he didn't declare once and for all, I'm me. I wasn't born yesterday. I am who I am, I belong to myself, and I'm the one who answers for my own life in the end, not you. He didn't plan to cross any boundaries, of course, as there was no need for that, but he did plan to push them back a bit.

And it was amazing—immediately after making that decision, Sanya had a stroke of luck. Back at the beginning of the summer Papa and Mama hadn't planned to go anywhere, but when Sanya returned from sports camp, where he had spent the month of June, he suddenly learned that they were leaving. They were flying to Leningrad, where they would get into a car with their friends and drive to the Baltic Coast, then to Kaliningrad, then to Brest and someplace else, and they would return only at the end of August, to take Sanya back home in time for school. "You'll be staying at Grandma's," said Mama. Papa sighed. August at Grandma's on Lake Baikal was always a golden month, with berries, mushrooms, fishing, and swimming, and if Papa had had his way, he would have traded places with Sanya without giving it a second thought. Except that Sanya, of course, would have refused to trade— and not because he didn't want to visit the Baltic Coast or see Brest. He did, and he especially wanted to go to Brest, but he preferred to be where Papa and Mama weren't, for even in Brest they would manage to shove him into some military ditch or trench and then not let him stick his head out just in case, God forbid, a bullet fired forty years ago might get him. If parents have only one child, they show every sign of lapsing into a second childhood themselves, continuing to play with him like a doll until he buys his freedom by making his own parental investment. Sanya was embarrassed for his parents and felt sorry for them when he saw that, even though they talked in regular, normal language with his friends, they would instantly switch to excessively flattering or excessively strict language with him, going to both extremes as if they were blind and didn't see him but merely sensed that he ought to be there, talking not so much for his sake as for their own, to prove something to each other. And so he'd learned to view the words they spoke when they were together as intended not for him but for them. Yet individually each of them could also carry on a serious conversation with him. This especially applied to Papa, and it was especially noticeable how embarrassed he was in front of his son over their three-way conversations with Mama, but when the next occasion arose, when the time came for another conversation, everything was repeated all over again. "You're like little kids, honestly, just like little kids," Sanya told them mentally, mimicking their tone of voice, annoyed and yet realizing that in this regard his parents were no better and no worse than others and that in terms of his weaknesses a person remains a child all his life.

At Baikal, where Sanya went to stay with Grandma, his luck continued. Three days went by—and suddenly Grandma got a telegram: come quickly, Vera's in the hospital, the children are alone. Aunt Vera,

Mama's sister, lived in the town of Nizhneangarsk on the northern tip of Baikal, and now it looked as though she'd become seriously ill. And her husband was a geologist who couldn't be reached out in the taiga. Grandma got all flustered and started to moan. She had a boy on her hands here, and who knew what was happening there. At that time Sanya's parents were traipsing around Leningrad or heading for Tallinn. Everything fell perfectly into place for Sanya, and he announced, "I'll stay alone." Aunt Galya, Grandma's neighbor, come to the rescue. She agreed not only to feed Grandma's piglets but also to keep an eye on her grandson and to have him sleep in her cottage at night. Grandma left, and Aunt Galya forgot all about Sanya. True, she did remember the piglets, and that was enough.

Sanya began to lead a happy-go-lucky life. He got to like going to the store, fixing simple meals for himself, doing the little jobs around the house that you can't get along without doing, and he even got to like weeding the garden, which he couldn't stand before. And he made one important discovery: he'd pulled a little ahead of everything that surrounded him in his own life and that he'd been constantly forced to stay even with in the past. Nothing seemed to have changed, and outwardly everything remained in its own place and in its usual order, except for one thing: he had acquired an amazing ability to look back at this world and at this order from a distance. He could enter it, but he could also step outside it. People remain in the common ranks only in someone else's view; individually each person, in his own view, moves out in front, for otherwise life has no meaning. A lot of this was still hazy to Sanya, but the sensation that he'd moved out in front was distinct and joyous, like the sensation of height when distant horizons open up. Sanya was struck most of all by the idea that he'd arrived at this sensation and this discovery thanks to such a seemingly trivial thing as the unexpected need he somehow felt to putter in the garden—extremely unpleasant work. This was neither a desire nor an obligation but something else: he got up in the morning, and while he was thinking about the best way to organize the day ahead, he was reminded of the garden almost before anything else, which met his requirement for movement and action perfectly, similar to the way you think of water only when you're thirsty.

Spending the night alone in an old cottage where something was constantly creaking or sighing wasn't much fun at first, but Sanya dealt with fear in his own way—before going to sleep he'd read *Evenings on a Farm Near Dikanka.** The book had been read and reread and was so com-

---

*A collection of tales written by Nikolay Gogol and published in 1831–1832.

pletely tattered that it made your heart stop from its terrifying stories even more effectively than if they'd been in a new book, where you could take them for inventions, which you couldn't with an old one. An old book made you believe against your will, but after reading these stories, which ascended to the very heavens in their beauty and terror, with voices straight out of the nether world, the nearby rustlings in the corner and behind the wall no longer carried any force or fear, and Sanya would fall asleep. In his conception, the ghosts and evil spirits that were there, in the book, for some reason did not associate with those that might be here, as if they didn't wish to acknowledge the present wasted and inglorious breed as their future. Putting the book down, Sanya would think about everything he'd been so afraid of earlier and feel nothing but pity and bewilderment, pity not for himself but for them: see what power they had and look what they've been reduced to! And then he got used to them. He got used to distinguishing the distant signals of the steamboats at sea, which sounded like groans; the noise of the wind, which built up during the day and howled in the walls at night; the heavy creaking of the old larch trees in the yard; and the mighty, muffled drone from Baikal, which called out in the dark for something it had lost and got no answer.

Sanya spent a week like this, secretly proud of himself, of his domesticity and independence, and he worried only that Grandma, from whom there was no news, might show up unexpectedly. A tear-off calendar hung on the wall in Grandma's front room. Sanya would remove the sheets and put them on the bedside table next to Grandma's heavy dresser, arranging them in a separate order of his own in which he saw some unexplained but significant meaning.

Mityay came over on Friday afternoon. He didn't know that Sanya was living alone, but he'd seen him at the store a day earlier and for that reason figured he'd find Sanya's father here. Mityay used to go to him for help, and now he sat on a stool by the entryway, confused and dismayed, and watched with an intent, vacant look as Sanya, using a needle, threaded sliced brown mushrooms onto a double thread. He watched for a long time, wrinkling his face with effort and worrying that the pieces of mushroom on the long, sagging thread might touch the floor, and then he asked, "You drying 'em?"

"Yes."

"Good for you."

It wasn't the praise that affected Sanya. No, he knew it wasn't worth anything and didn't come from the heart. He simply began to feel sorry for Mityay, recalling how Papa would pity him in such situations and take his side against Mama and Grandma when Mityay would just show up like this, sit down, and wait.

"Uncle Mityay, you probably need three rubles. I can give them to you. I've got some money."

Studying Sanya with a livelier expression, Mityay frowned harder than before and replied, "You don't call a cow 'auntie,' do you?"

"Why should I?"

"That's just it—why should you? 'Mityay'—that's an animal's name, like what you'd call a bull. Who sticks 'uncle' onto an animal's name? Call me 'Mityay' like everybody else. Go ahead. I won't gag."

"But what do people generally call you?" Sanya couldn't bring himself to use the formal Russian word for "you," as children usually address adults. But they actually had known each other a long time, and Sanya's informal, familiar "you" used to creep in even before this.

"Mityay. That's what they call me. Ask my ma if you want. She only died a hundred years ago."

Sanya was familiar with this, too, and Papa would talk about it, remarking that when Mityay felt uncomfortable, he'd get "carried away" in the opposite direction. But that's how it was with a lot of people, as Sanya knew from his own experience. "He didn't degenerate from a monkey—he came from the Devil," said Grandma sternly when Sanya once tried to explain the theory of evolution to her. "If he'd come from a monkey, he'd hold his tongue and not disgrace himself. But for him, you see, the worse it is, the better he likes it. That's where he gets it, from the Evil Spirit."

Sanya got a three-ruble bill from the bedside table, where he kept his money, and offered it to Mityay. He took it, glancing at Sanya with unusual severity for some reason, and instead of thanking him he said, "Your father's a fool. The berries are ready and he's gone off somewhere. Right now there's berries from here to there."

Ah, if only Papa could have heard this, if only . . . Even out there, in illustrious Riga, Kaliningrad, and Brest, his soul would have started moaning and groaning, begging to go back—that's how much he loved berry-picking time and how he waited for it all year, contriving every summer to make his vacation coincide exactly with the berry season. He'd guessed right this year, too, and had probably tried so hard, worried and fought so hard not to be too early or too late, and then it hadn't worked out. If only he could have heard that "from here to there," which in Mityay's speech meant the rare and total abundance that occurs once every five or even ten years. Mityay wouldn't say something without good reason—he had his faults, but lying wasn't one of them; on the contrary, like all the local residents who feared the Evil Eye, he'd rather understate something than exaggerate. That meant the taiga had come up with a wonderful crop. And as Grandma was leaving, she had sighed, "People say it's just loaded with berries out there now, but I can't even run off to my little hill. My berries'll weep."

When it came to berries, Papa and Mityay really hit it off. They'd gone out together for many years now, managing to get some even in bad seasons. If it wasn't red whortleberries, it was bilberries; if not currants, then honeysuckle; if not raspberries, then blueberries. Once they even went out late in the fall after buckthorn berries, but they had to travel a long way, to an unfamiliar part of the taiga, and they got caught in snow and came back empty-handed. Usually they had plenty of berries in their own part of the taiga, except for the rare years when there was nothing whatsoever. Grandma wouldn't be able to cook or crush them all. Sanya wouldn't be able to keep up as he repeatedly ran to the store for sugar. By winter two rows of the wide shelves down in Grandma's storeroom would be completely crammed with jars bearing labels in Sanya's large handwriting to indicate which ones were tart berries and which were raspberries, which were uncooked jam* and which were preserves. Half the jars would then be transported to the city and eaten with company and with everyday meals; half would stay at Grandma's, but Grandma, who was all alone, didn't need much and they'd last till spring and summer when, after the whole family had gathered again, they'd light into the berries—here's some more, coming right up!

Mama was from this town. She'd grown up here while Papa was from the city, but he was the one who dragged her back, and if Mama went at all, it was against her will. She didn't enjoy it and went only to avoid hurting Grandma's feelings.

Mama also didn't like Papa's friendship with Mityay. Mityay had once "done time," and besides that he "drank"—he did indeed have certain traits that scared off decent people. He didn't hide them either, and, sensing the hostility of Sanya's mama, he loved to tell prison stories in front of her when he got "carried away" or to talk about his drunken escapades, in which it turned out that during his two years behind bars he'd murdered no fewer than twenty men, and that no later than yesterday he'd held up five tourists on the shore by the cafe. Mityay greatly exaggerated, pouring on the prison-camp slang, and Mama didn't believe everything, of course, but she took some of it seriously, figuring

---

*This method of preserving berries involves crushing the fruit, adding sugar, putting the mixture into jars without special sealing, and storing the jars in a root cellar below the frost line.

that tall tales are told in order to hide some truth that has good reason to be hidden. As far as Mityay's present escapades were concerned, Mama couldn't help but know that, having once been convicted for drunken brawling, Mityay had been deathly afraid of rowdy men ever since and that he tried to keep his distance whenever a fight was brewing. Defending Mityay in arguments with Mama, Papa would start to get all worked up, but, because there wasn't much he could say, he'd simply repeat time after time that even in his most brutish state Mityay remained a human being and behaved like a human being, unlike certain teetotalers. Grandma, who didn't like arguments and who also feared them as much as Mityay feared brawls, would sigh, trying to make peace: "He's not a bad guy, no. He's just broken away from the fold." For some reason this "broken away from the fold" aroused Sanya's interest in Mityay more than anything else. It suggested that some people were in the fold while others were outside it—and he wondered whether Mityay could return to the fold or whether he even wanted to.

Mityay didn't put Sanya's three-ruble bill away. He turned it over and over in his hands, evidently considering what to promise, what date to set for returning the money. And suddenly he complained, "I already owe folks three pails of berries, Sanyok. Got to shake a leg tomorrow."

That meant that he'd borrowed money in exchange for berries. What made him different, and what Papa always gave him credit for, was that Mityay didn't beg the way some people in the town did who knew only one thing: how to take, cheat, and wheedle by every possible means. No, Mityay would immediately tell you when and how he'd pay back the debt, and then with rare exceptions he'd pay it back exactly as promised. The exceptions were when Mityay would come on an appointed date, drunk or sober, and say, "Couldn't do it today to save my skin, but I'll be able to by such-and-so a time."

He turned the three-ruble bill over and over in his hands and did some very complicated calculations but apparently couldn't come up with anything consoling, and suddenly he made an offer.

"If you want, you can come with me tomorrow and take your father's place. The berries are out there—I went and looked. You can stretch your legs instead of sitting at home."

And when Sanya, surprised and glad, agreed without hesitation, Mityay looked at him more sternly and attentively, as if only then did it register in his dense brain that standing before him was someone who had absolutely no experience in the taiga yet, or in anything else, for that matter, a tame city boy. Sanya noticed his uncertainty.

"What's the matter, Mityay? You think I can't walk that far or something? I can walk okay, don't worry."

"If you can't, you'll get left out there," Mityay muttered angrily and put the three-ruble bill into his pocket. "Just remember . . . We'll be gone overnight, so stock up. Main thing is, take warm clothes for the night."

Sanya gasped and involuntarily came to a stop when, after walking down the hill and coming out from behind the last house, he saw a huge crowd of people gathered that morning on the platform where the train would brake to a halt. In the gray, faded light of dawn, when it was neither light nor dark, the crowd did indeed seem huge— a lot bigger than the number of people who lived in the town, and they kept coming and coming from three directions. Out on the water, motors roared deafeningly one after another, and boats with guarded figures hunched over in them, like people in a race, were speeding along the shore to the right. Those waiting for the train stuck together in groups and for some reason were also uncommunicative and on their guard.

In this unfriendly and mostly unfamiliar throng Sanya didn't recognize Mityay right away. Today he was a completely different person from the one he'd been yesterday. His eyes gleaming confidently and somewhat slyly, with a cunning smile on his broad face, which had firmed up during the night, Mityay was sitting on the tracks, his short boot-clad legs tucked under him Mongolian style, and he was taunting a flabby guy, sullen and ragged from head to toe, who stood in front of him looking guilty. Mityay was telling him about something that he didn't remember and didn't want to remember. Sullenly refusing, the other guy looked hopefully in the direction of the station, where the train would appear. When Sanya walked up and said hello, he immediately took the opportunity to move away from Mityay, stepping back, back . . .

"Where you going?!" Mityay shouted after him cheerfully. "All right, Golyanushkin, you birdbrain. I'll find you in the taiga. You can't hide from me."

Sanya turned around to look, wondering why he was a birdbrain. But by now there was no trace of the guy. Sanya turned back to look at Mityay, who had on an old cloth cap faded to such a mournful color that it was impossible even to give it a name. But it was somehow wonderfully suited to Mityay, to his whole harmonious and appropriate appearance that morning. Everything taken separately looked out of place—the cap, the light-blue T-shirt under the dark jacket with the sleeves rolled up, the pants with legs as wide as overalls, which were a light color from frequent washing and were tucked into well-worn boots smeared with tar—and everything taken together seemed to be exactly what a person should wear when heading into the woods on serious business. This was either because of his face or his build or because of something else. Sanya already knew that some people are lucky that way and can wear any clashing combination so well that you envy them, but with Mityay it was something different. This harmony of his seemed to come from some kind of accord with himself, when a person doesn't care what he puts on as long as it's easy to wear, and for that reason everything he wears is made to look comfortable and attractive.

Mityay saw the backpack behind Sanya with the edge of a pail sticking out and asked, "So where's your father's wooden basket with the shoulder straps?"

"It's way too big."

"Berries won't fall out of a big one. Should've brought it. Main thing is, it's easy on your back. Okay, let's climb aboard. Look alive."

The train was approaching, and Mityay, aiming for the best place to stand, took several steps alongside the moving train and kept Sanya beside him by holding onto his backpack. As soon as an open door appeared opposite them, Mityay shoved Sanya through it swiftly and forcefully and jumped in himself, and while others were still wedged in the doorway, they were already sitting at a little table by a window. Pleased with his first success, Mityay kept looking cheerfully out the window at the crush, twitching and eager to shout something at especially interesting moments but refraining. And again Sanya marveled at the change that had taken place in him since yesterday, as it if weren't really Mityay beside him but his double, always cheerful and carefree. But even before this Sanya had begun to suspect that every person must have a double somewhere in the world, so that, as a result of there being two people identical in appearance and opposite in nature, one of them can always decide what to do next.

"What a horde! What a horde!" Mityay shouted in a loud, defiantly happy voice when the train started up and they were squeezed so tightly on both benches that they couldn't budge. "Hang on, taiga!"

"I'd say there's too many people," Sanya remarked cautiously as he looked around, his alarm at the throng still not having subsided. "They're not all going out to pick berries, are they?"

"There's enough berries if they get 'em like you're supposed to. Only a horde like this, they won't pick 'em so much as trample 'em. Now it's a stampede." Mityay stretched his neck out, studying somebody. "Not to worry, Sanyok. We're not their traveling buddies. They'll pour out of here pretty soon. They're all going out just for the day, but we're real berry-pickers. We're going where they've never set foot."

The train moved slowly and unevenly, jerking the creaky old car that had served five times its normal life span, a kind not seen on through trains for a long time. And only here did they still operate, surprising the stranger by their ordinary everyday appearance, crude by present standards: heavy wooden berths, small, opaque framed windows like those in a winter cabin, narrow aisles with corners jutting into them, and on the walls, window frames, doors, and berths, left there as a re-minder, a multitude of names and wishes carved by travelers thirsting for eternity.

This wasn't even what is commonly known as a passenger train. In-stead, it was a freight train to which sometimes three, sometimes four, cars were coupled on for passengers. Only one was enough in the winter. The antiquated, detachable monster would leave town early in the morning and return late at night with coal and gasoline; prefabri-cated wooden houses and crates of vodka; metal structures and cookies-candy-hardtack; huge, beautiful foreign-made automobiles with bright, shiny paint; and domestically produced portable generators, all of which would jostle around inside the boxcars and on the flatcars and the plat-form cars with railings. This freight would then be loaded onto ships waiting at the town and delivered to northern construction sites after crossing Baikal.

In the old days the famous Trans-Siberian Railroad used to pass through here. It went from Irkutsk along the left bank of the Angara River and at this point headed farther east along the shores of Baikal. The section of the famous Trans-Siberian Railroad known as the Baikal Shoreline Railroad was even more famous—for the difficulties in con-structing it and maintaining the route, but mainly for its beauty and for the special, uncommon spirit that, whether you were working on the line or riding on it, only Baikal could give. Now people travel to get somewhere, but in the old days they also traveled to see the sights, and on such a journey (now even the word *journey* seems as old-fashioned as, for instance, *phaeton*) these spots were the most important, the most eagerly awaited, and the most memorable. The train would stop not for its own sake but for the sake of the passengers at a kilometer marker on a convenient and beautiful stretch of shoreline, and the train schedules were set up so that it could wait there awhile and people could splash a little water from Baikal in each others' faces, ooh and aah at everything around them, and then travel onward with the secret dream of seeing and feeling all this again. At the Baikal Station at the source of the Angara they used to sell a type of salmon called omul all lined up in wooden rows, salted, smoked, dried, and fried, with distinctive con-tainers and a distinct smell. Life went on briskly and continuously, with whistles and honks, announcements over the loudspeaker, and shouting on the railway platform. Where has all this gone?!

"It was like a different life," Grandma would say, but she spoke without sadness, just as she did about her youth, which had come and gone in the proper sequence.

That former life came abruptly to a halt for a reason that is now quite commonplace. When they began building the Irkutsk Dam, the railroad had to be moved to higher ground, away from the banks of the Angara, which would be submerged by the new reservoir. They laid it in a straight line, with no zigzags, from Irkutsk directly to the southernmost point of Baikal, to the Kultuk Station, and the section of railway from Kultuk to the Baikal Station was thus deprived of traffic and became a dead end. They took out one set of tracks and left the other one just to be on the safe side. The smaller stations and whistle stops grew deserted, and people moved out of the towns that had become home to them over the decades, abandoning houses and gardens alike. Only the stations that had been fairly large at one time and whose existence depended on more than the railroad alone still held a glimmer of life. There, though, life consisted of old folks hanging on until the end.

But when they began constructing the celebrated Baikal-Amur Main Line* and needed an enormous amount of supplies, they were glad they hadn't destroyed the second set of tracks. And although the local train still made one round trip a day the way it used to, leaving early in the morning and returning late at night, it came back more heavily loaded and with additional cars. This schedule couldn't have been better for the berry-pickers who wanted to reach a particular spot, load up with as much as their luck would permit, sometimes working like draft horses throughout the long summer day, and take the same route home the same day. But every dark cloud has a silver lining—after those areas became practically closed to city folk, they were still thought to be choice spots. City folk did, of course, penetrate that far with the help of friends and relatives, but not like on the new line, where they'd attack everything from wild garlic to pine nuts and strip the woods bare like locusts.

Were it not for the wooden baskets, perhaps it would actually have been roomy in the car even with all those people. A person takes up twice as much space with a wooden basket, especially with clothing and a mess kit tied onto it. But Sanya, looking at the berry-pickers, was already sorry he hadn't taken Papa's basket—it was made out of bent plywood, it was light and comfortable to wear, and you could fall down,

---

*Baikal-Amur Main Line (BAM)—a second major railway running north of and parallel to the Trans-Siberian Railroad across eastern Siberia.

you could tumble into a pit with it, and the berries would remain safe and sound. He would have taken it, but the day before, when he was trying it on for size, he'd discovered that the straps were a little too long for him. But the straps probably could have been shortened, and Mityay would have helped. Sanya's new green backpack with the pail sticking out looked absurd among this compatible and harmonious equipment—as if the boy were heading for the market instead of into the taiga.

"Berezay Station! Everybody out who's getting off here!" shouted a sickly guttural voice from the nearest door.

Looking out the window, Mityay explained, "Kilometer eighty. Now it'll ease up a little."

The old kilometer markings had been preserved along here—at one time it had numbered eighty kilometers to this point from Irkutsk.

The train began to brake, and the baskets started to stir and sway, and then—shoving those who were staying on board to the sides of the compartment—they swam toward the exit, which channeled them like a funnel and forcefully drew them out into the open expanse where, dispersing in various directions, they finally acquired owners, who were calling back and forth to each other and forming groups again. Nearly half the people got off, which certainly did ease things a bit inside the car. When the train pulled away you could see that those who had gotten off, now lined up one after another in a long single file, were heading into a ravine past abandoned houses with cold and emptiness showing through their windows.

Seen from here, from the car window, this picture startled Sanya. The day was starting out gray and overcast, daylight hadn't warmed up the taiga yet, and the people moving off into the dark ravine, passing the uninhabited houses as if they were the graves of strangers, seemed to be going out in search of their own eternal refuge and carrying in those strange vessels the sum total of their lives. Who cared about berries?! Berries were just a pretext. Until the ravine became hidden from view, Sanya had a strong, vivid feeling that he was looking out at an old burial ground, and that somewhere on the other side tombstones stood over the houses just the way they were supposed to stand over graves.

Once while Papa was reading a book, he had uttered a phrase from it out loud: "the deathly terror of birth." "What's that?" Mama asked him to repeat it. Papa did. "What kind of nonsense is this?" asked Mama, all upset, to which Papa replied thoughtfully, taking his time, "It's actually not such nonsense at all. There's something here that's not for us to know. Maybe it's stated here just by chance, but behind this happenstance—there's an abyss." He put the book down and, even deeper in thought, continued in an unnatural, strangely remote voice, "We may think we're alive, but maybe we were buried long ago and don't remember a thing. We run around here, lashing out at each other . . . like werewolves. And we don't realize that we don't exist, that somebody just put all our sins and passions together to see what we were like." Mama got scared. "Stop it. At least don't talk about this nonsense of yours in front of Sanya. He'll remember it." Papa looked at Sanya and smiled. "That's true. It's all nonsense. Live your life, Sanya, as if this were the only place you were ever born."

But Mama was right. Sanya did remember. And now, at this stop, the phrase Papa had read from the book rang out in the voice of that unknown person who had said it first.

Time after time they went through the tunnels that the railroad was famous for, clean and not very long, with beautifully finished portals. There were haystacks in the tunnels on the side that used to be occupied by the other set of tracks; a slightly bitter dampness drifted in through the lowered window; white outgrowths flashed by along the walls, convoluted stripes that looked like veins in a belly; the roar of the train rose and swelled, muffling itself; and the car creaked and lurched with greater force. But strangely enough, Sanya liked the twilight of the tunnels. Just as it would begin to arouse in him a certain special, deep-seated instinct, time would run out and they'd burst into the broad, clear celestial twilight of day, where the train would pick up speed again. Sanya had never been here before and he was all eyes. In the dangerous places just beyond the tunnels were walls providing protection from falling rock and extending as neatly and evenly as if they'd been put up only yesterday. A boulder as enormous as a tank jutted out of one of them. He couldn't imagine how it had managed to jump onto the wall and hang on there, as though it actually intended to rise like a monument on a pedestal in full view of the gigantic cliff, confirming that the wall wasn't standing there without a reason.

Staring out along the track, Sanya didn't even notice when an older man, much older than Mityay, sat down beside them. He had a white, jowly face that marked him as a stranger to these parts, but, judging from his manners and his self-assurance, he was a local. Sanya heard Mityay's voice first.

"I kept looking and looking for you . . . Thought you stayed home. Or overslept."

"I got on at the very end. Barely shoved my way in," replied somebody unfamiliar, and now Sanya turned away from the window to face them. A man in a heavy flannelette shirt that bloused out above his pants was sitting beside Mityay and pulling tomatoes out of an open wooden basket, getting ready to eat.

"Didn't have time to drink any tea this morning. Is the boy going with us or something?" he asked, not looking at Sanya.

"Yeah."

"You didn't tell me."

"So what? When could I tell you?"

"Okay, you're the boss. He should've brought rain gear. It smells like rain."

Sanya pricked up his ears. He hadn't known either that he and Mityay weren't going by themselves. It was safer and more fun in the taiga with a third person along, of course, but for some reason it bothered Sanya that he hadn't found out about him until now.

At the ninety-fourth kilometer mark, where there wasn't supposed to be a stop but where maybe even yesterday the engineers, local guys, had been talked into putting on the brakes, people began dropping to the ground with their wooden baskets all battened down, like discarded parts of a single, huge dismantled creature. That's how it seemed to Sanya. Hurrying them along, the engineers made the train jerk, and the people on the ground, getting to their feet, laughed and shook their fists toward the head of the train. Only a few people remained in the car, but they weren't dressed for the taiga and were going on to the county seat. Making the rounds of the car, Mityay cheered up and, after returning to his place, said flippantly, "No gloomy forecasts out of you, Uncle Volodya. It shouldn't rain. Am I right, Sanyok?

The three of them got off at the 102d kilometer, and Mityay, clowning around, began waving his arm: Get going! We don't need anybody anymore.

"How come, you ask, they all stayed back there but we got off here? Because, Sanyok, back there it's easy walking. Totter along for an hour or so and you're there. But to get where we're going you got to change legs three times, like changing horses, plus shed tons of sweat. Got it?" Although addressing Sanya, Mityay was also talking to Uncle Volodya, who was out here for the first time, too, thus forewarning them of the difficult route.

Countless times they crossed back and forth over a small river while moving upstream along a ravine, sometimes jumping from rock to rock, sometimes balancing on tree trunks that had fallen across it, sometimes wading through it or stepping over deep, narrow holes where dark water gurgled. The path of dried-out, white stones would vanish, and no matter how hard Sanya looked for it, not the slightest trace remained. But Mityay seemed to see it on the surface and would come out precisely where it continued. At times they followed a steep slope where more effort was spent in getting a good footing so they wouldn't slide than in making headway. At times they went along such a narrow ledge next to a cliff that not only was it impossible for two people to pass but it was even a tight squeeze for one—they had to put one foot directly in front of the other and walk in a line. And sometimes they tramped through grass in marshy bottomland that was taller than a person. But then the path turned off into the woods, giving them a rest, and became wide and dry. Nothing slowed their pace, and following the path was pure pleasure.

The taiga was quiet and gloomy. Having already awakened and joined the day, it seemed to have dozed off against its will, anticipating some sort of change. You couldn't tell if the sky in the thick white murk was high or low, as if its skin had been pulled off and only an obscure, bottomless void remained. No sunshine penetrated it and there was no wind either—massive trees that had filled out during the summer stood straight and motionless, seized by lethargy, and only over the river did the leaves on the bushes and birch trees tremble now and then, obeying the noise and movement of the water. Birds would take wing from time to time, and once, as they were walking along the path, they flushed a covey of hazel-grouse, but the birds took off and flew away more calmly than usual so as not to destroy the overall stillness.

The farther they went, the more frequent became the stands of Siberian pine and the more often Sanya would crane his neck trying to spot pine cones. There were lots of them, and they appeared to be sitting on the thick dark branches, falling potbellied to one side in search of support. When Mityay, who was walking ahead, picked up several pine cones dislodged by a nuthatch, Sanya began bounding around under the trees and found a cone with half the seeds missing and a double cone that had been torn off by the wind without being damaged. How could you help but boast! Sanya ran up to Mityay, who nodded without breaking his stride.

"There's pine nuts now, all right. From here to there. But the nuthatch, the rascal, is already after them." And he added disapprovingly, "Don't go hopping around too much. Pretty soon our legs won't be enough. We'll have to start crawling on all fours."

That "pretty soon" began after they had rested and eaten something without bothering to make tea, when they headed away from the river and bore left. Until then, they'd been on an upgrade the whole time, which was sometimes gentle, sometimes steep; it continued now, too, but they tried to fool the hill by cutting across it diagonally, and they found it easy going at first. The stands of spruce and Siberian pine were left behind and an aspen wood began, with tall, bent grass leaning over the path from both sides so that they could only feel their way along with their feet. Then the aspen thinned out, too, and everything became jumbled together again—ordinary pine, Siberian pine, birch, and spruce—and the hill thwarted their efforts to go around it by unfolding before them and rising to its full height. They began to climb.

Mityay continued to lead, and only he alone knew what lay ahead of them. The woods kept thinning out more and more, freeing the sky, as though any minute now they'd finally get to the top and begin the steep descent, which was why the sky had opened up. Uncle Volodya was breathing hard, making whistling sounds. Sanya couldn't bring himself to pass him, and so they kept walking in the same order in which they'd set out. But now Sanya and Uncle Volodya were lagging way behind Mityay, whose wooden basket, hiked up so that it blocked his head from view, seemed to move along on legs of its own, knowing no fatigue.

The steepness actually decreased somewhat, and a fresh breeze blew in their faces. Sanya was walking with his head down, looking at his feet, when he almost ran into Uncle Volodya's basket. Mityay was standing still up ahead, facing them, and he was smiling expectantly.

"What're you up to? Where are you taking us?" asked Uncle Volodya, looking around fearfully.

"Smoke break!" Mityay announced. He sat down on the nearest fallen tree without any apparent pleasure, somberly satisfied with what he was about to show them. "It's a low crawl from here on in."

Sanya couldn't believe his eyes. They'd just been walking along a ridge through woods that were clean, cheerful, and as alive as ever when suddenly— From where they'd stopped to as far ahead as wherever it came to an end, some monstrous, diabolical force had demolished everything right and left in a huge strip of unknown length. Trees piled on top of each other held up nests of roots wrenched loose from the ground along with clumps of earth. The trees bristled with boughs whose branches, still yellow, hadn't fallen off, and cracked fragments lay scattered far and wide. Sanya could never have imagined such an obstruction. What hadn't been wrenched out by the roots—mostly spruce and Siberian pine—had broken off, leaving tall, hideously splintered stumps standing in a grotesque order that didn't appear to be accidental. Only here and there had a sapling escaped destruction, and in the midst of this general, all-too-clear defeat their green branches and green leaves, now emboldened and forcing their way upward, seemed an inappropriate game of getting on with life.

"What is it? What happened here?" asked Sanya, barely pulling himself together.

"A twister," said Mityay.

"What kind of twister?"

"The kind that comes off Baikal. Nowhere else it could've come from. First time I myself ever seen such ruin. Last year when me and your father come berry-picking, everything's normal. But in the fall when I

come looking for pine nuts . . . Main thing is, I might've been the first
one to see it. Go look at how even it cut from this side. Like it was
measured."

Sanya walked past them and took a look. The boundary between the
toppled trees and the live, standing woods was indeed remarkably even,
although the woods contained notches where trees had been thrown in
from the doomed strip of land.

"Somebody could've got killed that way," Uncle Volodya remarked
sullenly, looking out from under his eyebrows at the overthrown army
of trees.

Mityay began to laugh—and not without malice, which Sanya de-
tected in his voice.

"Could've? It couldn't help but strike you dead if you happened to be
here at the time. You'd never guess it now."

"I stay home. You're the one who runs around in the woods," Uncle
Volodya responded, not to be outdone.

"It's the greenhorns that take a beating. Main thing is, they're the ones
it lies in wait for. This happens on account of them. Look at how much of
the taiga gets destroyed on account of one of them greenhorns."

"On account of who?" Uncle Volodya lit into him. "What's this
garbage?!"

"How would I know who? I wasn't here."

"So don't go running off at the mouth. The lord and master of the
taiga has turned up! How you all hate newcomers—whether it's Nikolay
Ivanovich, or Lyokha, or you . . . Like it's your own garden . . . 'I'll let
you in if I feel like it. I'll kick you out if I don't.'"

Mityay grinned.

"Don't put me on the same level as them," he said after thinking
it over awhile, trying to make peace. "If I was like what you say, I
wouldn't've taken you with me. And I wouldn't've asked the boy along.
You're all wet about Lyokha, too. You don't know beans about it. Lyokha's
a careful guy—he likes order. But once you let just anybody into the
taiga, it only leads to destruction—it's already been destroyed enough
without that."

"I live right next door to you—how can you call me 'just anybody'?"

"I don't mean you, Uncle Volodya. I don't mean you," replied Mityay,
sounding sincere and still more eager to make peace. But even Sanya
sensed an emptiness and a lack of conviction in his voice, as though
Mityay had left something unsaid.

And so it took them about an hour and a half to fight their way across
this strip of land no wider than a kilometer. Mityay had already tried
to clear a passage here before—now, too, he walked along with an

axe, often stopping and hacking off boughs, throwing them to one side—and yet it was still hard going. At times they crawled under tree trunks, scraping their baskets and getting them caught, constantly falling clumsily and being forced back. At other times they climbed up on top and made their way over the trunks as if on a footpath of tangled, crisscrossed planks, picking their way from trunk to trunk just to get a few steps ahead. They went in complicated zigzags—wherever it was possible to go. Uncle Volodya groaned and swore, and streams of sweat poured off him. A big green bundle, which turned out to be a rain poncho that doubled as a ground sheet, was torn off his basket—Sanya picked it up, even though his own backpack kept tormenting him by continually slipping off his shoulder. Suddenly thinking of it and seeing part of his load in Sanya's arms, Uncle Volodya merely nodded his head feebly in approval: all right, carry it till we get out.

But when they finally managed to get through all the obstacles, when, after following a clear path for about another fifteen minutes, they reached the summit, which cut away sharply to the left and descended to the right like a paper streamer made of stone, when their eyes were unexpectedly struck by a limitless expanse opening up on two sides in the dark, glimmering greenery, victorious at this hour over the empty, whitish sky, it made up for everything, everything. Among huge boulders overgrown with red whortleberry bushes, standing highborn and important with no need to stretch upward—not merely standing but soaring into the air—were mighty spreading pines, as if they had every right to appear regal and mighty in full view of many, many unmeasured kilometers of unfettered land. Here was the boundary, the throne; down below and farther off, rising in waves toward the smoke-colored horizon with light and dark patches playing over its surface, seeming to slide down and dig in, there lay in mysterious attentiveness the broad sweep of the humble and powerful taiga.

After removing his basket, Mityay proclaimed loudly and cheerfully, "Well, now, Uncle Volodya, what were you saying? How come you said all those things that aren't true?!"

Uncle Volodya, groaning as he sat down heavily on a rock, didn't reply.

"Fa-an-tastic!" exclaimed Sanya, who had come up last.

"From here to there, huh, Sanyok?!" Mityay shouted to him. "Remember this—you'll dream about it later in your sleep!"

A chipmunk began to chirp somewhere nearby, angrily claiming his rights to this neighborhood. Mityay burst out laughing.

"Yeah, buddy, we're going, we're going. We'll set here awhile and then go. What's the matter? You such a fool you don't even remember me?"

It can't be, Sanya had reflected more than once, that a person enters each new day blindly without knowing what will happen to him, living through it only by a decision of his own will and making choices every minute about what to do and where to go. That's not like a human being. Doesn't his whole life, from beginning to end, exist in him at the very start and doesn't there exist in him a memory that also helps him recall what to do? Maybe some people make use of this memory while others ignore it or else go against it, but every life is really a recollection of the path put into each person at birth. Otherwise what's the sense of letting him into the world? Such a perfect creature, whose perfection Sanya had begun to marvel at more and more all the time, increasingly running up against some clear, imminent inscrutability in this wonder; so complete in his capacities and contours and so elevated in comparison to everything else in the world—and suddenly to hit the open road like a rolling stone, to go wherever the wind blows him? It can't be! Then what's the purpose of these persistent and remarkable strivings in him? To put so much on the inside and leave him without a path to follow? That would be too stupid and absurd.

Sanya felt that this was exactly how he'd seen this place before, the way you can foresee the coming day. All he had to do was strain his memory harder than usual. Only a couple of details didn't match up. Or more likely he hadn't made himself examine them closely once he'd seen the main thing and decided that that was enough. Within five minutes after they'd arrived at the hunting shack, Sanya no longer had any doubt that he'd been here before. He'd never been here in reality, of course, but he seemed to have arrived just where he was supposed to arrive, without deviating from the path that lay before him like a dotted line, and to have found just what he was supposed to find. But what he saw and found was a complete picture rather than a bare representation, one that contained every possible color and was filled with life like no other place anywhere.

It was a wonderful spot, on a small dry hill among spruce and Siberian pine. The hunting shack stood under the protection of a huge pine with thick, widely spreading limbs. It was covered with branches and bark, and the ground inside was carpeted with grass and an old bough. The blackened site of a campfire lay nearby, arranged neatly and economically and ringed with stones. A tripod was already there, with sooty, horn-shaped birch sticks for hanging pots over the fire, and a little farther away, in the direction of the river, someone had rough-hewn the surface of a tree trunk that had broken off high above the ground, making it into a table. It was clean here, all ready to be lived in: no papers, no bottles, no cans—even the taiga maintained the order that humans had introduced. Dry branches blown down by the wind seemed ready-made for kindling, so that a person didn't have to look for any, and they caught fire right away. Mityay, cheerfully and impatiently giving orders, chased Sanya off to get some water and, by the time Uncle Volodya had sliced the bread, by the time each of them had unpacked his food, spreading it out in a row on the long narrow table, by the time they'd done one thing after another, the tea was ready. After the difficult trip they drank to their hearts' content and then felt exhausted. Their full stomachs, the dense stagnant air, and the lulling gurgle of the water in the river made them sleepy—they wanted to rest. Yawning, Mityay gave them permission.

"Okay, half an hour for a nap—that's plenty. Only not a peep out of you guys. We'll still have time to wear ourselves out."

He lay down by the dying fire, putting his cap under his head and spreading out his quilted vest beneath him. This vest had spent more than one summer and winter out here with him and had begun merely to resemble a quilted vest, although apparently it hadn't lost its ability to warm and to cushion. Uncle Volodya went into the shack and soon began breathing noisily. Sanya sat on a rock by the tree trunk where they'd had their tea, and, thoroughly relaxed, drowsy, and with no will of his own, looking and not seeing, listening and not hearing, he became open to everything, everything all around. He was open to the broad, swampy bottomland beyond the river, completely overgrown with bilberry bushes and dotted with gnarled birch trees; to the low sky that was gradually beginning to accumulate a murky skin; to the muffled, quavering sounds that reached him like an unsteady echo from the depths of a world overflowing with stillness. All this entered the boy, was carried into him, poured into him consciously and unconsciously as he dozed in a sweet stupor. All this was searching in him for the right disposition and for an involvement that would unify and continue but on a different, non-human scale. Everything so entranced and ennervated him that he wanted to freeze right here like a stone statue and not budge.

It was hot and humid. A stream of sweat ran down Mityay's cheek as he lay motionless on his side with his eyes closed. A big blue-gray fly, alternately flying off a short distance and then sticking its velvety, segmented head back into the accumulating liquid, was lapping up the sweat and preventing it from rolling down his neck. This fly finally woke Mityay. He sat up, shook himself, wiped away the sweat with his jacket sleeve, and looked around.

"Cut the shuteye, you guys," he said in a low voice, yawning and peering intently at the sky. "You get your wish after all, Uncle Volodya. You're gonna get your rain. Have to finish before it comes."

And in a minute he was cheerfully and energetically giving orders once again.

"Come on, come on, Sanyok, get a move on. Main thing is, you got to get half a pailful today. Oho! You watch out—we got Uncle Volodya with us! Hang on, berries!" He saw Uncle Volodya, a pot fastened to his belt, standing at the ready and holding a special metal scoop with spikes on the end. "Let's make a bet, Uncle Volodya—I bet I'll get more than you without using no scoop. What d'ya say? Are you chicken? Why rip the berries to shreds with a scoop when they're like this?! You can shake a whole bunch off with your hand, nothing to it. And the berries'll be clean—good enough for the market. You just tear off leaves with a scoop. You'll haul 'em home with leaves on half of 'em."

Without replying, Uncle Volodya set off toward the river first.

"Let's go to it, Sanyok, let's go to it," Mityay repeated excitedly when they, too, had crossed the river and stood before the berry patch. Uncle Volodya went off to the left into the depths of the bottomland; water swirled and squished noisily under his feet. With a cluck of encouragement, Mityay bent over the bushes, and Sanya heard how sharply and nakedly the first berries fell into his can, and then, falling and falling, how they became a soft, rapid patter.

Sanya had never seen so many berries in his life. He'd never even imagined that there could be so many. He'd gone raspberry-picking with Grandma more than once, and last year he'd actually come with Papa and Mityay out here, to Wide Hollow, near Baikal in search of black currants. That had been his first major outing in the taiga, and it had gone well, but they'd gathered in places that had already been picked over, mopping up after others, and although they'd gotten a lot of berries, it hadn't been much fun. This time they were the first ones. No one had been here before them touching and squashing the berries, and they were magnificent. It was a rare year, in Mityay's words, when you got a crop like this. Now Sanya knew what "the bushes are breaking with berries" meant. They really were breaking, lying on the ground under the weight or standing all bent over as though supporting each other with their excessive burdens.

Sanya parted the bushes and froze at the sight of the dense fruit-fulness he'd disturbed by uncovering it. Quivering, smoky-blue berries sprang out, plump and dangling, and dazzled the eye, arousing wonder, and delight, and guilt, and something else Sanya didn't know by name, which impressed all this on him with a feeling that bound everything together—a vague, benevolent feeling. Taking hold of a bush all decked out with alternating round and oblong fruit and bending it toward himself, Sanya set to work, playing a game that arose spontaneously and that pleased him. "Don't take offense," he chattered, "because I'm going to pick you. I'm going to pick you so you won't go to waste for no reason, so you won't fall on the ground and rot without doing anybody any good. If I don't pick you and if you don't end up falling on the ground and rotting, some bird will get you or some animal will eat you anyway—so why is it any worse if I take you now? I'll protect you." Sanya didn't want to admit that he was going to cook or crush the berries—that seemed barbaric. "And in the winter a little girl by the name of Katya, who gets sick a lot—" It seemed crude and tactless to name himself, to acknowledge that he would be eating the berries, and Sanya recalled a cousin who actually had been nursed back to health with large quantities of preserves, so Sanya wasn't exactly lying. "—and a little girl by the name of Katya . . . she likes bilberries very much, she likes you, and you'll help this girl a lot. When we get home, you'll see her and realize that she needs you. Please don't be offended."

His fingers soon learned to sense the elasticity of the berries, their strength and state of ripeness, and to handle them sometimes with a single, light touch, sometimes with careful pressure, and sometimes with a slight twist so as not to tear the fruit when the berry didn't want to come off the branch. His fingers did their job quickly and with wonderful dexterity, which Sanya had never even suspected he had in him, as if this, too, had come to him like a recent, welcome memory. And pressing them down, being kind to each berry, coaxing them one after another into the palm of his hand and then pouring them into the large can hanging from his belt and dangling over his stomach, repeating the same motions over and over, he didn't even notice the monotony, just as he didn't notice the time, becoming totally absorbed in this brisk, sensual handiwork and losing himself completely in its rich, dense design. And when something brought him back to his senses—a strange sound or a careless movement—he would look around and have trouble orienting himself: so this was where he turned out to be, and he was the one who turned out to be picking berries. Yet it had seemed to him . . . But it was impossible to say what it had seemed like to him.

And how pleasant it was to feel the ever-increasing weight of the can without looking into it and then, while dropping in some berries, to run into its warm, rising contents with his hand as if by accident—so fast! And to walk to the shack with the full can, to stand there awhile by the pail before emptying the berries into it, carried away by the sight of the steamy, living blueness of the fruit, light and glossy, with each berry breathing drowsily on its own. As Sanya emptied the bilberries into the pail, he saw that the ones at the bottom were already dark and covered with moisture and looked as if they'd suffocated. Down at the bottom he could finally grab a few berries and pop them into his mouth, feeling faint for an instant as the fruit melted tenderly and the sweetness spread under his tongue. Smacking his lips, he would slowly return to the berry patch and forget all about the can for ten or fifteen minutes, as if he were drinking some drug and continually adding to the unspecified dose.

No, there are no berries in the world sweeter and more tender than bilberries, and a person has to be pretty determined in order to carry them out of the woods in a container.

It began to rain, but not one of the three showed any reaction. Nobody began hurrying for the shack, and all of them made their hands move even faster. Mityay and Sanya continued to stay fairly close to each other. Uncle Volodya was emerging from the depths of the bottomland, gradually working his way toward them. The rain fell on the berry patch with a dense resonance. It became hard to pick the wet berries as they got squashed and smashed, and leaves stuck to their hands. Darkness was falling quickly and only then did Mityay, suddenly realizing this, shout to them to beat a retreat. By that time Sanya had managed to empty three three-liter cans into the pail, filling it more than halfway.

They cut and lugged firewood in the dark and the rain, stocking up for the damp, restless night. Mityay swore at himself and Uncle Volodya for having played too long in the berry patch like little kids and being tardy, but Sanya sensed that he was swearing just for the sake of appearance, that he was pleased with himself because they'd picked right up to the end and had come away with quite a bit. They didn't want to mess around with fixing grub in the rain, so they boiled water for tea again and, getting inside the shack, drank tea by the firelight for a long time, savoring it sweetly, the way you enjoy tea only in the taiga after a hard day that ends well in spite of everything.

This was Sanya's first night in the taiga—and what a night!—just as if it had undertaken to show him one of its mighty extremes. Darkness had fallen—you could cut it with a knife. Neither the sky beyond the circle of fire nor anything to either side was visible, and the rain made a continuous noise. Sometimes it fell silent for a bit and sometimes it came down hard, and then the fire would hiss even more, resisting the water, shooting small coals upward in annoyance and murmuring warnings from time to time with angry puffs. But the fire burned nicely. Before turning in for good, Mityay had piled two dry tree trunks on the fire, laying them side by side—these would last a long time. Sanya sat and watched as little wood ants raced around on the trunks and splinters burned through and fell off, revealing a granular patchwork that had been eaten away by the ants and looked like sawdust. When he lifted his eyes to the sky, the gigantic darkness was still there, beginning right at ground level and rising to some unknown infinity. It seemed as though the rain passing through it could only be black. And how pitiful, helpless, and tiny this fire probably appeared from somewhere out there! But to whom, to whom could it appear this way? Who could see it besides Sanya, sitting next to it? But wasn't this the reason for the dark, the teeming dark, so that the fire could be seen from distances that were hard to imagine? And Sanya could be seen next to it—alert and ready for anything, waiting with certainty and impatience for something from the sky or from one side: no, something had to happen . . . A night like this was not for nothing. Mityay was already asleep, and Uncle Volodya had been snoring softly for a long time, covered from head to toe with his rain poncho. Why was he, Sanya, the only one who didn't feel sleepy? But wasn't this why they had fallen asleep, why they had been lulled to sleep, so that he could remain alone, in private? Who had suggested to him—and he sensed this suggestion in himself more and more distinctly, as if he hadn't caught it right away and only afterward had deciphered the message from the sounds that remained—who had suggested that precisely now something must be revealed to him? He grew more and more impatient—and that meant the fulfillment of his wish was closer, as though something all-powerful and unseen had bent down and was trying to make out whether or not that was him. No, it wasn't trying to make him out. Sanya suddenly realized that he was mistaken and that they couldn't make him out, but that there was something trying to home in on all his feelings, on all the unspoken, secret life emanating from him, to determine whether he had what it took for some kind of fulfillment and whether he had enough of it.

The rain began to grow silent again. The smell of wild rosemary and of pitch from the Siberian pines reached out to him tangibly through the rising air. Mityay rolled from one side to the other and muttered something in his sleep. The rain grew even softer, and it hung above the fire against the dark background in fine hovering beads. Sanya froze, bracing himself, with a premonition that right now— And suddenly the darkness heaved a single sigh, far-reaching and sad, having achieved something, and then it sighed again. Twice the resonance of some tremendously deep, suppressed anguish breathed on Sanya, and he seemed to recoil involuntarily and then start toward this eternity-bound summons from who knows where—he recoiled and then instantly started toward it as if something had entered him and something else had left him, entering and leaving so that, having traded places, they could communicate afterward without interference. Sanya lost track of himself for several moments, not understanding and afraid to understand what had happened. Then a pleasant warmth spread throughout his body in a continuous, gentle wave, tension and suspense disappeared altogether, and he got up and crossed over to the shack with the sense of a certain special completeness and ultimate consummation.

He quickly fell asleep after bedding down in the empty space between Uncle Volodya and Mityay, but as he was drifting off he heard the rain start up again and begin to drip through the branches and down the bark. And suddenly he woke up. Leaning across him, Uncle Volodya was shaking Mityay and whispering in a frightened voice.

"Mityay! Mityay! Get up! There's somebody walking around."

"Who's walking around? Probably a bear," replied Mityay, annoyed. "Who else'd be walking around out here?!"

"Hear that? Listen!"

Continuing to grumble crossly, Mityay got up and began to revive the fire. A shower of sparks crackled and then the flame started burning evenly. When Mityay returned to his place, Sanya was already asleep. The talk of a bear troubled him little—either he hadn't been completely awake or else Mityay's calm voice had had a soothing effect.

Once again in his sleep Sanya heard Uncle Volodya shake Mityay, but his words sounded very far away and were hard to hear. And out there, far away on the other side, Mityay explained grumpily, "Go to sleep and don't be scared. He'll come and go. He's just curious to see who's here, so he comes out. He don't need us for nothing. If you lived here and some bears showed their ugly mugs on your territory without asking—main thing is, wouldn't you be curious? You'd wander around like that, too."

By now nothing could awaken Sanya anymore.

◢◤   Mityay shook him awake. The first thing Sanya saw when he opened his eyes was the sun—it was no accident that it had come out from behind the storm clouds, wanting to show it was alive and well and the one and only object in the whole huge, clear sky, which curved from the hill past the river and beyond to make it easier for the sun to roll out into the open expanse. Shadows still lay near the hill, pale and beginning to melt a little. A slight dampness even seemed to be accumulating from them, but the entire bottomland was radiant in the sunshine, and evaporating drops of water sparkled explosively on the bushes in bright, starry bursts. And it was impossible to imagine where everything—the thick, infinite darkness in the sky, the rain, the nighttime fears and anxieties—had gone so soon.

Mityay had managed not only to make tea but also to cook some grub, which they decided by friendly agreement to save for dinner—just before they headed back. The fire was burning out; a thin, delicate strand of feeble smoke rose straight up in the air, pulled by a steady draft. Even Sanya's footsteps were somehow unusually elevated and light, as if he had to expend effort not to walk but to stay on the ground and not fly away. The trees were lifting their branches and the grass was straightening up, stretching to its full height.

They drank their tea and sat for a while enjoying the sunshine and waiting for it to burn off the moisture. Mityay was cheerful and loud, and he teased Uncle Volodya about his nighttime vigilance. Uncle Volodya said nothing, as usual, but this time he was visibly secretive and resentful. Even Mityay finally sensed this and left him alone. Sanya, though, was delighted by everything in this bright morning—the way the last large drops of rain were falling off a Siberian pine and plopping onto the shack and the ground; the way the fire was dying down, tranquil and sad, evoking an incomprehensible sweetness in his chest; the way the forest floor gave off a sharp, intoxicating smell after the rain; the way the bottomland, where they were about to go, kept growing whiter and whiter; and even the way a nuthatch started screeching unexpectedly in a nasty voice above their heads, frightening them.

The sun took effect, and the air warmed up. It was time to get down to business. Sanya glanced into his pail, which still stood in his backpack under a pine tree. The berries in it had settled and shriveled noticeably, yet even so, he guessed that no more than two cans would fill the pail. No need to hurry. But he had only to begin picking—to finger the first berries, even riper now and differing from yesterday's by having absorbed a certain complex power from what had happened the previous night—he had only to become engrossed again in their bright, joyful profusion when his hands began working by themselves and it became impossible to hold them back. The bilberries brightened up quickly in the sunshine and became the color of the sky—if Sanya lifted his eyes for a second, the berries would vanish completely, blending in with the blue of the air so that he had to look closely, straining his eyes, to find them again—dangling, plump, and distinctly visible as before.

He didn't even notice that he'd filled one can, then another. The pail was overflowing, but he'd just recently come to like berry-picking. After covering the top of the pail with the clean cloth he'd brought so that the berries wouldn't spill during the return trip, he began to walk back down the path, taking his time. Not letting up, Mityay was moving in spurts beyond the formation of widely spaced birch trees to the right while Uncle Volodya was nowhere to be seen, apparently wanting to be left alone. Full of happiness, Sanya gave a delighted sigh—everything was great, everything so radiant and calm in himself and in this world whose fierce, boundless grace he'd never even suspected. He'd only had a feeling that it might exist somewhere for someone. But for him!

And there turned out to be a lot inside him that he hadn't known about or suspected—this inhumanly strong, immense feeling, for example, that was trying to encompass all the radiance and all the movement in the world, all its inexplicable beauty and passion, all its plenitude deceptively coming together in a single vision. Sanya was bursting with this feeling. He was ready to leap out of his skin and take off, giving in to it . . . He was ready for anything.

Suddenly he felt thirsty, and, walking down to the river, he took a drink, sipping water from his cupped hand.

The sun rose high. The day slid farther away and became deeper and more spacious. Everything around him was somehow especially vivid and fresh, as if Sanya had just arrived from a completely different world, crowded and gray, or at the very least as if he had just emerged from winter. The sunshine, its mighty, flashing current falling cleanly and evenly, made the air hum. Now, after last night, the ground kept drinking it in, unable to satisfy its thirst or get its fill of sunshine, and this is how it would be until the next night, when the sky would again demand its share from the ground. Each sound, each tremble of a leaf seemed no accident but rather signified more than simply a sound or a tremble, more than the usual place each might occupy in the day, just as the day itself could not be merely the passing of time. No, this was a Royal Highness of a day, the kind that occurs only once a year or even once every several years, reaching the utmost limit of its significance, radiance, and grandeur. Somewhere on such a day—on the earth or in the heavens—something special happens, and from then on a different kind of reckoning begins. But where, what, how? No, such a day is too great, too unfettered by anything, too all-glorious and divine to yield to any rational deduction from itself. You can only feel it, sense it, hearken to it—and that's all. The inexplicability of the feelings it arouses merely confirms its own immense inexplicability.

Sanya got down to business again and went back to berry-picking. He still had plenty of energy, but he spent a long time filling the last can, upset and dissatisfied with himself, confused and vexed first by his clumsiness and then by his negligence, which had prevented him from understanding something important, something that had been right beside him and was ready to help him. "Something," "somehow," "somewhere," "sometime"—how dim and vague it all was, how smeared and smudged with hazy notions and feelings, and wasn't it actually the same for everybody? But he'd been closer to this "something" and "somehow" than he'd ever been before. He'd felt an inner warmth and excitement from their breathing and had shuddered at their touch. He'd opened himself in readiness and frozen in their promising presence.

And what did he lack in order to see and to understand? What being did he lack, what substance capable of detaching itself in order to receive and to draw inside, arising from what depths of what primordial origin? Or had they only been teasing him, playing hide and seek with him, once they noticed his trustfulness and curiosity? And who could tell? If he'd turned out to be fit to divine the enigmatic vagueness he longed for and to take it into himself, to discover it and to give it a name—wouldn't this have been roughly the same as a talking parrot among humans?

Seeing Uncle Volodya heading for the shack, Sanya followed him, wanting to empty his can into Uncle Volodya's wooden basket, which was far from full. But Uncle Volodya, showing unexpected crudeness and sharpness, wouldn't let him. Quite astonished, Sanya stepped back and set his can on the ground next to his backpack. There was nothing more to do. He sat down on a rock by the lifeless fire and, growing thoughtful and staring off into space, he again became absorbed in the warmth and radiance of the day, which lay completely wide open, standing still above him in all its grace and power, in its exposed fathomlessness and tenderness—without a doubt first and foremost among many, many days. He sat there and thought in feeble, sleepy, bewitched, and disjointed contemplation: "What more could I possibly need? Everything's great! A day like this and me existing at the same time . . . at the same time and place . . ."

And on the way back, when they'd climbed to the top of the pass with their heavy loads, to that rocky "throne" of the taiga from which waves of forest flowed off into the distance, when Sanya, standing on the edge of the precipice, took a last parting look around at this primeval expanse, majestic in its beauty and peacefulness, radiant in the sunlight and knowing no bounds, becoming blue right below him, his heart began to pound loudly and joltingly with an unbearably sweet pain and delight. Let anything, anything happen—he had seen this!

They came out at Baikal in soft late twilight, crossed the railroad tracks, and threw down their loads in the wooded strip, high and round like an island, between the railroad and the shore. The soft twilight was a sure sign that this day, with its pure, ringing power, would not be repeated tomorrow or the next day or for a long, long time. We know what earthly holidays are like. This had been a holiday of the heavens, which they could not celebrate only within the confines of their own expanses. This had been the lavish frontier between the two borders. And now it was over, and now it had passed. The daylight burned out, and the sky darkened and died away, giving off no depth. Pale, dull stars popped out stupidly over Baikal and then slipped out of sight, as if they'd been pulled down. The forest loomed dark, standing out sharply and distinctly without yet forming a solid wall, displaying varying heights and depths, and the wind rustled through the treetops in long, sad sighs. The distant shores on the other side of Baikal were sharply outlined in a rich blue. The water in the sea, muffled by the tedious sky, just barely glimmered with a quivering luminescence, as if its bent rays were trying to penetrate the water from the bottom up.

About forty minutes remained before the train was due. Stretched out on the grass at the edge of the steep bank, they didn't move. They had no energy. Their legs ached, their backs ached—this clearly applied to all three. First they'd dawdled at the berry patch because of Uncle Volodya, who wanted to finish filling his basket. And then they'd dawdled along the way, tempted to gather pine cones after Mityay had found a wooden mallet stashed away and had demonstrated how to bang it on the trunk of a Siberian pine to knock the cones down. So they came out of the taiga with two different kinds of crops. They didn't come walking out, but, having lingered longer than they should have, they ran the last kilometers at full speed in order to make it out while there was still some light. The Devil himself could break a leg on that path in the dark. Sanya's back burned. The hard bottom edge of the pail, bouncing with every step, had chafed him and left a bloody welt, and only now did he fully appreciate the true value of a wooden basket. By the end of the trip Uncle Volodya was gasping for breath. Even now he was breathing in sobs, trying to swear and choking on the words. Mityay was silent. Used to forced marches of a different kind, he was tired but not exhausted, and he lay resting, but not like Sanya and Uncle Volodya, who were flat on their backs, seeing and hearing little around them.

After catching his breath, Mityay got up, found a way down to Baikal to the right of the small woods, stripped to the waist by the water, and began splashing loudly, slapping his body several times and crying out. Sanya thought he ought to wash up, too, but he couldn't lift his legs. Mityay, invigorated and cheerful, came back with a pot of water and, undoing the bag with the leftover food, which was strapped to his wooden basket, he said, "Be nice to make some tea, but we don't have time."

Sanya reached for his backpack, took out some bread and some crushed boiled eggs, and somehow managed to pull a mug out of his pocket. What he wanted was a drink of water. Now, after they'd rested a bit and the harsh, bitter taste had left their throats, a deep, demanding thirst made itself known. He drank his mug of water in a single gulp and wanted another one. Uncle Volodya reached for the pot, too, and started drinking right out of it, his fat, creased throat working like bellows. Mityay waited until Uncle Volodya tore himself away, then dumped out what was left and held the pot out to him.

"Now it's your turn."

"The boy here'll go," Uncle Volodya wheezed, passing the pot to Sanya.

Sanya went down to the shore, made himself wash up, wiped his face on his shirt sleeve, and, freezing in place, listened. Everything around him was secretly living its own separate life without coming together as one whole. The weak, intermittent wind kept rustling in the tops of the trees; the water lapped feebly with a smacking sound; the profusion of colorful rocks on the shore caught the eye, giving off warmth; and round black beetles sailed through the air over the water with the sharp noise of a motor. From up above came the unintelligible and unfriendly voices of Uncle Volodya and Mityay. When Sanya returned, they fell silent. He poured some water into his mug again and began peeling an egg. He wasn't hungry the way he'd been before. He was still thirsty, but to earn the right to water, he made himself swallow the soft, warm, unappetizing egg.

The backpack had slipped down around the pail, which, with the cloth on top, stood out in the dark with a sharp whiteness that hurt the eye. Sanya wasn't too lazy to cover up the pail.

"So what do you plan to do with these berries?" Uncle Volodya asked all of a sudden, speaking softly but somehow meaningfully, with emphasis.

"I don't know." Sanya shrugged his shoulders. He decided that Uncle Volodya was asking because he wasn't sure that he, Sanya, would know how to prepare the berries without an adult around. "I'll probably make preserves out of half of them . . . and I'll crush up the other half."

"You can't make preserves out of them," said Uncle Volodya firmly and decisively. And he added even more decisively, "And you can't eat them."

"Why not?"

"What kind of fool puts berries in a galvanized pail? And even lets them sit overnight! And with this kind of berry!"

Sanya didn't understand a thing. What was so special about these berries? What did sitting overnight have to do with anything? What did "galvanized" mean? Was Uncle Volodya kidding or what?

Mityay didn't get up right away, and when he did it was with extra thoughtfulness and slowness. He bent over Sanya's backpack and pulled the pail out from under the cloth. And he saw for himself—the pail really was galvanized.

"You viper!" he started in, turned toward Uncle Volodya. "Why'd you do this, huh? Why'd you do it?" He made a move toward Uncle Volodya, who jumped up. "'Cause you saw, you knew—main thing is, you saw it out there! And you let the boy pick 'em, let him carry 'em out—well, aren't you a real viper, huh?! I'll show you!"

"Don't touch me!" Uncle Volodya warned, jumping back. "And didn't you see?" he yelled. "Didn't you see it out there? Didn't you know? How come you're playing innocent? It was in plain sight, standing there right out in the open! What are you, a little kid?!"

Mityay, taken aback, stopped.

"Yeah, I saw! I saw!" he yelled. "I knew! But the main thing is, it went right out of my head. I looked and I didn't see. But you, you viper, you waited around. I forgot, I clean forgot!"

"You won't forget again. Had to teach both of you a lesson. And the boy'll remember this all his life."

Mityay began flailing around, as if looking for something at his feet, and his eyes fell on the pail of uncovered berries. Beside himself, he snatched the pail out of the backpack and flung the berries down the embankment with a sharp, quick motion. They rustled through the grass as they rolled away and then lay still.

"Mityay, what're you doing?!" Sanya, who had been sitting down till then and still didn't understand a thing, jumped to his feet. "How come, Mityay?! How come?!"

"You can't keep 'em, Sanya," Mityay muttered hurriedly in a frightened voice, startled by the decisiveness with which he'd taken care of the berries. "You can't keep 'em. Main thing is, they gave off juice during the night . . . You'll poison yourself and everybody else . . . You can't ever put 'em in a galvanized pail. Well, I'm an idiot, I'm a real idiot. From here to there. To think of picking berries with such an idiot . . ."

He sat down and cooled off. Sanya picked up the pail and put it into the backpack, then neatly fastened all the buckles, watching himself with a strange attentiveness, as he would watch somebody he didn't know.

"Better keep an eye out now, Uncle Volodya, old pal," said Mityay with unexpected calmness. "To take such filth into the taiga . . . Isn't the town big enough for you?!"

"You'll do time," replied Uncle Volodya just as calmly. "You did time once and you'll do time again."

"I'm not gonna dirty my hands with you," Mityay declared confidently, as if the matter were closed. "The first tree trunk will fall on you all by itself, the first rock'll come loose and fall on you. You'll see. They don't like these kinds of tricks. Oh, no, they sure don't!"

They could now hear the clackety-clack of the train.

That night Sanya dreamed of voices. Nothing happened, but in the darkness and emptiness various voices reverberating in various tones sounded inside him. And all of them came from him and were part of his agitated thoughts and flesh. All of them repeated something that he might have said in anger, in alarm, or in dismay. He was also learning what he might say after many, many years. And only one voice uttered things—crude, dirty words spoken in a familiar, confident tone—that weren't in him and never could be.

He woke up in terror: What was this? Who was it? From where inside him had this arisen?

1981

WHAT SHOULD I TELL

THE CROW?

As I was leaving early in the morning, I promised myself that I would return that evening without fail. My work was finally coming along, and I was afraid to interrupt it, afraid that even after two or three days away from it I would lose everything I'd pulled together with such difficulty as I was getting into the right frame of mind for work—by reading and reflection, through long and agonizing attempts to find the voice I needed, one that wouldn't stumble over every phrase but, like a specially magnetized string, would attract to itself the words required for a full and precise resonance. I couldn't boast of "a full and precise resonance," but some things were turning out right; I sensed it, and for that reason I tore myself away from my writing table this time without the enthusiasm I usually felt on those occasions when I had to go into the city.

A trip to the city takes three hours from door to door and just as many back. So that I wouldn't change my mind or be detained there, God forbid, I went straight to the bus depot when I got to the city and bought a ticket for the last bus that evening. Practically the whole day lay ahead of me, during which I could both attend to business and spend some time, as much as possible, at home.

And everything went fine, everything proceeded according to plan until the moment when, having finished rushing around but still not slackening the pace I'd set, I stopped by the nursery school at the end of the day to pick up my daughter. My daughter was overjoyed to see me. She was coming down the stairs, and when she caught sight of me she gave a start and stood stock-still, her little hand gripping the railing, but then, that was my daughter: she didn't race toward me or hurry at all but, quickly regaining control of herself, came up to me with intentional deliberateness and restraint and reluctantly let herself be hugged. Her willfulness was showing, but I saw right through that inborn if still not hardened willfulness; I saw what an effort it took her to restrain herself from throwing her arms around my neck.

"So you've come?" she asked like a grown-up, and began hurriedly putting on her coat, glancing at me frequently.

We were too close to home to make a real walk out of it, so we went past our apartment building to the river embankment. The weather was warm and quite summerlike for the end of September, and it had been this way for some time now without any visible change, rising each new day with the regularity of what seemed like an unseasonable gift of grace. It was even pleasant just to be out on the streets, and all the more so here, on the embankment along the river, with the uneasy and pacifying power of the water's eternal movement, the unhurried and unheard footsteps of sober, cordial people, the soft voices, and the luminosity of the waning day, low in the slanting sunlight but full and warm and thus disposing one to harmony. This was the sort of magical hour that occurred with great infrequency, when it seemed that throughout the whole throng of strolling people, their souls, disliking solitude and having gathered here at an appointed time, led each person and spoke for each one.

We walked for about an hour, and, contrary to habit, my daughter didn't take her little hand out of my hand but pulled it away only to point something out or to gesture when words alone would not suffice, and then she'd slip it back into mine. I couldn't help but appreciate this: it meant she had truly missed me. Last spring, when she turned five, she'd somehow changed a great deal all at once—and not for the better, in our view, because she revealed a stubbornness that had gone unnoticed until then. Apparently considering herself sufficiently grown-up and independent, our daughter didn't want to be led by the hand like all other children. We'd have to struggle with her even in the middle of a raging intersection. Our daughter was afraid of cars, but, jerking away her little shoulder, which we'd grab out of desperation, she would still try to walk at her own pace. Blaming each other, my wife and I argued over which of us could have passed on to our little girl what seemed to us such fierce stubbornness, forgetting that neither of us, of course, could have done it alone.

And now all of a sudden such patience, obedience, and tenderness . . . My daughter was chattering away, finding plenty to tell me as she talked about nursery school and questioned me about our crow. At Lake Baikal we had our own crow. We had our own little house there, and our own hill, a rocky cliff rising almost straight up from the house. Our own little spring spurted out of the cliff, ran through our yard alone in a burbling stream, then disappeared back underground beneath the wooden planks near the gate, and never again appeared for anyone anywhere. In our yard stood our own larch trees, poplars, and birches and our own large bird-cherry bush. Sparrows and titmice would congregate in this bush from all over the neighborhood, then rise up and head for our water, our spring (the wagtails would fly in a long arc from the fence), which they seemed to choose because it matched their size, height, and taste; on hot days they'd splash around in it without fear, bearing in mind that after their swim they could feed on bread crumbs under the mighty larch growing in the middle of the yard. The birds would gather in great numbers, and even our Tishka, the kitten I'd picked up on the railroad tracks, became resigned to them, but we couldn't say that they were our birds. They'd fly in, and, after eating and drinking, they'd fly off somewhere again. But the crow was truly ours. The day my daughter arrived at the beginning of the summer, she spotted the shaggy cap of its nest high up in the larch. I'd been living there for a month by then and hadn't noticed it. A crow kept flying about, cawing as crows do—so what? It never once occurred to me that this was our crow simply because here, in our midst, was its nest and because in this nest it was raising its young.

Our crow, naturally, had to be special, unlike all other crows, and so it became. We learned to understand each other very quickly, and it would tell me everything it saw and heard while flying over regions far and near, and then I would relate its stories at length to my daughter. My daughter believed them. Maybe she didn't actually believe them; like many others, I'm inclined to think that we aren't the ones who play with children, amusing them any way we can, but that they, as purer and more sensible beings, are the ones who play with us to deaden the pain of our existence. Maybe she didn't actually believe them, but she listened with such attention, she waited with such impatience for me to continue when I was interrupted, and her eyes shone so, betraying a complete uncloudedness of soul, that these stories began to give me pleasure, too. I began to notice an excitement in myself that I picked up from my daughter and that in some amazing way made us equals, as if bringing us together on the same level, despite our age difference. I made things up, knowing that I was making them up, and my daughter believed them, not paying any attention to the fact that I made them up. Yet, in what seemed like a game, there prevailed between us a rare harmony and understanding that did not arise from the rules of any game here, but seemed conveyed from someplace out there where they alone exist. Conveyed, perhaps, by that crow. I don't know, I can't explain why, but for a long time I've lived with the certainty that if a link between this world and the next actually exists, then only crows can fly from one to the other, and I've been watching them for quite some time with secret curiosity and fear, trying and yet afraid to comprehend why only crows can do this.

Our crow, though, was completely earthly and ordinary, having none of these dealings with the other world, good-natured and talkative, with inklings of what we call clairvoyance.

I had stopped at home that morning and learned a thing or two about my daughter's recent activities, if you can call them activities, and now I related them to her as if I had heard them from the crow.

"It flew to the city again the day before yesterday and saw that you and Marina had a fight. Naturally, it was very surprised. You were always such good friends, wild horses couldn't drag you apart. But then all of a sudden you behaved like the worst barbarians on account of a stupid little thing—"

"We-e-ll, but what if she stuck her tongue out at me?" My daughter lashed out immediately. "Do you think it's very nice when people stick their tongues out at you, huh? Is that very nice, huh?"

"It's disgraceful. Of course it isn't very nice. Only why did you stick your tongue out at her, then? It's not very nice for her either."

"Did the crow see me stick my tongue out or something?"

"Sure it saw you. It sees everything."

"But that's not true. Nobody could've seen me. The crow couldn't have either."

"Maybe it didn't actually see you, but it guessed right. It knows you inside out, so it didn't have a hard time guessing."

My daughter took offense at being known "inside out," but, uncertain about whom to blame for this, me or the crow, she fell silent, further dismayed because something extremely secret had somehow been found out. A bit later she admitted that she had stuck her tongue out at Marina from the doorway when Marina had already left. My daughter wasn't capable of concealing anything yet, or, rather, she didn't copy us and conceal every trifle—those little things we could disclose and thus make life easier—but, as they say, she kept her own counsel.

Meanwhile, the time was approaching for me to get ready to leave, and I told my daughter it was time to go home.

"No, let's walk some more." She wouldn't give her consent.

"It's time," I repeated. "I have to go back today."

Her little hand trembled in mine. My daughter didn't so much speak as sing out.

"Don't leave today." And, as if that settled it once and for all, she added, "There."

And now it was my turn to tremble: this wasn't simply a request, the kind children make at every turn—no, it was a plea uttered with dignity and restraint but with her whole being, which cautiously staked out its legitimate claim over me, not knowing and not caring to know the generally accepted rules of life. But as for me, I was already more than a little corrupted and oppressed by these rules, and when the rules of others, established for everyone, fell short, I would make up my own, just as I did now. Giving a sigh, I recalled the promise I'd made to myself that morning and stood my ground.

"I have to, you understand. I can't stay."

My daughter obediently let herself be turned toward home and escorted across the street, and then she broke free and ran on ahead. She didn't even wait for me at the entrance to our building, as she always did in such situations; when I got up to the apartment she was already occupied with something in her corner. I began packing my knapsack, continually going over to my daughter and trying to start up a conversation with her; she'd become reticent and her replies were strained. It was all over—she was no longer with me, she'd withdrawn into herself, and the more I'd try to get close to her, the further she'd retreat. I knew this all too well. My wife, guessing what had happened, made the most sensible suggestion under the circumstances.

"You can catch the first bus in the morning. And be there by nine o'clock."

"No, I can't." I became furious because this really did make sense.

I still had some hope of getting a proper send-off. When it comes to parting, this is the way it's done in our family: no matter what might have happened, be kind enough to put all bad feelings, just and unjust, behind you and say good-bye with an unburdened heart, even on the most ordinary and nonthreatening occasions. I finished packing and called my daughter over.

"Good-bye. What should I tell the crow?"

"Nothing. Good-bye," she said with a certain glibness and indifference in a voice that sounded too grown-up for her, and she looked away.

The streetcar came immediately, as if on purpose, and I arrived at the depot twenty minutes ahead of the bus. I could have spent those twenty minutes walking with my daughter, you see; that probably would have been sufficient for her not to notice my haste and nothing would have come between us.

Then, as if someone wanted to teach me a lesson, I ran into a string of bad luck. The bus pulled in late—it didn't simply pull in, but lunged into view, screeching and grinding around the corner as if to say: Look how I've rushed. It was all ratty-looking and scratched up, with half the front door torn off. We got on and then sat there after mounting this skittish bus, suspiciously quiet beneath us as though it were about to buck again, while the driver, looking in at the dispatcher's office, vanished inside and didn't reappear. We sat there for ten minutes, then fifteen, inhaling the smell of the sacks of potatoes piled on the back seat; we were a silent lot, feeling sluggish at the end of the day, and no one let out a murmur of complaint. We sat mutely, content simply to be sitting in our places. How little, I've noticed on more than one occasion, our people need: scare them by saying there won't be a bus until morning and a furious outcry will erupt, until everyone is in a complete stupor, but rush the same bus in, load it up, and let it stand there until morning—and they'll remain satisfied and believe that they've gotten their way. Here the principle of one's rightful place is apparently at work: your place can be occupied by no one else and given to no one else but you, and whether this place takes you anywhere or not isn't really that important.

My common sense did indeed tell me to get up from this place that wasn't taking me anywhere and go back home. My daughter would have been overjoyed! She would never have let on, of course, that she was overjoyed, and, true to form, she wouldn't have come up to me right away, but then she would have latched on to me and not left my side until bedtime. And I would have been forgiven, and so would the crow. And how fine and warm the evening would have turned out, one to recall over and over again later on, during my days of solitude, to warm myself beside, stirring up and then soothing my soul, to make me feel tormented with joy by its full and happy conclusion. Our days don't coincide in time with the days allotted us for our activities; time usually runs out before we manage to finish, leaving the ends of the things we've begun and abandoned sticking out in an absurd way. It is not the sin of conception that hangs over our children like a great weight from their very first hours but the sin of what their fathers left undone. This day could have become uncommonly complete, consummated in all respects, and, like a seed, it could have been the source of other days just like it. When I speak of activities, of their completeness or incompleteness in terms of days, I don't mean all activities but only those in harmony with the soul, which gives us a special assignment, apart from ordinary work, and holds each of us accountable.

And I was prepared to stand up and get off the bus, fully prepared, but something held me back. The place where I'd been sitting such a long time held me back. It was conveniently located, a window seat on the right-hand side where oncoming vehicles wouldn't disturb me. And then the bus driver finally came running up almost at a sprint, demonstrating again that he was in a hurry. He quickly counted us once more, checked the itinerary, and stepped on the gas. I became resigned, and I even rejoiced that the chance to decide whether to go or not to go had been taken away from me. We took off.

We took off, all right, but we didn't get very far. Nothing else could possibly have been expected from our bus and from our driver. The driver, a small, fidgety, crafty little guy, resembled a sparrow—the same hopping and bobbing, the same jerkiness and lopsidedness in his movements, but with a craftiness that could be seen not only in his face, where it shone through openly, but also in his whole physique. And when he sat with his back to us it was clear even from behind that this guy would survive in any situation. I began to wonder why he'd stayed so long in the dispatcher's office. Perhaps this wasn't his route, and this wasn't the bus that was supposed to make this run, but because there was something in it for him, he'd talked somebody into switching and then talked the dispatcher into it. And there we sat again, a mere two blocks out of the dispatcher's sight, while our driver hopped around like a sparrow in the middle of the street with a pail in his hand, begging enough gasoline to make it to the gas pumps. That meant another stop; I began to worry in earnest about whether the ferry would wait for us as it normally did. We were already terribly late. It would be the last straw if, after enduring all this for the sake of being able to work in the morning, I had to spend the night in full view of our cabin on the other shore of Lake Baikal, and not simply spend the night, but be in an agony of suspense the whole time waiting for the morning ferry and thus spoil the entire coming day. And I still could have gotten off here, but I didn't get off here either. "Spitefulness, boy, was born before you were," my grandmother often used to say in such situations. In this case, though, it wasn't just spitefulness, but some other trait I'd acquired from earlier spasmodic attempts at building my character that still echoed in me from time to time. My character hadn't grown any firmer, of course, but the direction in which it had been bent sometimes manifested itself in the most unexpected fashion and made its own demands.

We just barely made it to the gas pumps at last, and from there we continued on our way. I was afraid to look at my watch; let come what may. It grew dark right outside of town; the woods, which hadn't lost a leaf yet, fell sweepingly away from where I was sitting like a solid black curtain. There turned out to be no lighting inside the bus—it would have been strange if there had been—but at least the headlights worked well: we rode in darkness and everyone dozed. The bus, meanwhile, was making a dash for it, as if it were hurrying home itself; glancing out the window in my semislumber, I saw the roadbed quickly slipping back and kilometer markers flashing by. The wind began to blow through the half-missing door, and the closer we got to Baikal the more we could feel the bus clank and sputter in infernal bursts under the driver's feet whenever he shifted gears; beyond that we noticed little and differed little from the sacks of potatoes piled up in back.

Good luck: this is not when you actually have good luck, but when, compared with bad luck, things change for the better. In this case it was impossible to determine the degree of divergence. I was so overjoyed when I saw the lights of the ferry as we approached that I didn't pay attention to the fact that it wasn't the *Babushkin*, the ship that functioned as a ferry from April through January and was equipped to handle passengers as well as cargo, but a small motorboat, barely visible at the base of the pier. Still going full speed, the driver hit the brakes sharply, making us feel that we were living people after all, and was the first to hurriedly jump out; he bent down over the boat, shouting something and waving his arms until they understood what he wanted, and then rushed back to hurry us along.

A rumbling sound was coming from Baikal, and quite a powerful one. The air, however, was completely still, even dead—that meant that Baikal had been stirred up somewhere to the north and that this billow had been driven for dozens upon dozens of kilometers. But even here it was moving with such force, delineating fiery streaks of foam time after time under the gentle new moon, and moving with such a roar that the night grew windy and chilly from the feeling of cold that rose up inside you. The poor little boat kept bobbing up and down next to the pier as if it were trying to leap on top of it. We were almost an hour late, and the boat's crew, four or five young guys (it was impossible to get an exact count), hadn't wasted any time: they were all at least three sheets to the wind. The driver nimbly carried the sacks of potatoes off the bus and handed them down, and the crew stumbled about and shouted in confusion as they took them, and you got the feeling that they were tumbling down right along with the sacks. The other passengers dispersed, and only we, the three unfortunate figures who faced crossing this Baikal in this boat with this crew, huddled together, not knowing what to do. The crashing water and the still air: it gave you sort of an eerie feeling—as if out there, beyond the end of the pier, was the beginning of another world. From out there, from the nether regions, the guys yelled at us, and after setting our sights and taking aim for a long time, in the last throes of gloomy foreboding, we awkwardly began to jump into the boat. I jumped first. From down below I could make out the driver's voice over the crashing water, cheerfully ordering the crew not to pull any tricks and to wait while he parked the bus, and I calmed down. We wouldn't perish with that guy along.

When I later recalled the return trip from beginning to end, and the boat ride in particular, I thought of it not as something awful or unpleasant but as something unavoidable that had occurred under all these conditions and in exactly this sequence only because of me, to teach me some kind of lesson. What lesson? I didn't know and perhaps I won't know anytime soon, and it's not really the answer that's important here but the feeling that I was to blame. These weren't accidents of chance. It seemed to me that even the people who were traveling with me suffered and faced risks only on my account. The last half hour, when we were crossing from one shore to the other, was, of course, filled with risk— there's no denying it! This half hour barely left a trace in my memory or my feelings. As our little boat alternately plunged into the water and leapt into the air, the guys in the deckhouse, and the bus driver along with them, let out one and the same cry of delight while I, wet and chilled to the bone, sat on a sack of potatoes that kept sliding around underneath me and apathetically waited to see how it would all end. I remember that we couldn't get close to the pier for quite a while, and that by the time we did I'd already regained my senses; I remember that when we finally caught hold and began climbing up onto dry land, one of the four or five brave lads rushed after us to collect forty kopecks from each of us for the ride. A crowd of people were waiting for our bus driver, and they greeted him onshore with a lot of noise and affectionate profanity, and then they immediately led him off somewhere.

The day had exhausted me so that, once I got to my cabin, I didn't bother to make any tea or even to unpack my knapsack but just collapsed into bed. It was already past midnight. At the last moment, when I was just on the verge of falling asleep, it suddenly struck me: Why, for what possible reason, was he bringing potatoes from the city out here, to the country, when everybody else, on the contrary, takes them from here to the city, the way they should?

I don't know if this is true of anyone else, but I lack a sense of complete and indivisible integration with myself. I don't have the feeling, as one is supposed to, that everything inside me matches up from beginning to end, that everything down to the smallest detail merges in a single whole so that nothing comes loose anywhere and nothing sticks out. Something in me is constantly coming loose and sticking out: either my head will start to ache, and not with a simple pain that you can get rid of with pills or fresh air, but seemingly because it is suffering from having been acquired by the wrong person; or I'll catch myself with a thought or feeling that never should have been in me in the first place; or I'll get up in the morning healthy and well rested without the slightest desire to go on living; or some other thing. Such things don't happen to a normal person, of course; they are characteristic of people who are either accidental or substitutes. Concerning "substitute" people, I've given the matter particular thought. Let's assume that someone should have been born, but for some reason (not for us to know) he lost his turn to be born, and then another person was quickly summoned from the next row to take his place.

And so that person was born, differing in no way from the rest, and grew to adulthood; it never occurs to anyone in this huge populace that something about him isn't quite right, and only he suffers—the further along he gets, the more he suffers—from his involuntary guilt and from his not matching that place in the world that had been set aside for someone else.

Similar ideas, no matter how foolish they might seem, have crossed my mind more than once in moments of discord with myself.

And this leads to my other abnormality: I'll never get used to myself. Having lived a good number of years, I discover with continuing amazement when I wake up every morning that I am really me and that I exist in reality rather than in someone else's recollections and imaginings (of things that might have come before or after me) that happen to have reached me. This occurs not just in the mornings. I have only to fall into deep thought or, on the contrary, to drift off in a pleasant absence of thought when suddenly I lose myself, as if I'm flying on ahead to some border region from which I have no desire to return. This not being inside myself, this straying from home, happens quite often; I involuntarily begin to keep track of myself, to be on guard so I'll stay in place, inside myself, but the whole tragedy lies in my not knowing whose side I should take, which one of them contains the genuine "me"—the one that waits for itself with patience and hope or the one that makes futile attempts to run away from itself? Does it run away to find something different, yet kindred and all its own, someone with whom it would make a complete and successful match? Or is it waiting to resign itself to its own likeness and to the impossibility of remedying anything even one iota? For "I" must be in one of them, the primordial, fundamental "I," so to speak, the one to whom something could have been added later rather than the one who would simply serve as an addition to someone else's incompleteness.

The morning after my trip to the city I got up late. I hadn't closed the shutters on the windows the night before, and the sunshine tortured me even as I slept. I lay there half asleep under its onslaught, tormented by wanting to wake up and not being able to. Everyone is well acquainted with this helpless state: you seem right on the verge of forcing your way through your oppressive body toward a means of escape where you can regain consciousness—but no, at the last minute some force hurls you back. Each time I'm in this situation I experience terror at the vast expanse that must be overcome in order to approach the line between wakefulness and sleep. And that's not all—once you've reached it, you have to calculate your final move in such a way that the oncoming gust won't pull you under again. There, in this numb state of consciousness that you can't control, everything has different dimensions: it's as though it might take a whole lifetime to wake up.

Somehow I managed to open my eyes—I opened my eyes and instantly felt my indisposition as though I could see it in front of me. A stifling emptiness in both my chest and my head weighed me down, something I knew all too well to just brush aside, for it came from the type of disharmony with myself that I've been trying to explain. But, oddly enough, I wasn't the least bit surprised at my condition, as if I should have known about it in advance but for some reason had forgotten.

The sunshine that had seemed strong and bright to me in my sleep lay on the floor of the room like a faded, washed-out spot; the window frames quivered in it like a barely noticeable, deeply sunken shadow.

My cabin was unpretentious: a small kitchen, a good third of which was taken up by the stove, and a small front room or parlor with corner windows on two sides, both with a view of Baikal across the road. The third wall, the one near the cliff, had no doors or windows and always gave off a coolness and a faintly discernible smell of rotting wood. Right now this smell was coming through more strongly than usual—a sure sign that the weather was taking a turn for the worse. And sure enough, as I was getting dressed, the spot of sunshine on the floor vanished altogether; perhaps I hadn't dreamed that the sun was bright after all, for it may well have been when it came up, but since then the sky had clouded over. It was still; after my agonized sleep I didn't realize right away that the stillness was absolute, which almost never happens in this bustling place where my cabin is located, next to the railroad tracks and the pier. I listened again: stillness—like on a day of celebration for old folks, if there were such a thing—and this put me on guard, and I hurried outside.

No, everything remained in place—the railroad cars that had stood on the siding not far from the house since spring, a long double line of them going nowhere, and the big heap of dry cargo on the lakeshore across the way with the motionless arm of a gantry crane poised above it, and an old woman sitting on a log by the road with shopping bags at her feet, observing me in silent reproach, not comprehending how it was possible to get up so late . . . Baikal was growing calm. Here and there on its surface a small wave would still tremble and break, then glide away before reaching the shore. The air dazzled the eye with the hazy brilliance of the ruined sunshine; the sun itself found it impossible to show through in any one place, and it seemed to spread across the whole smoky-white, drooping sky and to shine from all directions. The morning coolness had passed by then, but the day hadn't warmed up yet; it looked as if it never intended to warm up, being occupied with some other more important change, so it was neither cool nor warm, neither sunny nor cloudy, but somehow in between the one and the other, somehow oppressive and nondescript.

And once again I felt such restlessness and lucklessness inside myself that I almost went back to bed without doing a thing. Sleep, whose grip I hadn't known how to break, by now represented a longed-for liberation, but I knew that I wouldn't fall asleep and that I might get even more worked up in the attempt.

I sometimes managed to get the better of myself in these situations . . . I couldn't recall how this came about—by itself or with the help of my conscious efforts—but now, too, something had to be done. With exaggerated vigor I began lighting a fire in the stove and making tea, unpacking my knapsack in the meantime and carrying packages and canned goods out to the pantry. I love these moments just before my morning tea. The fire flares up, the teakettle starts to snuffle, and the tea concentrate, giving off a most agreeable aroma, languishes in the weak heat at the edge of the stove as it waits for the boiling water, while a breath of fresh air drifts in through the open door and goes back out again, as if it had gotten burned on the stove. In these moments I love to be alone and, keeping pace with the flaring fire, to savor my own ripening thirst for tea, my long-suffering and pleasant readiness for the first sip. And now the tea is brewed, now it's poured, the mug is giving off a fragrant, intoxicating steam, a violet haze hovers low over the hot, dark brown surface in a concealing, mysteriously stirring film . . . Now, at last, the first sip! . . . You can't help but compare it to the solemn stroke of a bell sounding forth in your lonely world, proclaiming the full advent of the new day, and, interrupted by nothing, continuing to ring until it reaches multiple reverberations, like a resonating echo. And the second sip, and the third—these are stentorian signals of the general readiness of the powers that were exhausted during the night. Then begins the nearly hour-long, work-related tea drinking, which gradually sneaks up on you and adapts itself to the business at hand. To start with, there's a lordly, superficial sidelong glance: What's this that you came up with yesterday? Will it do or not? Does it hit the mark or does it miss? You seem to have no interest whatsoever in yesterday's work; you simply happened to remember that you'd been doing something . . . This is attention focused in the right direction but still wandering. You drink your tea unhurriedly, with each sip pondering more and more deeply some vague and aimless idea that is lazily groping around in a complete fog for something unknown. And suddenly, heaven knows why, the first reciprocal idea will flash in this fog like an image, dim and flickering, which later will have to be discarded. But once it flashes it will indicate where to continue looking. Now you're getting close, you move from one table to the other, grabbing your mug of tea, and for the sake of routine you still look over your old work while its continuation impatiently begins to make itself heard inside you.

This time nothing of the kind happened to me. Even moving around required effort. I took pleasure in drinking my tea, as always, but it didn't help me in the least and didn't cheer me up; the causeless, cold weight had no intention of retreating. Out of stubbornness I settled down at the table with my papers anyway, but with the same effect as a blind person looking through binoculars: not a single ray up ahead and a solid gray wall all around. I sat there for half an hour like a perfect statue with a brick for a head, and then, thoroughly detesting myself, I got up.

Something seemed to squeak with malicious joy behind my back when I walked away from the table . . .

◢   Fretting, I wandered around stupidly and aimlessly—first I'd go outdoors and listen carefully and peer at something without knowing myself what it was, then I'd go back into the cottage again and stand next to the burning stove, torturing myself until I felt faint from the heat, and then I'd go back outside. I remember that I kept trying to figure out how such a complete and ancient stillness had built up and where it had come from, although by now the morning's earlier stillness was no more—by now something banged from time to time over on the dry cargo, a strong voice accustomed to commanding was giving orders through a megaphone somewhere on the water, and a motorcycle had roared past two or three times. But the air was growing softer and deader, as if the day were taking cover, trying to wrap itself up more tightly and guard against an alien spaciousness, and sounds died away and got stuck in the dense air, reaching the ear faintly and despondently.

After suffering like this for an hour or so and sensing that I wouldn't find any relief, I locked up the cottage and decided to go wherever my feet would take me. They took me through the gate and down the dry, well-beaten path along the railroad tracks, and in no time I had gone far beyond the town, to those sonorous and joyful spots along the shores of Baikal that remained sonorous, joyful, and fully distinguishable in any weather—in summer and winter, in sunshine and rain. But even here I could now feel almost tangibly how the day was sinking lower and lower and how much more tightly it was drawing itself in from the edges. Baikal is never without wind. It's as though it were breathing—calmly and evenly at times, a little more heavily at others, and sometimes with all its might, when you're just lucky to find a place to hide . . . A breeze was blowing now, too, but it seemed to fluctuate, as if it were trying to pick up speed and yet kept getting bogged down . . . The sun was finally overcome and was fading even from the atmosphere. Baikal was a solid deep blue.

I stood on the bank awhile trying to choose which way to go, down to the water or up the hill, without the slightest desire to go in either direction. Because the descent to the water was easy at this point, a gentle slope, while the hill was steep, as the hills are almost everywhere, abruptly rising to full height out of fear of Baikal, and because it appeared especially steep here, I began to climb, trying to breathe in rhythm with my steps in order to make my breath last over a greater stretch of the hill. Traversing the bare, rocky scarp, kicking gravel loose, I managed to reach the grass that poked out like long white tufts of hair from under the soil, which was still sparse and also white, and I turned to look back. The low sky circled above me, its broad rim curving downward toward Baikal—it was somehow completely faded and colorless, preparing for something from one end to the other but not yet ready. The wind was a little fresher at this altitude, but the breeze wafting from the rocks and the earth was deep-seated and dry, hastening to give off warmth as if it, too, had a purpose in mind. I went farther and, after the next change of terrain, came to a long and narrow winding glade that had been cleared to make a hayfield—the hay had long since been cut and carted away, and the glade seemed somehow very sad and solitary in its forlorn, harvest-home spentness. Feeling sorry for it, I sat down on a rock there and began to look down.

The sky continued to circle slowly and soundlessly, descending closer and closer all the time and acquiring a dry, smoke-colored, cloudless skin. Beyond the hill, beyond the sparse trees on the summit, there was no more sky, only a gray and unpleasant gaping void. The whole sky had girded itself tightly and come to a halt over Baikal, repeating both its contours and its color exactly. But now even the water in Baikal, submitting to the sky, started moving in slow and regular circles without splashing against the shore, as though someone had stirred it up like water in a tub and left it to settle.

The circles made me dizzy. Soon I could only poorly comprehend what I was, where I was, and why I was here, and I had no need of such comprehension. Much of what had troubled me only yesterday and today and had seemed important was unnecessary now and slipped away from me with great ease, as if this were an inevitable stage in some fixed sequence of renewal whose time had come. It wasn't renewal, however, but something else, something that was happening in a larger world, a world distant from me in breadth and height, in which I found myself by sheer accident and whose mysterious movement had inadvertently swept me up, too. I felt a pleasant liberation from the recent morbid weight that had tormented me so. It had totally disappeared, as if mentally I had half risen and straightened up inside, and, trying the feeling on for size, I somehow knew that this still wasn't a complete liberation and that something even better was yet to come.

I sat there without moving a muscle, watching the dark glow of Baikal before me with a diffuse significance that seemed to anticipate a special moment, and I listened to the hum rising from the depths as though it came from a bell that had been tipped over and aimed at the sky. You could sense anxiety and alarm in it and in the water's movement—whether the anxiety and alarm were dying down or, on the contrary, gathering strength was not for me to know: the instant in which they were born stretched out for me into a long and monotonous existence. And it wasn't for me to know whose strength it was, whose power—the sky's over the water or the water's over the sky—but I saw quite clearly that they were in an animate and divine subordination to each other. In divine subordination—for what reason, over what? Which side has height and which depth? And where is the boundary between height and depth? Which one of these equal expanses contains the consciousness that knows the simplest of the secrets, simple yet beyond us, of the world in which we are caught?

These questions, of course, were all in vain. Not only are they impossible to answer, they're even impossible to formulate. Questions, too, have boundaries that should not be crossed. It's the same as the sky and the water, the sky and the earth, existing in an eternal continuum and subordination to each other—which of them is the question and which is the answer? After using every ounce of strength to approach them, we merely freeze in helplessness before the inexplicability of our conceptions and the inaccessibility of the adjacent boundary lines; we are forbidden to step over these lines and send back our voices, no matter how faint and tentative they may be. We should mind our own business.

I tried to ponder these matters further and to listen, but my consciousness and feelings and vision and hearing kept growing dimmer and dimmer in me like a pleasant depression, receding into a kind of universal nerve center. And I kept growing stiller inside, more and more tranquil. I had no sensation of myself whatsoever. All inner movement had gone out of me, but I continued to notice everything that was happening around me, taking it in all at once and at a great distance around, but I did nothing more than notice. It was as if I had merged with the single nerve center that serves everything and had remained inside it. I didn't see the sky or the water or the earth, but an invisible road was suspended in the deserted, luminous world and it led off horizontally into the distance, with voices—now faster, now slower—shooting along it. The only way you could determine that a road existed was by the sounds the voices made—they came from one direction and whirled off in another. And strangely enough, they sounded completely different when approaching than when leaving: harmony and a faith happy to the point of self-oblivion could be heard in them before they got to me while beyond me they sounded almost like a grumble. There was something in me that they didn't like, something they objected to. I, on the contrary, felt more agreeable and lighter with every passing moment, and the lighter I felt, the fainter the departing voices became. I was already preparing myself and somehow knew that soon I, too, would begin to race off along this purifying road as soon as I was ready, as soon as it unfolded before me in reality, and I was impatient to be off. I seemed to hear an unbearable summons from the direction in which the road led.

Then I came to and saw that a lone spider's web hung swaying before my eyes. The air still hummed with the same voices (I hadn't lost the ability to hear them yet); they had encircled me, forming an edifying round dance of farewell. I was sitting in a completely different place, and, judging from Baikal's shoreline, it was a long way from the previous one. Next to me three birch trees were sadly tossing down their leaves just like fortune-tellers as they played some game. The air was absolutely still; it is in just such motionlessness, when everything, it seems, is left only to its own devices, that more things die away and vanish than in a wind, which is supposed to die away; this is the tranquillity of a cautious, divine presence gathering in its harvest. How joyful it must be for a free soul whose time has come to die in the autumn, in that radiant hour when the expanses unfold!

And, regaining consciousness, I again discovered that I was a long way even from the last place, the one with the birch trees. Baikal was nowhere in sight—that meant I'd managed to cross the hill and descend almost to the bottom on the opposite side. It was getting dark. I was standing up—either I'd just arrived or I'd gotten up to go farther. But how I'd come, where I'd come from, why I'd come here—I had no idea. Somewhere down below a river flowed noisily over some rocks, and, without actually seeing the river, I could see its course by its noise, lively and intermittent yet continuous—I saw where it turned and where it went, where it beat against which particular rocks, and where it grew still for a short time, trembling in foamy ripples. I wasn't the least bit surprised by this kind of vision, as if this were just the way it was supposed to be. But that wasn't all. I suddenly saw myself rising from my previous place beside the birch trees and heading up the hill. I continued to stand on the spot where I'd just discovered myself, clutching a thick bough that stuck up from a fallen larch tree for verification, and at the same time I was walking step by step, glance after glance, picking a handy trail. I palpably sensed every movement and heard every sigh I made. I finally drew near the place where I was standing next to the fallen larch and merged with myself. But even this didn't surprise me a bit, as if this, too, were exactly the way it was supposed to be; I only felt a certain excessive satiety inside that prevented me from breathing freely. And now, completely united with myself, I thought of home.

By the time I approached my little cottage it was already completely dark. My legs barely held me up—from the looks of it, all the crossings, those I remembered and those I didn't, had actually been made on foot. I found a jar in the grass by the little spring and set it under the stream of water. And I drank for a long time, returning to myself once and for all— to what I was yesterday and to what I'd be tomorrow. I didn't feel like going inside, so I sat down on a log, and, rooted to the spot from fatigue and from a peculiar spiritual fulfillment, I merged with the stillness, darkness, and immobility of late evening.

The darkness grew thicker and thicker, the air became heavier, and the damp earth gave off a sharp, bitter smell. I sat there in a mellow state and watched the red light from the little lighthouse flash on the retaining walls across the way, and I listened to the voices borne by the spring, the incoherent, wordless voices of friends who had died, trying to the point of exhaustion to tell me something . . .

O Lord, have faith in us. We are alone.

I was awakened in the middle of the night by the patter of rain on the dry roof, and I thought with pleasure that now the rain, which had been building up and anticipated all day, had set in. And yet, heaven knows why, I once again began to feel such anguish and sorrow inside that I barely refrained from getting up and tearing around the cottage. The rain fell faster and harder and I went back to sleep in this anguished state to its sound, suffering even in my sleep and realizing that I suffered. And throughout the rest of the night I thought I heard the crow cawing loudly and insistently time after time, and it seemed to be walking along the low earthen insulating wall in front of the windows and tapping its beak on the closed shutters.

And sure enough, I was awakened by the cry of the crow. The morning was gray and wet, it was raining incessantly, and drops large and white as snow were coming loose from the trees and falling off. I got dressed without lighting a fire in the stove and headed for the port dispatcher's office, where you could make phone calls to the city. For a long time I couldn't get through—the connection kept being made and then broken—and when I finally did get through to my home, I learned that my daughter had been sick in bed since yesterday and was running a fever.

1981

THE FIRE

My native town is burning, burning . . .
(From a folk song)

One

Ivan Petrovich had felt this way before, that his strength was giving out, but never so intensely, as though he'd reached the absolute limit. He parked his truck in the central garage and walked out through the empty passageway into the street, and for the first time the stretch of road from the garage to his house, which he hadn't noticed in twenty years—just as you don't notice your own breathing when you're in good health—for the first time this piddling stretch of road lay before him in complete detail, with every meter demanding a step and every step demanding effort. No, his legs wouldn't carry him any farther, not even home.

And the coming week, his last week of work, now seemed endless—longer than a lifetime. He couldn't imagine the great pains he'd have to take to get through this week, and whatever kind of existence might begin afterward completely resisted all envisioning and thought. Out there loomed something alien and forbidden—well-earned, but also un-necessary—and in these bitter moments it appeared no more distant and no more visible than death itself.

And how come he was so tired? He hadn't strained himself today, and he'd even managed to avoid a lot of shouting and stress. He'd simply reached his limit, the limit he couldn't go beyond. Just yesterday something had been waiting up ahead, but today it was all over. He didn't know how he would get out of bed tomorrow, how he'd get going again and drive off to work. It was even hard to believe in tomorrow, and he took a certain wicked satisfaction in his disbelief. Let the night be good and long, with no order or restraint, so that some people would rest, others would come to their senses, and still others would sober up. And then daylight again, with everyone recovered. That would be great.

The evening was quiet and gentle. The day's warmth had spread so far that it hadn't pulled back, and it seemed to have no intention of pulling back. The wet snow gave way underfoot, even on the blacktop road, forming deep tracks; rivulets continued to gurgle as they rushed down the incline. In the velvety twilight, thickened with pure blue, everything in this springtime flood seemed submerged, floating chaotically in slush, and only the Angara River, where the snow was purer and whiter, looked from a distance like solid ground.

Ivan Petrovich finally made it home, not remembering whether he'd stopped and talked with anyone along the way. He walked past the ruined garden in front of his cottage without feeling the usual pain (when his heart would either sink or rise up defiantly) and closed the gate behind him. He could hear Alyona's voice out in the cowshed in the back yard, gently coaxing the month-old calf. Ivan Petrovich kicked off his muddy boots in the entryway, made himself wash up, and then simply couldn't go on. He collapsed onto the bench in the back hall next to the big warm side of the Russian stove. "This is just where I belong right now," he thought, listening for Alyona to come, feeling distressed because he'd have to get up for supper. Alyona wouldn't leave him alone till she'd fed him. Not for the life of him did he want to get up! He didn't want anything. Like a man in his grave.

Alyona came in, was surprised to find him just lying there, and began to worry that he'd come down with something. No, he hadn't come down with anything. He was tired. She started to set the table, telling him something that he didn't listen to very carefully. Ivan Petrovich asked her to wait a bit with supper. He lay there and thought for a long time about the words *March* and *death*, which were inexplicably linked in his mind, mulling them over sluggishly and pointlessly as if these were somebody else's thoughts. The words had something more in common than just their sounds.* No, he had to overcome March, to conquer this last week with his last ounce of strength.

And then Ivan Petrovich heard shouting.

*In Russian, *mart* and *smert'*.

"Fire! The warehouses are on fire!"

Ivan Petrovich was in such a glum, depressed mood that it seemed as though the shouts were coming from him. But Alyona jumped up.

"Do you hear that, Ivan?! You hear that?! Oh, dear! And you haven't even eaten yet."

Two

The warehouses containing the logging town's entire stock of supplies were situated in the shape of a letter *L* whose long side ran parallel to the Angara—or, as they now say more accurately, parallel to the water*— and whose short side came out from the right on Lower Street. When viewed from the town above it, this weighty letter seemed to be lying down rather than standing up. The other two sides, of course, were closed off by a solid fence. There were two ways into this stockade full of goods: through the wide entry gate for trucks or through the nearby passageway for authorized personnel. To the right of the gate, closer to the warehouses, the line of fencing was broken by a general store, which stood neatly half inside and half out; it cheerfully faced the street with its large windows and green paint and had one front entrance leading to both halves—the grocery section and the dry-goods section.

Lower Street was densely populated to the left and right of the warehouses, since people are always drawn as close as possible to water. Consequently, a major fire could travel from cottage to cottage in both directions and might even spread to the rows of houses higher up. For some reason this was the first thing Ivan Petrovich thought about as he tore out of his house, not about how to save the warehouses. In such situations you start by imagining the very worst, and only later do thought and action begin to reduce the scale of the potential disaster.

Ivan Petrovich cast a glance in the direction of the warehouses from his front stoop and didn't see any fire. But the shouting, which could now be heard all around him, was more urgent and desperate over there. Taking the shortest route, Ivan Petrovich raced through the garden, and then, rushing out into an open spot, he became convinced— there really was a fire. A dull, intermittent glow was meandering off to one side and seemed far to the right of the warehouses. For an instant Ivan Petrovich thought that the dry slats of the garden fence and the bathhouse standing in back were burning, but at that very moment the glow straightened out and shot upward, illuminating the warehouse compound below it. Shouts were heard again, along with the cracking of

---

*When the Bratsk Dam was completed in 1961, it transformed the lower reaches of the Angara River into an immense reservoir.

wood being ripped away. Ivan Petrovich came to his senses. Where did he think he was going empty-handed? He turned around and ran back, yelling for Alyona as he went, but she was no longer there—she had already dashed off, leaving the cottage open. Ivan Petrovich grabbed an axe from the woodpile and began to scurry back and forth along the fence, trying to remember where the boat hook might be, but he never did remember because he was seized by the thought that he ought to lock up the cottage. Reflections of the fire had started to dance along the wall, hurrying him along, and Ivan Petrovich, forgetting everything, raced back the way he'd come.

As he ran, he noticed that the glow had moved closer to the street. So this was turning out to be no laughing matter. The logging town hadn't seen a major fire of this proportion for as long as it had existed.

Ivan Petrovich ran past the fence surrounding the warehouses and then walked slowly through the big gate, now wide open, into the grounds, looking around to see what was happening.

Three

From the looks of it, the fire had broken out in the corner or somewhere near the corner where the warehouses branched off in two directions, forming the long side, which contained foodstuffs, and the short side, which held the dry goods. All the warehouses in each row were connected by a single structural link. And they were constructed and situated in such a way that once they caught fire, they would burn to the ground. When it comes to building, to planning for the possibility of fire right from the start, Russians have always had twenty-twenty hindsight, and they've always constructed things for the convenience of living in them and using them rather than for protecting and saving themselves as easily and expeditiously as possible. And a great deal was poorly thought-out here, all the more so because the town had been thrown together in haste. While escaping from water, who thinks about fire? But regarding the corner where the fire had broken out, someone had certainly shown a lot of foresight—or if it were not some person's doing, then it was simply rotten luck.

The corner had burst into flame and the fire had immediately spread in both directions. In the food part, the flames were moving along the roof as quickly and with as much crackling as if the top had been sprinkled with gunpowder. They hadn't had time to cover that part with the slate roofing that had been delivered way back in the fall and that they'd piled up along the fence, where it was lying even now. But the dry-goods part had been under a slate roof for about two years. It was one thing when crates of canned goods or some old hardtack or candy got wet, but quite another if those fancy Japanese clothes that people came to this region all the way from Irkutsk to get and that held some special value apart from their cost ended up in the rain. It wasn't the slate, of course, that prevented the fire from racing along the roof in this direction, but something else. Here the inferno was inside the end warehouse, where common sense said that the whole business might have started.

One other warehouse also had a slate roof—the far one in the row of food warehouses near the fence, where they kept the flour and groats.

When Ivan Petrovich zigzagged his way across the illuminated grounds, not knowing where to run, people had begun to gather in two places. One group was wheeling motorcycles off log pallets near the fire on the right, while the second group, consisting of four or five men, was taking the roof apart in the middle of the long row of buildings that formed the other section—to cut off the fire on top. They were already roasting from the nearby heat—the men were shouting furiously and furiously ripping up planks, broken and blackened by time, and shoving them off onto the ground. Ivan Petrovich remembered the axe in his hands—he ought to help them out with the axe—and, running over to them, he began dancing around down below, hopping away from the falling boards, unable to figure out how or from which side to climb up. His head wasn't working at all. Nothing whatsoever came to mind. And when he saw someone else walking rapidly along the roof, coming from the fence on the left, his legs wide apart as he straddled the peak, only then did Ivan Petrovich also start running in that direction, no longer cursing himself with words—no words came to him—but searing and punishing himself for his mental slowness with a desperation that he seemed to inhale from the surrounding heat. Not too long ago he'd been a real man, you see—now only the shell of a man remained.

Up on top Afonya Bronnikov was in command. As Ivan Petrovich came running over, he heard Afonya's voice ordering somebody to go down and find a crowbar or, if worse came to worse, any piece of metal they could use for ripping. And somehow Ivan Petrovich's spirits rose immediately: thank goodness Afonya was here. There was one other dependable person—a tractor operator named Semyon Koltsov—a newcomer, it's true, but Ivan Petrovich happened to work with him, and he knew the man was reliable.

Seeing the axe in Ivan Petrovich's hands, Afonya rejoiced.

"Well, now, at least one guy with some brains has showed up! They all come running to a fire as if they're running to the table—with empty hands."

He put Ivan Petrovich on the edge facing inside, and, after getting his bearings for a moment, Ivan Petrovich set to work ripping out boards. Standing on a block at the other end of the slope, Afonya himself was working his way down from the ridgepole, jumping off the block each time and shifting it as he struck the roof from below with a wooden mallet, using it like a sledge hammer. Semyon Koltsov was in the middle, and he, too, was wielding an axe. He was demolishing both this side and the other side of the roof, the one facing the Angara, and, usually a reserved man and not very talkative, he was now shouting something wildly nonstop, flying into a rage, hacking and smashing boards right and left. Despite how busy he was, how preoccupied with the matter at hand, Ivan Petrovich still managed to think that a person could act this way, tearing, screaming his guts out, only when rushing to the attack, when rushing to kill, or when forced to destroy something, as they were now, and that it would never occur to a person to scream at the top of his lungs like a wild animal while planting crops, for example, or while mowing hay for livestock. We can count the centuries that have passed since primitive times. Centuries have indeed passed, but the primitive state is still right here with us, in our souls.

When Ivan Petrovich leaped onto the roof, about four meters of it had already been opened up. With him there, they began to move faster—and they succeeded. The fire, which had run along the inside of the roof, winding its way with greedy, impatient hunger, suddenly hit empty space and flew upward, forcing them to crouch down from the extreme nearby heat. But by now it couldn't bridge the gap, and it turned back and went to clean up the dry, pliable odds and ends left behind in its haste. The rafters began to smoke, but they didn't burst into flame, and where they threatened to, Afonya attacked them and smothered the fire with his quilted vest.

And once again Ivan Petrovich became convinced that this Afonya was a fearless creature. He was one of Ivan Petrovich's folks, one of the boys from the old village before it was flooded, and no longer a boy for quite some time now but a grown man.

They got down to business again, glancing over their shoulders more warily and more often. The boy who'd been sent after a crowbar came back, and instead of bringing a crowbar he brought some news: they'd wheeled out a scorched Ural. A Ural was a motorcycle with a sidecar, something more coveted in a logging community than Zhiguli cars. The boy looked vaguely familiar; there were lots of this type now, people who had poured in from various directions and had lived here quite a while but who had simply never become acquaintances. Indignant, the boy cried out, "So there was one after all! There was a Ural! But who was it for?! Who were they hiding it for?! I asked Kachaev the other day. 'There aren't any,' he says. And it was standing right there all along!"

Afonya brought him back to the present.

"Did you look for a crowbar or not?!"

"There aren't any. There isn't anything," the boy shouted. "You go take a look. The women all came running with buckets, but they can't find the water truck. They're hauling water from the Angara with their buckets on yokes. Using yokes against a hellfire like this! They might just as well line up and sneeze at it. It couldn't care less."

And shouting all the while, the boy began to tell them how, being one of the first to arrive, he'd tried to use the fire extinguishers.

"You hit them like you're supposed to, but all you get is 'poof.' Poof— that's it. No foam, no shmoam. They either dried out or got used up."

He was shouting from behind their backs. Afonya had the boy using the quilted vest to maintain the defense in the rear. This leaping, stac- cato voice amid this unrelenting, nonstop activity made it all somewhat terrifying. To Ivan Petrovich, the voice seemed to resound and to burst not out of someone nearby who was choking from the smoke and heat but out of the walls themselves. And afterward, throughout the long, hot evening that later turned into night, whenever Ivan Petrovich heard voices shouting something and passing on information or demanding something, he always imagined that the walls, the earth, the sky, and the river banks were calling out in human words—so that people could understand them.

After ripping out the last plank and shoving it off the roof, Ivan Pe- trovich turned and looked around. The flames at the back were rising high and hotly lighting up the grounds, their reflections leaping along the roofs of nearby houses in broad bounds. Kids were tearing crazily around the compound in silence. Near the dry-goods warehouses, un- recognizably illuminated figures that looked transparent were screaming and rushing about in front of the fire, performing some stately dance. Over there the fire was terrifying because it was lashing out from under the roof in long, furious tongues, forcing people to step forward and back again just like in a dance: "And millet we did sow and sow . . . And millet we will trample, trample."*

But by now the bosses had come running, too. Kozeltsov, the chief engineer of the logging operation, stood in the middle of the grounds next to the district manager, waving his arms and constantly pointing somewhere in the direction of the town. Boris Timofeevich, only half- listening to him, kept giving someone signals that could mean just one thing: keep on, keep on . . . And suddenly spotting a caterpillar tractor barging into the grounds, he rushed off to intercept it.

The place was crawling with people, for practically the whole town had gathered, but so far it looked as if no one had turned up who would

*From a Russian folk song traditionally sung during the harvest season.

be able to organize them into one rational, solid force capable of stopping the fire.

The houses and cottages of the town, lit up for quite some distance by the glow sweeping across them like an intimidating search light, pressed themselves timidly into the ground. Ivan Petrovich picked out the roof of his own little cottage, trying to gauge how far away it was, and then he remembered. The boat hook, which might have come in handy here, was lying in the entryway where he'd stashed it two days ago when the snow had melted.

Four

This was a bleak and untidy town, neither a city nor a village. It was more like a camp site, as if the residents, migrating from place to place, had stopped to wait out a storm and to rest up and had simply gotten stuck. But they were stuck in anticipation—waiting for instructions to move on—and for that reason they seemed to be here just for the summer, and then just for the winter, never putting down deep roots, sprucing things up, or making improvements for the sake of their children and grandchildren. Meanwhile, children were born and grew up and were now raising children of their own. Alongside this lively encampment there developed another camp to which people migrated for good, but it, too, was still like a stopping place, a temporary refuge that they'd vacate any day now. And it seemed to Ivan Petrovich as he listened to the electric power plant working all night, its machinery clanking away around the clock, that this town, never shutting off its motor, was keeping itself in a constant state of readiness.

A diagram of the town hung in the town hall: straight streets, a nursery school, a grade school, a post office, a timber industry office and a Forest Service office, a recreation center, stores, a central garage, a water tower, a bakery—everything considered necessary for leading a normal life, everything people should have. The streets actually were straight and wide; at one time the line along which cottages were built had been strictly observed. But here all semblance of order came to a halt. These wide streets, nothing like those in the villages, were all torn up by heavy equipment, which created a kind of unearthly disorder. In the summer during bad weather the caterpillar tractors and timber trucks churned the mud into a black-sour-cream foam that got pushed to the sides in ponderous waves and that later dried in waves, turning into rock-hard ridges, which for the old folks became insurmountable hills. Every year the town council collected one ruble from each household for wooden sidewalks, and every year sidewalks were laid down; but spring would come, when people had to haul in firewood, and after logs had been dragged across them and rolled along them, all that would remain of the sidewalks were splinters. During the summer they never got around to putting in new ones—nobody felt like it in the summer; toward winter the "sidewalk" crew would make its appearance, the virgin boards would lie under the snow for three or four months scarcely touched by anyone's feet until February or March, and once again they'd perish senselessly under the treads of the caterpillars and the sheer weight of raw timber. And oftentimes people even used the remains of these little three-plank sidewalks as chopping blocks—they sawed and split wood on them. And no amount of orders or edicts did any good.

And the town stood naked, defiantly exposed, repulsive, and nondescript. Rarely did a birch tree or a mountain ash in some flower garden warm the heart and gladden the eye. Back in the old villages where they'd come from, people couldn't have imagined life without some greenery under their windows; here those same people didn't even have flower gardens on display. And the whole street howled and looked through their windows without interruption. And once again none of the town ordinances about planting trees and gardens got any results. Or to put it more precisely, when you're cutting down thousands of hectares of taiga every year, when you're opening up huge expanses right and left, it's pointless to try to take cover from the penetrating winds and the penetrating view behind a bird-cherry bush. This is the way we live . . .

Two words: timber industry—the State procurement of wood for commercial purposes. This explained much of the sloppiness and disorder in the town's layout. Cutting timber is not like planting crops, when the same tasks and the same worries are repeated season after season and no matter how long you live, you'll never finish tilling the soil. Once timber has been clear-cut, it takes decades and decades to grow back. With today's technology they can clear-cut a forest in a matter of years. And then what? Then pack up and move on. Leaving behind your little houses, cowsheds, and bathhouses, leaving behind the graves of your fathers and mothers and years of your own life, get onto the caterpillars and into the lumber trucks and go where the forest still stands. And start all over again. Every time Ivan Petrovich went past Beryozovka, whether boating by it in the summer or driving across the ice in winter, he couldn't help looking at the boarded-up, abandoned cottages with anguish and dismay. The timber industry had been there, too, done its work, and left—and there wasn't one living soul in the deserted town except for the insane backpackers who would build campfires in the houses, letting smoke out through the doors.

Sooner or later the same fate awaited them, too. They were postponing it as long as possible, but they couldn't put it off forever . . .

They'd already harvested their allotment of timber from their assigned sections seven years ago. Then they'd extended their area beyond the Angara. There, too, they'd taken out everything they could in five years. After that the question had arisen in earnest: would the town continue to exist or not? Government authorities considered the matter on the district level and on the regional level and finally decided that it would exist. They went back over their old assigned sections, over the clearings, but if before they had taken only commercial-grade timber, only pine and larch (there was a time when they destroyed birch and aspen with herbicides to keep them from cluttering up the forest), now they went over the clearings with a fine-toothed comb. And the machinery had become so advanced that it didn't leave a single shoot behind. In order to creep up to a good-sized trunk, a tree harvester tramples and squeezes the life out of everything around it.

And there was enough "fine-toothed combing" to last about three or four years. And beyond that? Beyond that they predicted that crews would go out on long tours of duty dozens of kilometers away, like seasonal workers in the old days, and then, after finishing a job, they'd drop in at home to rest up. People would divide their work lives and home lives into shifts. One week they'd belong to the logging operation and one week to their families. Strictly according to the work schedule. No intermingling, like now, of one life with the other.

And that's how it is.

Besides, how could it be any different if there was no other work to be had? The construction of the hydroelectric power plant had flooded the fields and meadows that once provided people with a livelihood—and that left only the forests.

And so the diagram in the town hall showed a recreation center, but for twenty years now this recreation center had been located in a public bathhouse brought here from one of the old workers' towns. They should have built a new one, but how could you build anything when nothing was visible up ahead until the very last minute? There was also a nursery school on the diagram, but it was not in operation since nobody knew whether it was worth renovating. And it became clear that they were in no big hurry. Nobody held anybody responsible for these plans.

So how could the town look pretty—especially in the glow of a fire?!

Five

Ivan Petrovich jumped down to the ground and ran to the spot where he'd just seen the district manager. Five days ago he'd had a huge falling out with Boris Timofeich, when the district manager had refused to sign his resignation papers. But Ivan Petrovich knew that if anyone could do anything right now, he, the district manager, was the only one. Not the chief engineer, who had transferred here six months ago from a neighboring logging operation, where he'd been in charge of safety; and not the director of the logging operation, should he make an appearance (but he wouldn't because he'd gone off to a meeting); and not his deputy directors—no one but Boris Timofeich, a hot-tempered man, no longer young, who'd become a real bastard in this crummy job and was counting the days till he could retire. He didn't get along well with many people, just as few were on good terms with him. He ran around in a foul mood and was just as likely to give a tongue-lashing as a compliment to whomever crossed his path, but all that was like a smoke screen that confused only the beginners who didn't know Boris Timofeich very well. And those who knew him didn't pay too much attention to the fleeting outbursts and injustices, remembering that Boris Timofeich Vodnikov was one of their own kind, a man who deep down inside had a firm grasp of who's who and what's what, a man who carried out his duties as best he could. Vodnikov had been the district manager, without rising or falling in rank, from the day the town was built, and, considering that he had no higher education whatsoever, this alone said that they couldn't get along without him. To cope with the central district while under the scrutiny of the timber industry management, which meddled in everything and denied itself nothing, was no easy task!

Ivan Petrovich saw that after Boris Timofeich had turned off the engine of the caterpillar driven in by a drunk, he'd gone over to the pile of stuff in the middle of the grounds, to which people were dragging the goods salvaged from the warehouses. But now he wasn't there. Ivan Petrovich looked vacantly at the pile: felt boots scattered all over, as if they'd been kicked off in a hurry by those who'd come running to the fire, school bags and school uniforms tied up in bundles, wool scarves, quilted pants, boxes of something or other, and, a little way off, some Java motorcycles stacked on top of each other and an actual Ural with a scorched sidecar. Oh, yes, the men would make the head of the workers' supply department answer for that Ural; there'd be a big fuss. What would happen to the head of supplies anyway, after the fire? And, not doubting the outcome for a moment, Ivan Petrovich smiled slightly at his own naïveté: he'd get off the hook. Those guys never came to a bad end, so they didn't give a damn about anything.

"Ivan! Ivan!" He suddenly heard Alyona's voice. She had run up with an armload of boxes. She had run up full speed, but she set the boxes down on the ground carefully, picking a clean, dry spot. "Ivan, what on earth is going on here, huh?!" Her voice was excited and raised to a feverish pitch of liveliness, and her unnaturally rounded, frenzied eyes seemed wild. "It's all gonna burn up! And everything's there but the kitchen sink! Ivan, why are we like this?!"

And without waiting for an answer—she didn't need one at all—she swung around and began to hurry back, rocking slightly from side to side like someone no longer young, as if she were stumbling with each step and quickly catching herself on the next one. Ivan Petrovich took a moment to glance at her as she was leaving, but everything was so mixed up in his head, so topsy-turvy, that he was on the verge of thinking, "Who's that? She looks vaguely familiar!" But he managed to snap out of it and forced himself to recognize Alyona, to observe that the woman shouldn't be tearing around like a maniac, and then he instantly forgot about her.

He caught sight of Boris Timofeich. But before seeing him, he'd heard him shouting and had tracked him down by following his shouts through the illuminated, strangely paralyzed crowd near the first food warehouse from the corner. They were used to the district manager's continually soaring voice, but this was the shouting of a madman and therefore unintelligible. Judging from the distinct though also heated replies—the fire had raised everybody's temperature—Ivan Petrovich realized that it was Valya the storekeeper who stood before the manager.

"I won't do it!" she shouted angrily. "Put out the fire. I'm not going to unlock it."

"What in the f------ hell?! It'll burn do-o-own!"

"Put out the fire. You think I'm a little kid or something? You think I don't see how they're ripping off Klavka's stuff?! Everybody's ripping us off. And I've got more than a hundred thousand rubles' worth in there. Where am I going to get that kind of money?! Where?! Where?!"

"It'll burn do-own!" The manager was straining his voice to the utmost.

"Put out the fire. I don't have to open up so they can rob me blind. Put out the fire."

She began to sob.

Ivan Petrovich was about to rush up to the manager, but Boris Timofeich turned toward him instead. Not to him but toward the heap of stuff from the dry-goods warehouses where Ivan Petrovich was still wandering around. Right behind the manager, anticipating a command, were several figures belonging to the gang of roughnecks,* as the townspeople called the work crew sent from the job recruitment center. And sure enough, before he'd taken five steps toward the heap, and without turning around, knowing they'd hear him and understand, Boris Timofeich shouted, "Break it open!"

---

*In Russian, *arkharovtsy*. The term originally referred to the unbridled plainclothes policemen in Moscow whose notoriously zealous chief was Nikolay Petrovich Arkharov (1742–1814). It gradually became a colloquial term for rowdy, violent thugs.

The roughnecks raced back. This sort of work was to their liking.

"Where's Kachaev?" Vodnikov began to yell in Ivan Petrovich's direction. "What the Devil?! F----- son of a bitch! These are his warehouses. Where the hell is he?!"

Kachaev was in charge of all the supplies. Boris Timofeich knew better than anyone else that two days ago Kachaev, along with the director of the logging operation, had gone to the city for a regular meeting. Yes, Boris Timofeich was at his wit's end, too, or else he wouldn't have been shadowboxing like this. And once you lost control, you'd never find yourself, much less Kachaev: this had never happened to him before.

And glancing at his blackened, dried-out, scorched-looking face with its extremely pointed nose and sucked-in cheeks, Ivan Petrovich completely forgot what he'd wanted the district manager for, why he'd been searching for him, and instead told him what was needed now more than anything else.

"Timofeich, put Uncle Misha Khampo at the gate. Have him stand guard, since that's what he does. But it's got to be Khampo. He's here. I just saw him over there, to the right."

Vodnikov charged off in the direction Ivan Petrovich was pointing without even turning to look at him, maybe without even realizing that he was following somebody else's lead rather than acting on his own initiative. Ivan Petrovich saw him find Khampo and lead him quickly to the gate, explaining what was required of him as they went. Uncle Misha Khampo responded with a sweeping nod of his big gray head, throwing it way back and lowering it in a deep bow. He was already peering into the crowd near the fire and picking out the people who would require special surveillance. Uncle Misha would be right at home there, of course, and you could count on Khampo. Valya the storekeeper knew what she was talking about. And now, when they were about to open up the food warehouses . . .

And just then came the grating sound of bolts being wrenched out. Valya began to wail in despair, driven completely out of her mind by the disaster that had befallen her and unable to see salvation anywhere—neither in having her inventory burn up under lock and key, certainly, nor in having it carried outside. They opened one set of doors, then another, and, on the third set, where the bolts wouldn't give, they smashed the huge padlock with an axe. The roughnecks acted quickly and deftly—as if they'd done nothing all their lives but break locks. When Ivan Petrovich came running up to the open doors of the building on the far right, he bumped into one of them, Sashka the Ninth ("the Ninth" was his last name, not a nickname; only every second roughneck had a normal, human last name—everything about them was out of whack).

Sashka, merry and sweating with excitement, clapped him on the shoulder with a skillful twist that swung Ivan Petrovich around in his tracks and shouted right in his face in a jaunty, almost friendly manner.

"Don't go in there. Don't go in there, Mr. Law-Abiding Citizen. If you burn up, who's going to read us the riot act?!"

Familiar with life behind bars or imitating those who were, they called him "Mr. Law-Abiding Citizen" in prison-camp style. He'd gotten used to this, too. The times were such that you had to get used to lots of things that not too long ago would have been unthinkable.

That the earth itself, for example, was slipping out from under your feet. And how back home this had happened to them literally.

Six

Twenty years had passed since they had moved here, twenty years and more, it must be. The earth itself had managed to tilt in the direction they'd been pulled, but not a single day went by in which Ivan Petrovich didn't recall his old village. He recalled it every time he deliberately or unintentionally cast a glance at the water covering the spot that his village had warmed for three centuries. He recalled it fleetingly, nodding a greeting in its direction while on the go, and he recalled it during frequent, painful periods of reflection when he tried to understand things by drawing comparisons, to figure out what kind of life they'd led back there and what had become of them here.

Even his last name had been part of the village and was derived from it—Yegorov. Yegorov from Yegorovka. Yegorov in Yegorovka, to be exact. Only once had he left his village for a long period of time—when he'd gone off to war. He'd fought for two years, and, because of his bachelor status, he'd spent another year after the victory holding the fort in that same Germany where fate had taken him in a T–34 tank. He'd returned home in the fall of '46. To this day he still keenly felt the sensation he'd had back then when he first saw his Yegorovka after being away: good Lord, it wasn't even standing up—it was lying down! That's how cheated and unsightly it had appeared. He'd seen his fill of everything imaginable during the war—misfortune, poverty, and ruin. Everything around him had cried out in suffering and begged for help, and a great deal had been overturned and disfigured, but even in the most frightening havoc hope had peered through. Given time, given willing hands, it would all come to life and be rebuilt, because people couldn't stand destruction. Here, though, everything had remained unchanged, as if it had come to a halt for good. Nothing had been taken away, but nothing had been added either, as though adding something were not even permitted. That's just what happened later on. People lived there for another fifteen years after the war, but since Yegorovka had been cut out to have forty households, that's indeed all it ever had, and not a single bathhouse or cowshed was tacked on to what had been comfortably broken in. They'd known about the flooding in advance, of course, and then they couldn't have cared less about new buildings. Then they had to shake a leg and figure out where to go—whether to take their cottages and head for the high ground where they picked mushrooms or whether to follow their sons and daughters to the seductive city.

Then, he recalled, after his discharge and after his homecoming reception, the dashing sergeant in the tank-crewman's helmet who was decorated with medals and had seen the world began to feel depressed. Your homeland was your homeland, nobody could deny it. There every stone had foreseen and awaited you even before you were born and there with each new spring every blade of grass brought you something from bygone days either as a warning or for support. There everything kept a quiet, ancestral eye on you. But it was just the way you'd imagined it . . . everything the same, the same, the same . . . just the way you'd imagined, and even in the beginning it seemed as though you'd come back from war only to die a natural death.

But as Ivan Petrovich reflected in uncertainty, he lingered on, and that meant making a choice in favor of Yegorovka. Famine set in soon after that, and at least it was easier to escape it here, next to the Angara and the taiga. Soon after that he spotted Alyona in a neighboring village, and she goggled at him so awkwardly and innocently with eyes that were naturally enormous, and she got so scared the first time he took her arm that he never looked for anyone else. Soon after that the kolkhoz got a new truck, and he turned out to be the only one they could put behind the wheel. Soon after that his mother took to her bed with a serious and prolonged illness, and fate itself had blocked his way out. And so it went, the same as with everybody: children, work, a slow and cautious shift toward a life that was a little easier and more cheerful.

Ivan Petrovich didn't exactly get used to it, but he seemed to have escaped the Devil, who lurked on the sidelines and kept pulling him, pulling him somewhere with a vague promise, and he sighed with relief. The grass is always greener on the other side. Perhaps the most important thing in life is for each person to stay headed in the right direction within his assigned place and not to veer off in vain or run around in circles on ill-defined quests.

That's what he'd come to believe. And that's what he believed now, but what could you do if in old age and against your own convictions and desires you were nevertheless forced to prepare for departure? And "forced to" isn't just strong language. That's the way it actually was.

Yes, and there's more. The Devil, whom he'd once escaped, didn't leave the house unaccompanied but enticed away his younger brother, Goshka, instead. Goshka went off to work in construction and, with the big money he made, became a hopeless alcoholic.

Who could have warned us in time where these paths of ours lay?!

Ivan Petrovich remained in Yegorovka, settled down, and grew content without suffering in the least from living in an out-of-the-way spot, which was gradually brightening up over the years. Electricity was installed, white steamboats began to dock at Yegorovka more and more often, and a well-heeled logging operation appeared eight kilometers farther up the Angara like a threat hanging over Yegorovka, luring the young folks away. And here, like everywhere else, life changed from a whole number into a fraction with a numerator and a denominator, and it became difficult to figure out what was above the line and what was below it. And here everything would have slowly straightened out, if indeed the times were such for everybody nowadays . . . And when they were hit with news of the flooding, when the time came to move, Ivan Petrovich had to admit that he found it hard to part with Yegorovka, as it must be for any person with a heart and a memory. And at the same time he felt secretly satisfied that he hadn't been the one to decide but that it had been decided for him. He moved his cottage and set it up in the new place. It was fine back there, but here as the years went by things should have gotten better. It had seemed, after all, as though Yegorovka would never get back on its feet by itself.

The name of the new town, which combined six such victims of misfortune as Yegorovka and where a logging operation immediately took hold, was derived from the vast forests, or, according to the current attitude, from the raw material—Sosnovka.*

Seven

If they were going to break the locks, they should have done it sooner. When Ivan Petrovich dashed into the food warehouse on the far right, it was completely ablaze. A terrible hum was coming from above the cracked ceiling, a single, mighty drone that drowned out all the lesser sounds. Several ceiling beams had broken off at one end near the corner wall, and flames fell through the opening like furious bursts of exhaust. The corner wall was burning from top to bottom—it was impossible to approach it—and the other walls were smoking, too. Strips of fire

---

*Literally, "Pineville."

were sweeping down through the cracks in the ceiling where it still held together, strewing sparks with a crackle. Everything gave off a red-hot glow, and the whole place could have burst into flame all at once. The smell of roasted meat permeated the fumes, along with the bitter, acrid smell of something edible that didn't call for such blast-furnace temperatures.

Ivan Petrovich had never been inside before, and now, with what feelings of amazement he still had left, he was staggered by the abundance. A good-sized mound of pelmeni* was heaped on the floor, and next to it were fat, hideously bloated rings of sausage strapped together with coarse twine, lying right on the dirty floor and already scattered around by people bursting in. Heavy bricks of butter were melting on a low platform by the back wall, wrinkling their wrappers and sucking them in, and next to them cartilaginous fish peeped out of crates stacked on top of each other. There'd been something in wooden barrels, something in cardboard boxes, something in paper bags. So there'd been food, there'd been plenty of food after all! And where had everything gone? Not just to the camp kitchens at the felling sites, that's for sure. Tell that to somebody else—as if he hadn't eaten at those kitchens and didn't know what was actually served there and what was only a pipe dream! And Ivan Petrovich smiled or at least chided himself with the charred thought that in this place he ought to smile at his own foolishness: trucks coming from the county seat, from all over, every blessed day, turning in at the supply department headquarters and getting Kachaev out of his office! That must be why they'd been agitating for all three logging communities to have common, centralized warehouses, which naturally ought to be located in the county seat! And Ivan Petrovich nodded his head, or thought that he should: now if these were to burn down, the largest warehouses in the largest logging town, it'd be easy as pie to get their way.

How much paraphernalia there is in the world, and how many brazen souls! And how did it happen that we surrendered to them? How did it happen?!

Pulling his quilted vest around him and dancing away from the heat, Ivan Petrovich took the slippery-slimy rings of sausage, which were starting to shrivel, and tossed them through the doorway. Somebody outside was catching them and carrying them off somewhere. All Ivan Petrovich saw were feet in canvas boots running to and fro. Other people were also nearby, but he didn't recognize them. From time to time they'd bump into each other and step back. The heat was becoming more and more unbearable as the fire moved swiftly along the ceiling

---

*Pelmeni—a kind of Siberian meat pie resembling ravioli.

and walls to the left; their eyes watered, their throats tickled, and it seemed as if even the smoke they had to breathe was on fire. Something was sizzling loudly, as if it were in a skillet, and something was exploding like artillery shells. The partially burnt end of yet another overhead beam broke loose and began swinging back and forth, strewing flames everywhere, and then the other end broke loose. It was time to retreat. It looked as though all the sausages had been tossed outside and all the crates of fish had been dragged out, but when Ivan Petrovich glanced at the platform by the back wall where the crates had been, he spotted the butter there and rushed back, groaning because it wasn't the sausages they should have been saving but the butter. He picked up one of the shrunken bricks, burning his hands, and butter began to ooze over his stomach like dough, running down his legs in a single mass. He set it on the floor and picked it up again, hoisting it onto his chest and leaning backward—and he carried it out and transferred it to somebody else's hands. Those hands had choppers* on them, and Ivan Petrovich was sorry that he hadn't thought to bring his choppers from home—they really would've come in handy! He went back inside, pulling his vest around him the way he had earlier and peering out from behind it as though it were a shield, heading for the far wall again where there was still more butter, but halfway there somebody collided with him and, half screening him and half using him as a screen, dragged him back. Ivan Petrovich didn't resist, realizing that, yes, that was enough.

Outside, that somebody turned out to be Sashka the Ninth. Sashka bared his teeth and hoarsely uttered the same words as before.

"You'll burn up, Mr. Law-Abiding Citizen! Oh, you'll burn up!"

And he pushed Ivan Petrovich away.

Eight

Nobody seemed to be fighting the fire anymore—they'd given up and were just dragging out whatever could still be removed. The water truck stood by the gate with its engine running while water trickled out of its dangling hose. The entire grounds were brightly illuminated, and Ivan Petrovich, instantly catching sight of the small puddle under the hose, rushed toward it, feeling that he couldn't take any more of this without water. He splashed some on his face, which began to sting even more, and took a few swallows out of his cupped hand, only two or three swallows, before the water stopped. The hose gave a dry snort, began to

*Choppers (in Russian, *verkhonki*)—leather work mitts usually worn over knitted liners.

hiss, and fell silent. He shook the hose once more and tugged on it, holding his hand underneath—empty.

No, the dry-goods warehouses couldn't be saved. Emitting a powerful, satisfied drone, the fire had reached the middle, completely girdling the warehouses, and was advancing. The slate on the roof was disintegrating from the searing heat, and small pieces were shooting all over, the way nuts jump and shoot around in a red-hot skillet. Smoldering chunks of wood were also flying everywhere. It was dangerous to stand too close, and one of the men kept shouting at the kids to stay back. They would jump away at the threatening gestures and then be drawn close again, having lost their senses, their eyes wide, mesmerized by the fire. Ivan Petrovich tried to pick Alyona out of all the figures who were rushing around the grounds and continuing to drag stuff out and haul it to the pile—she was nowhere to be seen. The heap of salvaged goods was growing. They'd reached the warehouse containing household items. Scythes, sauce pans, and pieces of crockery clattered, and sheet metal clanged. Good Lord, did they really need to save that stuff? Or maybe people were right when they said that you can get along without a refrigerator and a TV but not without a tea kettle and a skillet.

The fence between the warehouse and the general store began to screech and sway, and it crashed to the ground with its nearest section falling inward, exposing the street and the cab of a logging truck, which was retreating and swinging around for another assault. "That's right," Ivan Petrovich noted. "We can't recapture the warehouses, but the store can be defended—it's quite a ways from the warehouses." Kozeltsov, the chief engineer, was bustling around by the truck. He was probably the one who'd thought of knocking down the fence, which could otherwise become a pathway for the fire.

Yes, the dry-goods warehouses were weeping, Japanese blouses and Soviet-made skillets were weeping—could there actually be as much left inside, in that inferno, as they'd already carried out?! Except for the one on the right, the dry-goods warehouses could still have been saved even now if there'd been a fire truck and a little more order. But about two years ago the only hook-and-ladder for the whole logging operation had been cannibalized for spare parts, so it existed only on paper.

Ivan Petrovich was still hurriedly looking around, still hoping to find Alyona before diving back into the fire, when Uncle Misha Khampo tapped him on the shoulder.

"Khampo-o . . . khampo-o!" He struggled to get the word out, pointing to the far end of the grounds with his left hand, his good one. A man was standing back there in the left corner, illuminated from the side and from behind by the glow, unnaturally animated and resembling a gigantic ghost, and he was tossing bottles over the fence like hand grenades.

Ivan Petrovich began hurrying toward him, but Boris Timofeich, popping out from somewhere on the right, got there before he did. Charging at him with a shout, he yanked the man around, nearly knocking him off his feet, and quickly got ready to charge again. The other guy raised a bottle threateningly. He might actually have hit him—anything could have happened at that moment—were it not for Ivan Petrovich, who ran up and managed to grab the bottle. This was one of the roughnecks, one of the most hard-core, who for some reason had the woman's name "Sonya" and who Ivan Petrovich had already tangled with before. Sonya pulled the bottle out of Ivan Petrovich's hands, threw it off to one side, and wailed out a threat in the strange lingo he and his buddies used, pointing past their heads.

"Oh, how hot it's bu-urning! Oh, it's ho-ot! Ow, it hu-urts!"

And he began wobbling off to where everything was burning.

"And where were you?" The district manager could think of nothing better to do than light into Ivan Petrovich. "Where were all of you? You should all go to hell! What are you looking at?!"

"I went to the bathhouse," Ivan Petrovich replied, adopting the manager's tone of voice. "You ought to go, too. Rinse off and cool down or you'll attack somebody! You should at least watch who you're attacking!"

The moon was coming up over the hill, a huge moon. Rolling out from behind the forest, it was moving to the right, and, just like in the movies, the tops of the trees floated into it and burned up there in cold excitement.

Nine

Now no one is ever likely to find out how and why this shift to the present free-and-easy life came about. But it wasn't this way in the beginning. Even in the new town people didn't go their separate ways like this, and they didn't turn their backs on each other and break away from the communal, harmonious existence that had stood firm because of laws and customs that hadn't been thought up overnight. And remember, wasn't it those very laws and this single source of protection that sustained and saved people in the old village during the war and during those troubled postwar years so warped by excessive harshness, when, not bothering with trifles, they gave ten-year sentences for the disappearance of ten ears of grain? When they piled on the taxes, when they cut back the size of private gardens, leaving idle plots overgrown with nettles, and when they wouldn't let anybody cut hay for their cow, the sole source of food for their kids, till after the first snowfall? When people not only had to stick together but also had to apply their cunning together in order to survive? There were all sorts of people in the village, too, and some were probably itching to denounce their neighbors, allegedly to maintain order by adhering to the letter of the law, and to do the bidding of the authorities whenever asked. There's no doubt that some folks were just itching to do these things. But they knew there would be no place for them in the village after that. Yegorovka would never forgive them.

But now it was Ivan Petrovich who had to move away—and how greatly everything had changed! You might say that everything had been turned on its head, and that what people had held onto quite recently as a whole community, what had been the general unwritten law, the very earth under their feet, had changed into a vestige of the past, into some kind of abnormality and almost into treason. And Sosnovka didn't care. Maybe it would even feel more comfortable and at peace if Ivan Petrovich just went away and stopped muddying the waters. Or better yet, yes, of course, better yet, he should never have started flailing his arms in the first place, like some senile old man recalling the clean water of his childhood, trying to keep it clean nowadays, too, when everything around him had gotten muddy. When the question of water comes up, everybody knows that it's clean not when it's actually clean but when people want to see it as clean. And to do that you must be willing to fasten some clever optical device over your eyes.

No, things didn't get off track right away, as soon as they moved. The new work, of course, took its toll: cutting down timber, just cutting and cutting, not worrying whether anything would remain or grow there after they'd gone. Only now were they making them replant where they'd cut, but what was meant by *make?* It was like a feeling of obligation, the way you feel obligated to think about death from time to time so you can lead a cleaner life. You can also not think about it, just live and that's all, but then life amounts to felling trees. If you didn't replant your quota, they'd bawl you out a little; if you didn't cut your quota of timber, they'd tan your hide. That became customary and over the years things hadn't changed: the Forest Service was supposed to play with this toy of reforestation, but it had five pairs of hands for every fifteen work orders, and it lacked the manpower to see a single job through to the end.

At first each village was reconstructed on its own street in Sosnovka, and people planned to live in the same communal groups as before. The whole so-called kolkhoz worked together, according to long-standing tradition, to get the widows and old men settled in, helping them transport their cottages and break ground for their gardens. Paths were beaten through these gardens so they could run over to see each other by taking short cuts, avoiding the street, whenever they needed something, or even when they didn't, when they simply had a free moment for tea and conversation. And at sunset you could hear all over the neighborhood:

"Darya-a! Marya-a! The samovar's ready! Natalya-a! Aren't you going over to the Krivolutskies'?" That meant to the street closest to the hill, which the village of Krivolutskaya occupied.

Then everything got mixed up. It wasn't so bad when one village started penetrating another through deaths, weddings, property divisions, and trading—life is impossible without such penetrations—but things began to go wrong when lax people started settling in place of those who passed away or who left, people who didn't set up households and didn't even plant gardens, who knew only one route—to the general store. That's where they ate and where they whiled away the time when they weren't at work. At first they spent their leisure time there, but then they took work time, too, replacing it with hanging out at the store. And the longer this went on, the more it happened, the sweeter and more irresistible it became. The workplace didn't appreciate this, of course—and they got into trouble at work. And they even formed communal groups of a different stripe, a kind unheard of in the past. There had always been drunks, of course—when hadn't there been drunks in Holy Russia? But to huddle in a circle, to grow into an unconcealed force that feared nothing and was ashamed of nothing, with its own ataman and council exercising power—such a thing had never happened before. This is something we have accomplished all by ourselves.

Yury Andreevich, the school principal, who had even taught back in Yegorovka, recently undertook the task of counting how many people out of the six villages that formed Sosnovka had perished during the war and how many had died an unnatural death during the last four years. An unnatural death meant drunken shootings, knifings, and death by drowning, freezing, and getting crushed at the cutting sites through your own or somebody else's carelessness. As it turned out, there was very little difference. Ivan Petrovich gasped when he heard the results—so that's peacetime for you! He'd known about all these incidents; he'd suffered on their account—something always changes and seems to grow dim in the world when someone you know departs this life, and something inside you weakens with his departure even if he's a good-for-nothing three times over. Ivan Petrovich had known about each separate incident and had grieved over every one, but taken all together, as one statistic, and put beside the other statistic, they left him stunned. He wasn't himself for several days, trying to grasp something and realizing only that it was impossible to understand, impossible to grasp even a portion of what he was trying to derive from this terrible equation. And another thing—someone who perished at the front made an appeal for justice and goodness and left them behind, along with his soul and the memories that live on among his relatives, and he left them behind to be acted on and fulfilled. Without suspecting it ourselves, we were sustained for perhaps twenty years after the war by this legacy from the dead, by their single behest, which we, in keeping with our human nature, could not fail to honor. This was something beyond us and stronger than we were. Somebody who just throws away his life for no reason—out of stupidity and blind despair—leaves behind only stupidity, dissoluteness, and despair. Death is a powerful teacher, and no matter whose side it takes in carrying out its duty, that of good or evil, that side increases fivefold.

In the earliest years the entire logging operation consisted of one area alone. Then they opened up a second area, then a third, then a fourth, and today the tree-harvesting business extends a hundred-odd kilometers in a straight line just along the river bank alone. Nowadays over one hundred thousand cubic meters of timber are clear-cut in a single area each year. They've jacked up the quotas and pushed the use of machinery, applying it with ever-increasing force, cleverness, and craftiness, until it can no longer be operated by the local folk. Seasonal workers and moonlighters have come in, some looking for an extra ruble, some after an extra day off, which they don't care how or where they spend as long as it gets spent. In more recent years a special breed has appeared, made up of people who aren't totally worthless or lost for good, who are after something other than money in their endless migrations, and who readily and easily squander what money falls their way, seemingly driven by a fanatic rejection of and indifference to absolutely everything. Such a person accepts no help for himself and won't offer it to anybody else. He goes through the motions of living in an abbreviated way, having no family, no friends, and no attachments, and he acts as if it's a burden, as if he's serving out his life like a prison term. They used to say that such a person was touched in the head; nowadays you could say he's become wrapped up in himself, that he's taken a vow of solitude. And what's going on in their souls, who their souls belong to, is anybody's guess.

And so in the spring, when the timber hauled down from the hills during the winter has to be sent off, and in the autumn, when it has to be cut and hauled down again, they pour in and out, in and out without sticking around, not because of any intolerable inconveniences but simply because they're incapable of staying, not understanding why or what they should stick around for, urged on by a vague, unbearable restlessness. And they leave—with bitter longing in their eyes, wondering where to go and for what purpose. But they leave, and those who stay behind remember them only for their eccentricities and for the parlor tricks at which they're old hands, like one artist who could lift any table of hors d'oeuvres with his teeth, or another who would make a soup out of bread and vodka and spoon it all down without wincing, or a third who loved to send telegrams that looked like coded messages, frightening the girls who worked at the post office. "Three days of rain—what should I do?" Or, "December comes after November. Don't mix them up." Or, "Don't wait for me, but I'll return." In all the three hundred years of its antediluvian existence, old Yegorovka never experienced one one-thousandth of the miracles and magic that Sosnovka has seen in twenty. And from the looks of it there's no end in sight.

Out of everything that might be remembered, these, of course, are the most innocent things and the easiest to recall. But people might also remember what happened to Andrey Solodov, the forest ranger. Two years ago Solodov, using the authority vested in him, fined the logging operation for leaving behind tall, nearly waist-high stumps. To avoid having to remove deep snow, they'd been felling trees the easy way, breaking regulations, and after repeated attempts at persuasion and after making repeated threats, Andrey, normally an easygoing man, lost patience: "There you are, since you don't understand plain language." On Friday the payroll clerk went to pick up the wages and came back with nothing. Because of the fine, the bank had frozen the logging operation's assets. On Saturday Andrey heated up his bathhouse as usual, took a sauna, and went to bed, and during the night his bathhouse burned down. You had to suspect carelessness or negligence on the owner's part—he'd heated it up and taken his sauna, and then he'd collapsed into bed and slept like a log. On Monday the payroll clerk set off for the bank again, and once again she returned with an empty bag. She'd been told to wait till Wednesday while they reached a final decision about where to get the money. But on Wednesday they said wait till Friday. On Wednesday Andrey Solodov's Forest Service mare disappeared—it was the sole workhorse for the whole town, which they used to plow half the gardens and which was indispensable in forestry work. Only in the spring did its bones show through the snow melting in a thicket, and a rotting rope lay beside them.

Ivan Petrovich had a talk with Andrey, and they agreed that this couldn't have happened without their own folks taking part. It would be ridiculous to blame only the newcomers. No, even their own people, with whom they'd lived side by side and pulled together in the same harness, even they had learned to frown on anybody who held the law up to them as in the old days and who repeatedly brought up conscience. And his own folks threatened Ivan Petrovich when, unable to keep quiet, knowing he would tan his own hide later if he kept silent, he'd get up at a meeting and state out loud everything that was going on at the felling sites, at the lower landing, in the storehouses, and in the central garage. He spoke of things that everybody knew about and that were gradually becoming customary—how they needlessly and mercilessly abused the machinery in the forest or drove vehicles for dozens of kilometers on drunk and sober errands of a personal nature; and how they ripped off stuff from the sawmill in broad daylight; and how goods listed on invoices vanished mysteriously on the way to the logging operation while money immediately appeared in their place, to make doing business easier; and how, in violation of safety standards, they made the caterpillar operators haul timber down onto thin ice; and how . . . It had gotten to the point that on the morning after payday Boris Timofeich himself would sneak a couple bottles of booze to the felling site in his canvas bag to stop the work crew from falling apart. And they had learned to take this for granted, like they did those three packets of tea that the union gave out free of charge.

Ivan Petrovich got all worked up as he mulled everything over. The world doesn't get turned upside down instantly, in one fell swoop, he concluded, but this way, the way it happened with us—what wasn't permitted, what wasn't done, has become permissible and commonplace, what was forbidden has become allowed, what was considered a disgrace, a mortal sin, is now revered as clever and valiant. And just how long are we going to keep surrendering the things that gave us everlasting support? What rear guard, what reserves will provide the help we long for?

"How come your eyes are all over the place?" Boris Timofeich would thunder, but there'd be no urgency in his voice, no question that required an answer. "How come you're always harping on one and the same thing? We can't live without quotas, you see—"

That's where Ivan Petrovich would blow up.

"Quotas, you say? Quotas?! We'd be better off without them! We'd be better off setting up different quotas—not just for cubic meters of timber but for souls, too! So we could keep track of how many souls have been lost, have gone over to the Devil, and how many are left! Quotas! You remember how it used to be . . . why, even five years ago—"

"What about five years ago?" Boris Timofeich played dumb. "Back then we didn't have any tree-harvesting machines or knuckle-boom loaders. You didn't have that Kraz truck of yours that holds thirty or forty cubic meters at a time."

"Numbers, numbers, numbers! In those days you didn't take vodka up the hill at your own expense on account of quotas. You just remember that. Meeting our quotas—that's simple. You don't need any farming expertise for that."

"Simple?" Nobody understood better than he, who knew the quotas backward, forward, and inside out, who had devoted his life to quotas, waking up in the middle of the night over them when he'd managed to fall asleep, fearing the quotas like the plague, dreading the last days of each month when the quotas were ripening amid technology more complicated than anything a wheatfield ever dreamed of—how well he knew not just that it was a complex business but that it required a good deal above and beyond mere resourcefulness. He couldn't possibly explain all this, and, hiding his hurt feelings, he said, "You ought to be in my shoes once."

"No, thanks. My own are tight enough."

Afonya Bronnikov, a Yegorovka man who worked on a logging truck, took a different line of reasoning.

"How come you're getting all excited, Ivan Petrovich?" he chided with a reproachful smile on his broad, hardened Old-Believer's face.* "What are you going to prove? I look at it this way: I work honestly and live honestly, I don't steal, I don't cheat—and that's enough. Anybody with eyes can see how I live and how other folks live. Whichever way people are inclined, that's the way they'll go. Our job is to live right, to set an example with our own lives and not try to drive others into our fold with a stick. You won't get anywhere using a stick."

"But we're a little late, we're a little late with setting these examples! It's too late!"

"It's never too late."

But Ivan Petrovich was made of different stuff. Under daily pressure, some kind of spring would seem to grow tighter and tighter inside him, and it would get so tightly wound and coiled that he'd finally find it impossible to endure. And Ivan Petrovich, after pledging more than once to keep quiet, having persuaded himself that silence was also a means of action and persuasion, Ivan Petrovich would stand up again and begin to speak, his voice sinking, feeling terribly nervous and hating himself as he realized it was all in vain.

Something had happened even before the arrival of the roughnecks who grouped around Sashka the Ninth. When Ivan Petrovich showed up at the garage one morning, the connecting brake lines to the trailer on his Kraz truck had been cut. That meant, "You won't get your way, you plush truth-seeker." He'd once been told, "You're like a plush teddy bear that's had two words drilled into it: good—bad, good—bad. You think about that a little."

So, then, good is bad. And so, then, bad is good. You couldn't help tripping over your tongue and getting lost among three little words.

Ten

The fire had been completely forced out of the first food warehouse. They moved on to the second one. It was a good thing the roof on the second warehouse had been torn off, because this held back the fire,

---

*Old Believers—descendants of seventeenth-century Russian Orthodox schismatics, in this case from the Volga region.

which was trying to spread from the upper corner on the far right across the ceiling boards. When Ivan Petrovich dashed into the building for the first time, it was white hot and smoky in there, too, but bearable without any actual flames, and the place was still held up from the inside by four walls. This warehouse turned out to be surprisingly crowded. People were shouting gleefully and calling back and forth, and there was a constant ringing and banging. Ivan Petrovich didn't immediately spot the human chain they'd formed, which was passing along crates of the most popular item—vodka. The chain included both his own people and the roughnecks. After distractedly marking time for a moment and grabbing one crate so he wouldn't be empty-handed, Ivan Petrovich ran back out convinced that even without him they wouldn't let this item perish. Outside, a red-hot glow poured down around him from above and from somewhere came the shouts of Valya the storekeeper, demanding and begging someone to salvage the vegetable oil. Valya was shouting that there wouldn't be any more vegetable oil till autumn, that they'd cleaned her out, and Ivan Petrovich, turning back at these words, couldn't get his aching head to remember which season it was—winter or summer.

He'd dashed out for just a second, but by now the fire was breaking through in the right-hand corner.

The fire was breaking through in a roaring blaze, the voices from the human chain were growing more gleeful and disjointed, and bottles were clinking dully, but there was also another repetitious sound amid this medley of sounds—as if something were warbling melodically or gurgling drily. It gurgled or warbled in soft undertones. Ivan Petrovich charged over to the burning-hot wall where the noises were coming from, and, reaching the crates of imported wines, he guessed what it was: corks shooting out of bottles. He didn't try to track down the undertones, figuring that they most likely originated in a similar salute from vials of triple-strength cologne or something on that order. Some time ago, triple-strength cologne had joined the ranks of foodstuffs—it was used to flavor dry Hungarian or Bulgarian wine, whose own taste the men rejected as too sour and strong.

Ivan Petrovich expected to find the vegetable oil in bottles, but it turned out to be in a metal barrel. It was a huge thing with bulging sides that had been in more than one scrape, and he had trouble tipping it over, burning his hands in the process, but he couldn't roll it outdoors; it only rocked back and forth with his exertions. He hurried over to the human chain, and, without taking a close look or choosing anyone in particular, he snatched out the first link he came to. It materialized into the same boy who'd helped them tear off the roof and who'd brought them the news about the Ural motorcycle. The boy smelled of boiled vodka; without understanding a thing but without protesting, he began bounding along behind Ivan Petrovich. Using their hands and feet, the two of them working together rolled the barrel outside.

"There's one more in there! Ivan Petrovich, there's still one more in there!" Valya the storekeeper shouted and rushed over to show them. "There it is! Right over there!"

Ivan Petrovich caught Valya and pushed her outside, away from the door. With her vested interest, which might prove stronger than common sense, she had no business being there. No reason for her to see what was going on inside. Ivan Petrovich's partner, the one who'd helped him roll the barrel, had disappeared in a flash; the boy had naturally gotten back into formation without delay. While trying to find him, Ivan Petrovich noticed that it wasn't just crates moving along the chain but open bottles as well, which gleamed under the flames like flashlights.

"March! March!" someone began, rashly throwing a crate to his neighbor, and the chain joined in: "March! March!"

"March! March!" A bottle shot up over a tilted-back head. "March! March!"

But the fire kept marching, too. After bursting in, it seized half the back wall and spread to the ceiling, from which it lashed down in long, falling tongues according to some rhythm of its own. It was getting harder and harder to breathe. They were no longer breathing air or their own breath but quick, irregular gulps of burnt emptiness. Somebody, and you couldn't tell if it was a man or woman, called out anxiously in a naked, straining voice.

"Petka! Petka! Are you in here? Where are you?"

"We ate your Petka—he was the hors d'oeuvres!" somebody shouted from the chain. This voice seemed scorched, too, like a wire conducting nothing but words through the heat.

And once again Ivan Petrovich tipped over a barrel of oil, which was in better condition than the first one and seemed more pliant, and again he tried to roll it by himself. Somebody gave him a hand. When they got outside, Valya the storekeeper, seeing the barrel, started wailing and broke into a howl—the barrel had lost its stopper. Stunned, Ivan Petrovich looked first at the trail of oil winding out of the warehouse, then at Valya, who was grieving as if two or three liters of spilled oil were her greatest loss that day.

Somebody grabbed Ivan Petrovich from the side—Afonya Bronnikov. Walking quickly away from the fire to the left-hand corner of the grounds and pulling Ivan Petrovich after him, Afonya explained.

"We've got to get the flour out, Ivan Petrovich, before it's too late. All this—" He made a disdainful gesture backward, where the fire was burning. "But if we end up with no flour . . . We can't get along without flour."

Women and kids were carrying cans of condensed milk out of the third warehouse, along with boxes containing some kind of tiny, toylike jars and something in neat boxes strapped tightly around the middle with metal bands. The flour was kept behind the third warehouse in the low building closest to the fence, where there were no log pallets.

The doors, as wide as a gate, had been thrown open.

The shadows cast by Ivan Petrovich and Afonya, growing longer and longer in ugly contortions, leaped over the fence and rose above the town.

"We're on fi-i-ire!" These words rang out somewhere in the streets above them.

Ivan Petrovich jumped in fright and began peering toward the voice.

"So you woke up!" Afonya replied with gleeful malice. "We're about to burn up, and you just noticed. Come on, pal, run on down here before it's too late. Tomorrow's the Sabbath. Tomorrow you won't be able to get the hair of the dog that bit you."

Eleven

Disorder all around is one thing, and disorder inside you is quite another. When it's all around, you can find as many people to blame as you wish, and sometimes completely extraneous forces are even capable of entering the picture and, as they say, playing a role. In short, that kind of order or disorder has many masters who find it hard to agree on anything. They have differing concepts of an orderly world, and what is a sensible arrangement of things for one person is a total mess for another.

In everything concerning only yourself, you, of course, are your own boss. In the domain located inside you, no one else can be held accountable. And even if this domain seems to rest on many external factors and causes, these factors and causes do not escape your supreme authority before they flow across your secret, precious boundaries. Consequently, in this instance, too, you alone must answer for yourself.

And there's nothing simpler than getting lost in yourself. A sensitive person knows this. He views himself not as a doctor would, seeing primarily organs fulfilling specific functions, but as the powerful, weak-willed sovereign of an immense, incomprehensible kingdom miraculously granted to him by nature and requiring a special kind of ruling authority.

You think you know where your conscience is located in you, where your will is, where memory is, where desires spring up, and where prohibitions and limitations come from. You don't know their exact locations, but you can visualize the lines of communication needed to send the signals for them to respond. Conscience begins to speak in you not by itself but at your beck and call. Perhaps it can also raise questions on its own—of course it can, but it doesn't have time because, you believe, you appeal to it first. You imagine that this is how things should be within the borders entrusted to you, so that you can intervene in advance when an objection is about to make itself heard or when there's a weakening consent, so that you can step forward first and speak ahead of it rather than simply appear on command.

You and they. You are the ruler, carrying in your body a kingdom with all its cities and hamlets, all its institutions and means of communication, all its vices and glory. And they are what form the secret life of your world. You and they are both a single entity and entirely separate. You and they are a single, indissoluble entity when peace and harmony prevail, when the occasional misunderstandings that no life lacks crop up and continue only until reason passes judgment. Exactly in this way: from misunderstanding to reason. And you and they are separate when discord arises and when the realm that belongs to you refuses to obey you. Only then comes the inkling that they are stronger than you. Because they are what determine your thoughts and actions, what direct your movements, and what get sounds out of your voice. Because you, after all, are mortal while they are not. They were placed in you at the behest of some vague, powerful force that you simply could not distill into an image. And this force, not you, was their ruler, while you were merely their temporary dwelling place, the weak shell for everything that they, taken together, represented and from which they sought harmony and union with the world. You didn't live up to their hopes, and you didn't deliver or demonstrate what you were commanded to. And this means that you weren't yourself. You were anybody you please, only not yourself. And when they give you back, they will say good-bye not to you but only to your name.

◢ Disorder all around is one thing, and disorder inside you is quite another. Ivan Petrovich felt a terrible desolation in himself—as if a foreign host had marched through him and trampled and desecrated everything, leaving acrid smoke, melted shards of crockery, and sharp, formless pieces of what had been, after all, a stable life. This doesn't mean that he had lived in complete harmony with himself before. In every person, even a completely satisfied one, something always goes beyond the bounds of obedience and begins to whine or to make demands. This would happen to him, too. But routine repairs, so to speak, was all it needed. Ivan Petrovich knew what would cure this illness— work or a good deed. He didn't do good deeds only for the sake of rubbing them into an aching wound like ointment. They would be done on their own, and the pain would gradually subside. After that the pain would seem to spring up from time to time first in one spot and then in another to show that these places hadn't lost the ability to feel and to hurt.

And what was going on now? How did it happen that his whole being, built up with such care, had suddenly rebelled against him and grown bitter? No matter what he did, it was never right; no matter where he went, no matter what he undertook, some force stopped him and whispered with vindictive correction in its voice, "And couldn't you come up with anything else?" But he really couldn't come up with anything else; he'd lose heart, and a pervasive hollowness would envelop his whole body.

He didn't remember how this discord with himself started. It must have started somewhere; there must have been a first time when his soul not only disagreed with him but also cried out in protest and refused to understand him. The way he lived ran counter to his soul. But the catch was that he had always tried to live by his conscience. He'd always measured his actions against fairness and usefulness, against the common good as he saw it. And aren't the soul and the conscience sisters? Doesn't conscience nurture the soul, and can there actually be strife between them? When it was necessary to speak the truth, he spoke up. When action was required, he acted. And he always made sure he was not turning his back on truth and action. And isn't it important for truth and action to stay inside the boundaries in which they've been presented to a person? Truth is a river whose bottom is covered with solid rock and whose banks are clearly delineated with sand and stone, a river with clean water hurtling forward, not a buttressed mass with an overflowing level of rotting liquid and muddy, washed-out banks. Truth flows from nature itself, and neither public opinion nor orders from above can improve on it. So then why had he, a man living by the unswerving truth, become engaged in a war not only with those who didn't want the truth or who only partially accepted it but also with himself? Why was he certain that it didn't pay to live by only partially agreeing with the truth or by rejecting it altogether (better to reject it outright than in part), yet at the same time why was he uncertain in his own mind as to who stood at the opposite extreme from those who were clearly wrong? They were wrong, and he, in saying they were wrong, in sticking to the truth as though it were law, he was wrong, too. What was this all about, anyway?

Is it that conscience and truth either confer with each other and supplement each other or that they are not independent and bow before something more important? Before what? Before the soul? And does this mean that the soul, eager to bring about a reconciliation, is ready to serve both your kind and ours? But if it will serve your kind, too, if it seeks truth and conscience where they've never spent a single night, then truth isn't truth and conscience isn't conscience, and there's only the searching, suffering soul. And how does the soul fare if conscience and truth are skewed on its account? Where can it find support? All right, let's suppose that the soul doesn't like one-sidedness and can't abide arbitrary judgment, that it's made to get satisfaction from looking for pearls in slag heaps; but while it's digging around there, you see, nothing remains on its side. Well, but what do "its side" and "the other side" mean? Who drew a boundary line between these two sides, and why is a person so tempted to cross this boundary? Isn't this a person's general destiny—to leave his own side and go over to the other one?

And, after chiseling his way into these endless "hows" and "whys" that held no answer, that slid down any answer as if it were a perpendicular wall, after chiseling his way into a remote dead end, into a patch of some sharp-edged, lifeless tormentil, Ivan Petrovich retreated. He didn't understand a thing.

Twelve

Not only were flour and groats kept in the last building, in the flour warehouse, but sugar was kept there, too. Amid the flour and groats, the sugar was stored in lordly fashion: the sacks of flour and groats, thrown on the floor helter-skelter, looked swollen under a coating of gray dust, but a platform had been constructed over on the left side for the sugar and a tarpaulin had been spread under it. And the bags containing the sugar stood out for their cleanliness and well-sewn seams, and they'd been neatly arranged, as if it hadn't been local men who'd carried them in and laid them there but some work crew called in from abroad.

Because he was accustomed to grabbing the heaviest objects first, Ivan Petrovich's feet took him toward the sugar. But Afonya Bronnikov stopped him.

"Ivan Petrovich, let's get the flour. All this—" And once again, as he'd done at the other warehouse, he dismissed everything else with a wave of his hand.

At least it wasn't quite so hot in here. But they still had to hurry, since the fire was less than one entire building away. The huge, shapeless psuedo-pile, psuedo-stack of flour rose to one-and-a-half or two times a man's height. There were enough sacks to keep two people carrying them out till the next fire. Ivan Petrovich didn't let the work scare him— this was no time to mull things over and make calculations—so he hoisted the first sack he came to, one that lay off to the side, without wondering why it had been put there and tackled the flour head on. The sack came apart at the seams as Ivan Petrovich heaved it up onto himself by its gaping side—when it burst in a spray of white, flour stopped up his mouth and poured down his collar. Afonya, unable to restrain himself, began to guffaw in a mighty rumble.

"Now, Ivan Petrovich, into the Angara, then under the fire—and the pie'll be done."

Spitting and brushing himself off, Ivan Petrovich didn't bother to hide his irritation. But what he said made sense.

"Instead of cackling, you should've figured that what you and I can carry out of here won't amount to a drop in the bucket. Not enough for one batch of bread. Where are all the people, anyway?!"

"The boss was going to round them up—"

"Yeah, that boss of yours has forgotten all about it! They whisked him off somewhere—and that's the end of that! He doesn't have his head on straight today."

Rising up in a state of readiness that showed he was about to grab anybody he met by the collar and hurl him this way, Afonya took off.

Ivan Petrovich stopped at the doorway with a sack slung across his shoulders. Where to? It was a long way to the gate, and carrying the flour through the gate would mean creating a path that they were better off without. The fence was nearby, but the fence was still standing; it was maintaining the defense against those who would love to get at all these goods scattered around in the mud and snow. And yet the fence would have to come down. And suddenly it struck Ivan Petrovich: where was the axe? Where was the axe that he'd brought from home and used to tear off the roof? Where had he thrown it? Ivan Petrovich was on the verge of rushing back toward the fire, but he suddenly remembered that he hadn't needed an axe in the last warehouse, where he'd rolled out the vegetable oil, and that he'd left it somewhere before that. And the axe had burned up. He'd let something burn up that was now more necessary for the fence than hands were. He'd brought the thing from home and destroyed it.

Once again he remembered Alyona, and this sudden vision of his wife was disturbing. Maybe she'd gotten herself into trouble, the scatterbrain. For some reason there now seemed to be an enormous distance between them. Nearby, yet far away. This sort of distance was marked off with a different set of paces, a set unknown to him and one he'd never used.

Before rushing off somewhere, Ivan Petrovich glanced once more at the warehouse that Afonya had dragged him away from. They were no longer diving in and out of the doorway over there but were flinging the last bottles and jars through the pattern of fire that covered the doorway like a curtain. What an absolute fool you had to be, totally crazed with heroism, to hold out in there by the skin of your teeth! And in front of the door somebody in a white rabbit-fur hat was performing tricks that even a circus acrobat never dreamed of, catching the stuff in leaps and sprints as it flew through the air. He'd catch something and toss it over his shoulder without looking back. Not far away Boris Timofeich was standing in the bright illumination and watching him. The blaze suddenly splashed high above the middle of the dry-goods warehouses and lit up the whole compound, where everything seemed to stand still and marvel at the dexterity of the fellow in the white rabbit-fur hat. And Boris Timofeich stood and marveled, too. Then the blaze subsided and the district manager dashed off, and everything else dashed off and began rushing around again, too.

During the brief moment when the whole compound had been lit up all at once, Ivan Petrovich had managed to spot a wooden mallet leaning lengthwise against a fence post. It was the same mallet that Afonya had wielded on the roof and that had now been left here as if on purpose, where it could come in handy. Ivan Petrovich grabbed it as he ran, and, aiming close to one of the fence posts, he struck first the upper and then the lower crossbeam with a bang. The boards came down, opening up a view across the sunken road of the garden and bathhouse owned by One-Armed Savely, a native son of the Angara. Ivan Petrovich knocked away the other end of the section, and, just as it fell down, somebody showed up to help him. Nothing should have been surprising that night, and yet Ivan Petrovich couldn't hold back his amazement. His helper was none other than Sashka the Ninth, one of the roughnecks. Together the two of them lifted the fallen section of fencing and hauled it down the slope onto the road. They couldn't have come up with a better arrangement if they'd tried: it made a platform to keep the flour off the ground.

"Let's get another one, Ivan Petrovich," commanded Sashka cheerfully and impudently. It turned out that he did know the polite form of address, not just "Mr. Law-Abiding Citizen."

They tore off a second section and laid it down beside the first one. And they'd just climbed back up the slope when the first dry-goods warehouse after the bend sank with a heavy groan, spewing sparks. Sparks kept pouring out of it, muffling the shouting and blocking the light. Sashka raced over there, and Ivan Petrovich saw how the men Afonya was bringing rushed back. And he couldn't bear it any longer. He had to find Alyona.

Alyona was standing five steps away from the heap of goods, to which she'd brought something and let it drop with a crash. Only the crash confirmed that she hadn't run up empty-handed. Now, stopped in her tracks by the burning-hot wave flowing backward from the collapsed warehouse, she didn't remember where she'd come from and what she'd brought and lost, and she didn't know where she ought to run now. Others around her were shouting and waving their arms, all facing the direction where everything was still crackling and giving off sparks, but the shouting was dry, and the arm-waving accompanied by jumping and stooping looked like a mechanical game. There was something unreal in the way people were behaving—the way they formed chains to pass bundles and packages from hand to hand; the way they ran around the grounds turning away from each other and colliding; the way they teased the fire, taking incredible risks; the way they'd start yelling first in unison, then separately—there was something stupid and unreal about all these activities, which were done out of excitement and disorderly passion. Only the fire was real, pulverizing everything that turned up in its path with an unimaginative relentlessness.

The incessant, explosive shower of sparks finally stopped, and the fire picked up again, starting at the base of the caved-in building. It burned in the jagged corners like tilted, outstretched torches. The neighboring dry-goods warehouse seemed to be swaying and creaking under a lofty crown of flame, trying to break loose—and it couldn't break loose because the wall it shared with the next building kept pulling it back. Apropos or not, Alyona recalled a story people used to tell about how some submerged islands with woods on them rose up from the bottom of the Angara below Ust-Ilim and floated around until planes dropped bombs on them. In the food warehouse nearby, some sweet product was glowing rather than burning—as if an electric current ran through it. Now they could plainly see that, no, not a single warehouse could be recaptured.

Alyona stood where she was till Ivan Petrovich reached her. Frightened by her immobility in the midst of all the running and shouting, he'd crept up on her the last few steps of the way and now approached her from the front.

"Oh, Ivan, look!" she said with a start, not knowing what to say. And at that very moment something especially interesting came into view. "Look!" She pointed at a figure weaving over on the right some distance away and yet still illuminated. After flinging off its winter jacket, it was hurriedly pulling something on. This was one of the roughnecks; Ivan Petrovich could tell who they were by their short, jerky movements.

"What in the world is going on, Ivan?! What's going on?! Everybody's stealing! Klavka Strigunova stuffed her pockets full of little boxes. I daresay they don't have irons in them! I daresay there's something else inside! People are shoving things down their pant legs and under their shirts! And these bottles, these bottles!"

"Don't you get any ideas about taking something." He said these words only to expel the ball of fumes that had accumulated inside him.

No, an Uncle Misha Khampo wouldn't be any help here. Khampo was keeping watch so they wouldn't carry off anything big and noticeable, but look what was happening here . . .

"Why, what do you mean, Ivan! What do you mean?!" Alyona responded rapidly without taking offense, seeing that he wasn't serious. "Why are you saying this to me? Have I brought home a lot of stuff since we've lived together? Was it all that much?"

They could go to the Devil. Let them choke on it.

He didn't walk over and straighten out that roughneck.

Thirteen

Two years earlier Ivan Petrovich and Alyona had celebrated their thirty years of life together. They celebrated by taking their vacations at the same time and going to visit their grown children, all of whom had left their place of birth. But there were only three of them—two daughters and a son. They went from the closest to the farthest, first visiting the daughter who lived in the county seat, where she taught in a grade school, and then moving on to the second daughter, the older one, in Irkutsk, where they nearly cut their travels short on learning only when they arrived that their daughter was in the hospital. Her family had been allotted an apartment on the top floor of a nine-story building, but the elevator didn't work, and during their move, while she was lugging up not just light objects but heavy ones as well, she'd strained herself to the point that right after the house-warming party she landed in the hospital. Just like her mother—she didn't know when to stop either. Naturally it was awkward to leave after this turn of events, but Tanya, their citified daughter, insisted that they go. And even Ivan Petrovich, who was used to all sorts of things and wasn't a worn-out man, even he, after making a dozen trips to the ninth floor, his arms and legs giving out on the last few flights of stairs, swore a blue streak and was more than happy to get away from these urban conveniences that turned city folk into beasts.

And that elevator stood idle to this very day, according to their daughter, and somebody had already been badly injured falling through the smashed door into the shaft. What could never happen in other places was possible in Irkutsk.

And only at their son's place, where they went by plane, did Ivan Petrovich recover his spirits. Borka, their son, met them in Khabarovsk. He was tall and strapping, like all these well-fed kids nowadays, very grown up, and wearing a uniform that set off his masculine build and accentuated the high cheekbones he'd inherited from his mother. And he was no longer "Borka" but "Boris Ivanych." Since flight school he'd been working as a mechanic at a small airport, and, much to Alyona's relief, his work was done on the ground. That same day all three took another plane, a small one, to this place—a beautiful, prosperous town filled with greenery and decorative touches. True, they'd come at a good time, in the dry month of September. Boris had his own house, which his father- and mother-in-law had turned over to the young couple after building a separate, sturdier one for themselves across the street, and next to his house was a garden with various kinds of berries and honest-to-goodness apples. Boris had written about all this and had told them in person, but until he saw it with his own eyes, Ivan Petrovich had regarded it as some storybook tale. And so he picked an apple from a living tree, walked around the town, looked into people's faces and saw that every other one wasn't ruined by heavy drinking, went fishing and was amazed to find more fish in the little stream than in the Angara, and he was happy for Borka. They say that the grass is always greener on the other side, but here things really weren't bad at all. It wasn't a matter of apples and warm weather, for every place has its own climate, but life didn't feel hectic here. More order was evident, and this order was maintained not by threats and penalties but by communal laws established ages ago among the people themselves. That's what it was. And even if Ivan Petrovich were exaggerating, although he believed he wasn't exaggerating in the least, Sosnovka still could never compare with this.

Their son and daughter-in-law pressed them to move here. Boris's father- and mother-in-law echoed them; they'd taken a liking to Ivan Petrovich and Alyona, apparently because of their simple-heartedness and congeniality. "We'll be on the lookout for a house and clinch a deal for you; there's a big State farm here, so you'll be able to find work. You'll come see us and we'll come see you, because you'll need somebody to lean on no matter what. Nobody in Sosnovka is holding you back."

Nobody was holding them back, but what about Sosnovka itself? And the land they'd given their lives to? And the lives of all the ancestors who'd gone before them? Should all this really be left to the roughnecks, who, on their way home from work, would turn off into the cemetery to relieve themselves, which Ivan Petrovich once caught them doing? Should somebody man the barricades or not? We've stood up to foreign enemies in the past and we'd do it again; the enemy among us, like the thief among us, is more frightening.

Ivan Petrovich resigned himself to this, too, after he returned from visiting his son and got back into the joyless harness of life in Sosnovka. But now he knew that people didn't live the same way everywhere and that there was some place to turn for support. And he did his job with this in mind, too, continuing to toil like the local winner in a competition for outstanding work performance even though there wasn't a shred of such competition left; instead you were either a worker or you weren't, or you were a born tiller of the soil, or a habitual loudmouth. And he would interfere, and he'd ask for trouble, and he'd practically have a heart attack again and again—and it always came back to this: it wasn't everywhere that nobody gave a hoot. And he would come out of his despair and admonish others who were prepared to stay in theirs, having built a wall of despair behind which they'd just let everything go up in smoke.

It always came back to this.

During the last year, however, things had become completely unbearable—ever since the present crew of roughnecks had arrived and become firmly entrenched. These work crews had been here before—too many to count. They'd stay awhile, toot their own horns, show off in front of the local folk—and then head back where they came from, to tempt their restless fate somewhere else. And the cemetery already held almost a dozen graves of those who had met their fate by accident and dropped anchor there forever. All kinds of them had come and gone, but never any like the present crowd. These guys made their appearance already organized into a single force, with their own laws and seniority system. They tried to break them up—it didn't work. They tried sending them to a felling site across the Angara—nothing doing. The roughnecks remained at the lower landing next to the town, where the timber was brought for trimming and piling, jobs requiring skilled hands. But their skills lay in other areas. And so it went. There was such a tangled mess of timber all around that you couldn't drive your truck up close; good stuff would be mixed with scraps, and both tops and trunks would be burning in the fire. You'd sit there with your truck for half an hour at a time until you yourself would help clear away the obstruction. If you couldn't hold back and yelled at them, you'd get nowhere with these guys. They'd just have a good laugh and make nasty remarks and then you'd yell at Boris Timofeich and he'd yell at you. For Ivan Petrovich, going to work had gotten to be like going off to hard labor.

And in town. At the recreation center they'd shoot pool for money, and at the store everybody else would wait in line—but make way for them. And if you said anything, they'd shut you up so fast that it would take over a week to pick up all the pieces. When people encountered this unprecedented, tightly joined raft that seemed held together not by the best in human nature but by the worst, they lost their nerve and tried to steer clear of the roughnecks. There were hundreds of folks in the town, but ten had seized power—that's what Ivan Petrovich couldn't understand. But after giving it some thought, he guessed that people had gone their separate ways even before this and that the roughnecks had simply stepped in and taken up the slack. He granted and even believed that the roughnecks could prove to be human beings during a large-scale, general disaster—this breed wasn't all bad—but in better times, when things were fair to middling, they would be drawn together and grow conceited in their devil-may-care attitude because of the lack of order they scented, flocking to it through their keen animal sense of smell. There was a reason why they'd settled in Sosnovka; they would never have lasted in Syrniki, where his son was living. And only two of them had moved away in the past year. One, who looked as if he came from the Caucasus and who had been in command at first, was evidently overthrown and dismissed by his own buddies, after which Sashka the Ninth took charge; the other one, maimed in a drunken brawl, never came back from the hospital. And one more, a guy named Somov, broke away from his pals and moved in with Nadya Pochivalova, whose husband had drowned.

One day in December Ivan Petrovich cruised away from the lower landing after work and was heading for town when halfway there he was stopped by Sashka the Ninth, who was walking along with one of his buddies. Ivan Petrovich put on the brakes. Sashka got in, but his pal stayed on the road, even though there was room in the cab. This Sashka was a good-looking guy—tall, well built, with light blond hair and a radiant complexion—but his good looks seemed eaten away by something. You couldn't put your finger on it at first. It was as if his good looks were drying up from the inside and getting wrinkled, as if they remained only on the surface.

They rode in silence all the way to town. But as he got out at the dormitory, Sashka said with a casual smile, "You better get one thing straight, Mr. Law-Abiding Citizen, Hero of the Struggle, Hero of Labor . . . What you do is none of our business, and what we do is none of yours. But if you're going to make us your business, we'll make you our business."

And soon after that the store ran out of booze. They were out everywhere—there wasn't a drop on either side of the Angara. And the roughnecks, dying for a drink, outfitted their buddy Sonya with a backpack and sent him to the city. For the week that he was flying and sitting out bad weather in airports, they covered for "that guy" at work, not letting on that he wasn't among them. And there was the timber, there was the end-of-the-year deadline for their annual quotas, and everybody's nerves were on edge day and night. Each pair of hands was worth its weight in gold. And when Sonya arrived with the goods, the ranks of the roughnecks thinned out by half. Ivan Petrovich brought the director and showed him: look what's going on. The director removed the work crew from the lower landing. Then Boris Timofeich sent them back because somebody had to do the work, after all, but nobody wanted to take the roughnecks' place, where the work had been neglected and where it was also dangerous simply because this place belonged to the roughnecks.

In January, on a snowy, windy day when you couldn't see a damn thing two steps in front of you, Ivan Petrovich drove up to the lower landing and got out while the truck was being unloaded. The man who did the unloading walked up, sank his hook into the timber, and pulled it down onto the ramp. You couldn't get all the timber in one try, so he grabbed the remaining logs with his hook and pulled it toward himself again. Without wasting any time, Ivan Petrovich began picking up the vertical support beams for the truck bed. Each one weighed a considerable amount; you'd never jump clear if your mind was wandering. He hoisted the first one into place and paused to catch his breath. And no sooner had he taken a step, no sooner had he gotten his head out of the way when the heavy metal support suddenly snapped. It just snapped by itself even though it was mounted leaning inward and shouldn't have fallen backward, which had never happened before. Some roughnecks— two of them—were fussing with something on the other side, where the timber had been pulled off. Ivan Petrovich stood beside them for a moment, looked at them, thought about it a bit, and didn't say anything. What could you say? And he drove off mulling over his fate.

Several days later his engine started to cough. Ivan Petrovich checked the ignition and the carburetor—both were okay. He tinkered and tinkered, but it turned out that somebody had poured a bunch of sand into the gas tank. The driver on the next shift, Petya Razborov, who'd been in the army, said thoughtfully when they were draining the tank, "Sand—that's no big deal. It doesn't last long. But if they dump salt in our tank, Ivan Petrovich . . . then we're in real trouble. Then we'll have something to worry about."

And Ivan Petrovich, a country bumpkin, had never suspected either sand or salt. They didn't pour salt into the tank, but they did slash two tires at once. Petya Razborov stopped driving the same truck as Ivan Petrovich and got a different Kraz.

At the meeting where they summed up the year's achievements, Ivan Petrovich received a bonus, a gift certificate for a rug. He stood up and, throwing a wrench in the works, refused to accept the gift certificate. He didn't need a rug. Bonuses and honors weren't what he needed. He needed the kind of work that they didn't attack from the other end in order to bring it to a halt, and he needed the kind of life that didn't include getting kicked in the shins. That's just what he said. But he said it nervously, almost in tears, trying to find out why people pretended that everything was fine and even splendid as long as the quotas were met, trying to find out how much longer these quotas would conceal and

justify everything going on because of them. Ivan Petrovich's resentment was not against the roughnecks—what could you expect from
them?!—but against his own folks, who'd grown accustomed to all this
and simply looked the other way, believing that any change was always
for the better. Becoming agitated, Ivan Petrovich got choked up over the
same thing that gnawed at him during his late-night meditations: could
he really be the only one who saw and understood these things while
nobody else saw and understood? And if he was the only one, then
why? Why see and understand? Was this true vision and understanding? Hadn't he himself become warped precisely because he was too in-
sistent on sticking to the straight and narrow?

More recently, even after Ivan Petrovich had given notice, they'd
wreaked havoc with the garden in front of his cottage. Most likely one of
his own folks had dug it up while three sheets to the wind. It wouldn't
be difficult to discover whose work this was if he asked around. But he
didn't want to ask. And Alyona kept quiet even though she must have
been informed. His resentment against other people, both guilty and in
the right, had boiled down to his being furious only at himself.

There was just one way out—to leave.

Fourteen

At some point Ivan Petrovich had unintentionally started
watching Alyona more closely. Not even watching her so much as keeping his ear cocked toward the place she occupied beside him. Every husband undoubtedly keeps two images of his wife before him—the way
she is and the way he'd like to see her. At times the images coincide, at
times they diverge, at times they speak with one voice, at times with different voices. They seem to have one face with different distinguishing
marks, and they don't necessarily get along with each other. A husband,
naturally, can always tell which one is approaching him just by listening,
but a wife also knows where each is located inside, and she senses in
herself a disparity between the person and the wife. The same can be
said of husbands, too, of course, but that's a different story.

And who knows when it happened, but his Alyona had merged into
a single whole. What perplexed Ivan Petrovich the most was that he
hadn't noticed when this occurred, when he'd stopped dividing her into
the Alyona that existed for herself and the Alyona that existed for him. It
was clear that, after spending thirty-odd years with each other, they had
flowed together to no small extent and had become more kindred as
each acquired some of the other's flesh, which couldn't help nestling up
to its original shelter. All this was true, and all this should apply to every
couple who has slept in the same bed for decades. But there was also

something quite special about Alyona. Her voice had changed. It seemed as if she were not the one speaking but a unified woman, the mother of all earthly women, who spoke through her. Her voice had grown deeper and richer and it steered a middle course in the stream of sound without being cast up on dry land. And she'd begun to speak less rapidly, and her words had begun to carry more weight—she used to waste a tremendous number of words before extracting the right ones, the main point, for whose sake she had started a conversation; now it would turn up more quickly, without any preparatory bombardment, as he liked to kid her, and it would be phrased more precisely.

Without his noticing, Alyona had begun to occupy the place that she hadn't measured up to in her youth and that may be defined as feminine repletion. This means that there was exactly as much of Alyona as was necessary—no more and no less. Perhaps there was a bit more, but a little excess could always be corrected. Whether he was at home or away, he constantly sensed Alyona in himself as she continued her tireless service. When need be, she would add to or subtract from his character, find patience in him, and lead him home. On long trips in the truck by himself, he would often hold conversations with her, knowing how she would reply, and, after talking things over, after consulting her, he'd arrive at some decision. Over the years that tidy, soothing world that was Alyona not only had not grown cold but had even expanded in understanding and warmth. The husband who doesn't hear his wife's voice inside—"Wait a minute, Vanya or Styopa"—soon throws off the normal garments of life, and even while he's still alive his life fits him like a big, loose robe that once belonged to somebody else.

Petite and shapely, with a girlish figure, she didn't simply move from place to place—she'd shoot straight up like a bird and fly. And that's how it was to this day, even though she should have slowed down some by now. Looking at her, Ivan Petrovich had brought himself up short more than once with the terrible and perhaps prophetic thought that people like Alyona, impetuous and all wound up, are cut down instantly, without complaining or gradually cooling off. One time, having completely worn herself out monitoring production rates while also working as an accounting clerk, having heard her fill of obscenities and frozen long enough out in the open air, she'd half-asked, half-told him that she planned to go work at the library, and Ivan Petrovich had started to laugh. "And what are you going to do there? Beat against the windows like a butterfly?" He couldn't imagine her sitting down, which working with books required. And she didn't sit down. She even wrote out catalog cards while standing up, bending slightly over a table or a windowsill. And she traveled to the far corners of the district pushing books even on people who didn't know which way they opened. And how many books had he, Ivan Petrovich, repaired—nearly a hundred! At first he repaired only the ones he read, and then he repaired all the rest—not just once but several times—and yet she kept bringing him more and more.

So now she, too, would have to leave work she loved.

Nobody praises wives these days, but what could Ivan Petrovich do if he couldn't imagine even God himself finding any fault with Alyona? And when he thought about her—here she comes running, now she's running into the house in the evening, impatient and dying to see her husband right away, now she's calling out something apologetic and disjointed even as she runs—his soul would immediately stretch out in peacefulness. Now the two of them are sitting together over tea, he's silent while she's speaking for him and for herself, and he doesn't know which words belong to whom; all he knows is that they've talked to their hearts' content and are better off because of it.

A wife is something separate. Given to you for your shared life, but separate. Some couples spend an entire lifetime trying to get close to each other and can't do it. Alyona was more than a wife for Ivan Petrovich. Everything a woman can be had come together in this quick-witted little figure, as in the Triune God. People usually don't appreciate those who spend their whole lives rattling pots and pans day in and day out; they take these efforts for granted, like air and water, and keep trying to get something more without knowing what they want. Russian men aren't used to living in harmony with their women. But for Alyona all this came without sacrifice and strain; it emanated from her nature and soul, and she would have withered on the vine if she hadn't had somebody to hover around and fuss over. She put everything down to the last drop into their shared life, leaving nothing for herself, and, drained, relieved, her face and body sagging, she would smile so happily and blissfully as she got into bed to replenish her strength during the night that there could not have been the subtlest doubt that this was genuine.

Every husband probably retains in his memory a single incident that says everything about his wife. Ages ago, when they still lived in Yegorovka, Ivan Petrovich was once tinkering under a truck with the hood up and the engine running. The truck was an old one, a ZIS–150. Only afterward did he find the gas leak, which he hadn't known about at the time. Suddenly the engine burst into flame. Spread-eagled on the ground and panic-stricken, Ivan Petrovich froze. He was able to dash to safety only when something rained down on him. A box of sand, set aside for winter, was standing in a corner of the entrance to the shed, and Alyona had grabbed it in a flash and dumped it on the fire. Later, after they had filled the box back up, Ivan Petrovich had great difficulty just getting it off the ground. No sense in Alyona even trying.

"It wasn't me," she concluded simply. "It was somebody else grabbed my arms and put their strength into them to save you. I don't remember a thing. And it didn't seem heavy a'tall."

And how many others times had it happened that somebody used her arms to lift something way too heavy for her?

When Ivan Petrovich came home and said that that was it, that was the end, he'd decided to turn in his resignation, she agreed.

"Well, so be it, Ivan . . . Of course you want to go to Borka . . ."

He'd also learned to hear what she left unsaid. You want to go to Borka, but it shouldn't be like this, not like this . . .

Fifteen

Now they could only keep carrying and carrying. Ivan Petrovich would position his shoulder, pull a sack down from one of the top rows of the pile, adjust it more comfortably with a movement of his shoulder, and swing around in the direction of the raging, fiery flashes of light hurtling through the doorway. And he'd walk down to the road, beating a single path. This was nothing new, for he'd done a lot of carrying in his lifetime, and if there hadn't been any fire, any catastrophe, this work would even have brought back pleasant memories—physical rather than mental—of his youth, when the whole village had fussed over the crops. And later on, during his life as a logger, there'd been countless times— whenever he got the chance—that Ivan Petrovich had taken a pinch of flour, crushed it in his fingers, and waited: after the bitter-tasting guilt, like after reveille, scenes of working in the fields would come to him clothed in sweat, dust, and sunlight.

At first there were about ten of them carrying out flour. And in the excitement and general enthusiasm they made such good progress, with two or three of them throwing down the sacks and the rest carrying them, that during the short interval when all hands were on deck they removed the whole top layer. Ivan Petrovich was already sizing up the sugar: pretty soon they'd start on that, too, though this customer was sweet to the tongue and bitter on the back. But Ivan Petrovich, scarcely lifting his eyes and seeing nothing except sacks of flour and the road, began to meet fewer and fewer figures coming from the opposite direction, and they were doing a poorer and poorer job of removing the stuff from the warehouse. Ivan Petrovich straightened up. Only four of them were left: he and Afonya, and One-Armed Savely, whose place was next door, and some half-familiar young guy who'd stripped to his shirt and was unsteady on his feet.

"Afonya!" shouted Ivan Petrovich. "What happened this time? Where are they?"

"It's more interesting over there, Ivan Petrovich," he replied as he ran past. "More interesting, know what I mean?"

Onto his shoulder. On his shoulder. Off. A short run that let his leaping heart just barely get back into place, and once again: onto his shoulder, on his shoulder, off. And he wasn't so young anymore. He squatted lower and lower as he danced along, his feet stumbled more and more often, and his heart never had time to find its nest. Even Afonya, strong as a bull, who at first had taken two sacks crisscrossed on his shoulder each time, now ran with his head down while carrying only one.

Boris Timofeich appeared and also joined in the carrying, having relinquished his authority to spontaneously occurring events. But Afonya and Ivan Petrovich unanimously demanded that he stop straining himself and go round up some men. Vodnikov left and then appeared again, bringing several men with him. One of them, a half-drunk roughneck, set about organizing a human chain so they wouldn't have to carry the sacks the whole way but could pass them from hand to hand. Afonya sent him and his chain packing, a task the roughneck didn't waste any time fulfilling, and they didn't lay eyes on him again. The new roundup added two reliable men—Semyon Koltsov and a metal worker from the garage named Teplyakov. There were fleeting glimpses of Sashka the Ninth, his brazen face flashing briefly about three times, and then he disappeared.

You couldn't tell where there were more sacks—in the warehouse or in the pile on the road.

Ivan Petrovich noted that Teplyakov had started on the groats. He was probably right: they ought to recapture at least some of the groats, too. They ought to recapture all of it, but the fire in the neighboring warehouse was pressing forward, crackling in preparation, and the common wall, where the groats were stacked, was becoming noticeably hotter. To help Teplyakov, Ivan Petrovich decided to alternate sacks of flour with sacks of groats. It was dim and deathly still inside, the air was thick with flour dust, and the flashes of light from the doorway died down and flared up only on the sugar. And the hot, roaring gusts, which were on the right as they ran in and on the left as they ran out, kept surging more and more forcefully.

From underneath the sacks Ivan Petrovich didn't see or hear a thing. His heart was pounding, and all other sounds were muted or seemed like weak undertones among the breakers lacerating his chest. The real fire and the fire inside merged before his eyes—flames from both of them were seething and spreading at the same time. Ivan Petrovich's lungs were ready to burst. Dropping a sack, he collapsed after it onto the wooden platform and fixed his gaze on the first building he saw, gluing his eyes to it so he wouldn't lose consciousness. This building turned out to be a bathhouse, from which a person suddenly emerged. It looked like the owner, One-Armed Savely, who then followed some tracks down to the road. Everything was lit up for a long way around, but Ivan Petrovich's eyes saw only darkness, and he couldn't say whether somebody had really come out of the bathhouse or whether he'd merely imagined it.

And he imagined something else: an old woman in a short fur coat with the collar turned up was walking along picking flowers at the edge of the road. She walked and walked, looking carefully, bent down, hurriedly plucked something, and put it into her bag. And on to the next snowy slope. Ivan Petrovich recognized her when she turned around, and he was sorry he did because then and there he guessed what sort of flowers these were, what sort of snowdrops. The old woman, who'd never done anything like this before, was picking up the bottles that had been tossed out of the compound—and, naturally, not the empty ones. But then until this night an incident like that one had never happened before either.

Fire leaped out around the corner facing the Angara—and it was above the last warehouse, where the flour was. Ivan Petrovich jumped to his feet. So that was why nobody had brought down a single sack after his last one. Now they were just carrying them out and dropping them five steps from the doorway because there was no time to take them the full distance.

At the other end of the fire, where the dry-goods warehouses stood and where the blaze was going full force, an uneven formation of people seemed to reel back and forth from the heat. And Boris Timofeich's shrill voice could be heard from that direction as it drowned out all the other unsynchronized shouts. People were standing there on purpose—to keep the fire away from the store. If the store remained intact, then they'd believe they'd almost won, that they could be completely victorious with just a little more effort.

Waving his good arm, Uncle Misha Khampo was hopping lopsidedly around the heap of salvaged goods in the middle of the compound. Seen from a distance, it looked as if he were rounding up baby chicks that were fleeing in all directions from a hen.

He had no reason to stay by the gate because the whole place now stood wide open.

Uncle Misha Khampo, that spirit of Yegorovka, had been disabled since childhood. His right arm, which was just barely capable of simple nudging and grasping, hung like a whip, and he spoke with such difficulty that outsiders found him impossible to understand. "Khampo-o! Khampo-o-o!" he'd drawl for a long, long time, trying to elicit the right word from his rigid depths, and if he managed to get it out, he'd hurriedly nudge this word along with an "aha" from some-where not too far off and light up with a happy smile. Those who knew Uncle Misha Khampo would hasten to help him and put in the next word, and then he would just nod and say, "Aha," his big, dark, leath-ery face shining. "Khampo-o!" he'd begin as he crossed a doorstep, and, without finding it the least bit difficult, the man or woman of the house would reply, "Hi, how are you? Come on in. You've been to the store, you say? Was there a line? And have you made dinner yet? Well, in that case sit down and have tea with us."

People don't need a lot of words to understand each other. It takes a lot of words to prevent understanding.

Uncle Misha lived alone. He'd buried his wife, who had been re-settled here during the war, a long time ago. The nephew they'd raised was sent to work in the North after military service, and, because he was good with his hands, had a quick mind, and had been trained to do all manner of things from an early age, he made big money up there. But he didn't send home a single kopeck. Uncle Misha did his own laundry, fixed things himself, kept a piglet, and at the age of seventy still chopped firewood for other people. He had tremendous strength and was used to doing everything under the sun with his left hand alone. But his tremen-dous strength was a thing of the past; now, of course, it had waned somewhat, and when he was puttering around with firewood he'd sink the hatchet into a block of wood more and more often and gaze steadily for a long time at the frozen or open Angara.

Sometimes he'd try to say something about the Angara, or most likely about Yegorovka, which had disappeared underwater. He'd extend his arm in that direction and choke out "khampo," but in this case people couldn't supply any words except the name of the old village. Uncle Misha would get upset and walk away.

He was struggling to say something important, you see.

Khampo was a born watchman, a self-appointed watchman. Not be-cause of his disabilities—no, he could do any kind of work, and he'd done a great number of things without a hitch. He was simply cut out to be a watchman. Out of the hundreds and hundreds of rules that were way over his head, the rule he placed first was, Hands off what isn't yours. Perhaps he even linked all the discomforts and disorder in the world to one thing only: people didn't keep their hands to themselves. Uncle Misha undertook any kind of watchman's job with great willingness. In the old days he would guard the Yegorovka pea crop for the kolkhoz, riding a mare through the fields year in and year out, he would spend nights on the threshing floors, and during the day in his spare time he'd pace back and forth in the stable and the dairy barn, keeping watch. And he never charged a fee for his sharp-eyed vigilance, considering his protection of society an obligation placed on him at birth. In the new town, when everybody was building and moving in, Uncle Misha could have been taken for a commandant at first. He kept an eye on everything and had a hand in everything that required security. They were used to this, and none of his people would ever dream of scolding Uncle Misha for not minding his own business. But during the first few years even theft rarely occurred. And when it did, Uncle Misha would become terribly upset. In his view, the established order of daily life could suffer no greater misfortune or greater loss than stealing. "What's the matter with you, Uncle Misha? Where were you?" people who weren't too sensitive to the pain of others would ask, knowing very well what would follow. What followed was always the same: Uncle Misha, unsuccessfully trying to articulate something, to justify himself in some way, would start to sob. "Khampo-o! Khampo-o!" His soul would be torn to pieces, his huge body would tremble, tears would stream down his face, and his right arm would try to rise and point to something.

Stealing gained a firm hold in time, and Uncle Misha wouldn't have lasted long if he'd reacted to every theft with such violent emotion. He, too, had to adapt. Whenever he heard rumors about someone's loss, he no longer shuddered as though he'd been struck, and he didn't run off to his cottage to hide the weakness of an invalid. Only his face would grow numb, expressing an enormous concentration that encompassed all of life, and it would take a long time for a guilty smile to appear there again.

But nowadays even the thief has degenerated into the Devil only knows what. Now grown men, trying to impress young female teachers on some holiday, will break into somebody's chicken coop and tear off the roosters' heads. Or, even though they're wallowing in luxury, they'll clean out some kind old woman who's taken great pains to acquire store-bought refreshments for the workmen who've agreed to saw up her firewood. This sort of thing happened in the past, too . . . But it never happened that one of the hoodlums who delivered the birds for cleaning was a brother of the teacher with whom they were celebrating the holiday, or that the other hoodlums, after taking stock of the old woman's pantry, suddenly turned out to be the very workmen for whom the refreshments had been prepared and, having helped themselves, then refused to do the job for her.

These aren't thieves—they're dirty scoundrels.

Sixteen

Having made up his mind to move away, Ivan Petrovich began to ponder more and more often and in ever greater detail, What does a person need in order to live in peace? If he has work that he doesn't regard as hard labor and a family he feels close to, what else is required so that when he wakes up unexpectedly in the night he won't lie there waiting for morning in desperation, wishing for the ice to start breaking up?

Let's begin with prosperity . . . Prosperity—yes, it is necessary, for without it a person begins to come apart, like a bone coming away from a piece of meat. But prosperity is not only having enough inside you, on you, and in reserve for you; it is not only what's required today and what will be required tomorrow for the satisfaction of the stomach as well as for the satisfaction of going out and getting the better of somebody else. If it were that way, how simple everything would be. But a hog in a warm pigsty can't help but know that it's being fattened up for meat, because it does have eyes, after all, and, even though they're small and bloated, they are capable of seeing that the work of those who aren't being fattened up for meat is more than simply gorging themselves and that life is more than just waiting around to gorge yourself. Human beings, having surrounded themselves with a whole host of support systems that produce prosperity, are obligated to maintain something special within this prosperity, something that comes from themselves and not from shortages alone, something causal and controlling that forces prosperity to feel ashamed of its full coffers in spite of itself.

All right, more about prosperity later.

Work is performed not only in the name of His Royal Highness the Belly. How many there are who barely work or don't work at all but stuff their bellies every bit as well as those who do. This is easy nowadays.

Work is what remains after you're gone. You are no longer there, you yourself are already becoming work for others, but those who come after you will still be reminded of you for a long, long time by your work. So they say. And so it is, especially if your work flows into a useful river. There are two rivers, one with a useful current and the other with a useless current, and community life moves toward whichever of these is the more powerful. But, again, this happens only in general, on some vast, superhuman plane. What is he, Ivan Petrovich, supposed to feel when he goes out tomorrow at daybreak and drives twenty or thirty kilometers in order to haul back his hundred cubic meters of timber per shift? Of course, even the language itself—"kilometers," "cubic meters," "timber"—seems designed to determine your feelings, pushing them in the direction of rubles. But this isn't what happens. Not entirely. It's not the thought of rubles that urges him on, making him overload his Kraz and squeeze in extra trips, but the work itself, which encompasses hundreds of people at the same time. When he's working, he doesn't remember that it's kilometers, cubic meters, and rubles; he rises above them into a totally different world of fantasy where there is no book-keeping, only movement, rhythm, and celebration. There his movements are always in step, and for that reason moving is easy. In step with what he couldn't say, though it looks as though his movements are in step with his soul, with its primordial inclination. Up there he is wholly transformed into the response to someone's urgent summons, and his soul becomes a finely tuned stringed instrument that begins to resound freely and openly.

Yes, he's a real worker—he knows this in his own mind—and life looks the most secure from the height he soars to when he's working.

Each person's life has four structural supports: home and family, work, the people who share weekdays and holidays with you, and the land your home stands on. And each of these four is more important than the next. If one goes lame, the whole world tilts. It's only through a child's eyes that the world looks like a marvelous gift, radiant with sunshine and filled with human kindness. The farther you get from birth, the more the rising sun exposes the world's disorderliness and discord. In his early years Ivan Petrovich believed that this was a temporary incompleteness, an unfinished stage in a long, difficult job that required more work, but later it became clear that the world, not being finished, had grown rickety even on its old foundations, and yet people were hastily putting in more and more new ones that swayed on unanchored bases.

There was probably never a time when people came close to an overwhelming inclination toward good. And for every person so inclined, there were always two or three who went the other way. But there was a distinction between good and evil; each had its own well-defined image. People didn't say that evil was the flip side of good, that it had the same face looking to the left rather than to the right. Instead, evil was considered a force that, like paganism, had not yet converted to a better, moral religion, a force that did bad things because of its undeveloped, bestial nature, not realizing that what it did was bad. If a line could have been drawn between good and evil, it would have turned out that some people had crossed the line while others still hadn't, but all were headed in one direction—toward good. And the number of those crossing over increased with each generation.

What happened next is anybody's guess. Who frightened the ones who had already crossed the line and tasted goodness? Why did they turn back? Not at once and not en masse, but they did turn back. Traffic across the line became two-way. People started sauntering back and forth, joining up in a friendly manner first with one crowd, then with the other, and they trampled and rubbed out the boundary between them. Good and evil became mixed together. Later on this foul-smelling mishmash was set aside once and for all, so it wouldn't get in the way. In their pure forms, good turned into weakness and evil into strength. But they have barely even survived in pure form; they've ceased being a way of life and have become a point of view that can change every day.

What do we mean nowadays by a good or bad person? Nothing whatsoever. These are obsolete terms that remain in the language as a reminder of our grandparents' time, when people simply and naively judged others by their heartfelt gestures, by their ability or inability to feel another's suffering as though it were their own. In current everyday practice a good person is one who doesn't do any evil, who minds his own business and doesn't interfere with anything unless asked. The measure of a good person is not his natural inclination toward good but rather the convenient position he chooses between good and evil, the constant, steady temperature of his soul. The attitude "It's your funeral," with the pallbearers facing in two directions, has marched from the outskirts to the center of town.

What used to happen out of ignorance has become the test of an enlightened mind. What people fled for centuries they have come back to once again. And instead of walking back, they've raced up in a motor vehicle, declaring the supreme victory of humanity to be the very fact that they fled on foot but have returned by vehicle.

So, then, concerning prosperity. We have prosperity, even great prosperity, but a person still can't live with any confidence in either today or tomorrow, as if he's still shivering out in the cold, and he keeps looking around anxiously. Despite all this prosperity something is lacking. He himself is lacking—the self he might have been with a better outcome—and this difference between what a person has become and what he might have become calls him to account for every degree of divergence.

Pondering life in all its twists and turns during long, disjointed periods of reflection, Ivan Petrovich came to one conclusion. For a person to feel fairly good about life, he must be at home. That's right, at home. Above all else, he must be at home—not just housed somewhere but at home within himself, in his own inner domain, where everything has a fixed, long-established place and purpose. Then you're at home in your house or apartment, from which you go off to work on the one hand and return to yourself on the other. And you're at home in your native land.

And he never felt at home anywhere. Not in his native land—what wasn't flooded had been emptied out by logging, with neither concern nor regard for this land. Inside him there was total pandemonium, like in a smashed-up, overturned wagon. And if there's no refuge in either the one place or the other, there won't be any in the middle either, no matter how hard you try.

◢◢   "So you're leaving, then?" asked Afonya as they walked out of the garage together after work. Rumor had already got around that Ivan Petrovich had turned in his resignation.

"Yes, I'm leaving."

"And what's there, where you're going?"

"Crops. They plow, they plant, and after that they harvest. Remember how it was in Yegorovka?"

"And what's the pay like?"

"Probably a little less, but I don't need much now."

Afonya wasn't asking the right questions, and Ivan Petrovich wasn't giving him the right answers. They hadn't hit the right ones—until Afonya said, "You'll go away, I'll go away—who will be left?"

"Somebody will."

"Who? Who is that 'somebody,' Ivan Petrovich?" Straining his voice to the limit, Afonya didn't so much speak as let out a moan. "Ah! Are we really going to just abandon it?! Clean it out completely and abandon it! And then say, 'Here you are—whoever wants it, it's all yours!'"

"I'm tired, Afonya. I've become a real son of a bitch. You can see for yourself that I don't make sense anymore."

"And what about Yegorovka?"

"What about it?"

He thought Afonya would say, "It's in us, in us." He thought Afonya would start to say, "If we leave this place, our Yegorovka might as well never have existed, but as long as we're here, its memory still lives on." Because that's the way he himself reasoned. But Afonya said, "Can you find the spot on the water where Yegorovka used to be?"

"I don't know. I guess I can."

"This summer I want to put up some kind of marker on that spot. Saying, 'Here stood Yegorovka. It wasn't the worst worker in the world. It worked hard for Mother Russia.'"

"How can you do that? Who'll give you permission?"

"And who'll stop me? There's no law against it, Ivan Petrovich. I haven't heard of any such law. Never. If you can put something on land, why not on water?"

Ivan Petrovich came to his senses.

"All this is just child's play. What are you, a little kid playing with toys? Who's any better off because of them?"

"Ah, Ivan Petrovich." Afonya burst out laughing. His laughter came easily but from the bitterness in his soul, and somehow it brought no relief. "What's your guess? There are so many toys all around . . . you think mine would be one too many?"

He had to turn off into his narrow back street—and so he turned off.

Seventeen

This is how it went: as long as there was no fire, he and Afonya exerted themselves alone, just the two of them; but once the fire rushed in, other people came running, too. And now a whole crowd was in desperate straits in the last warehouse, from which a whitish dust was spraying out—sacks of flour, groats, and sugar were flying every which way. And everybody was heading there, into the heat and incandescence. This wouldn't have been bad—it was their daily bread, after all, that they were salvaging—except that drunks were turning up among the rescuers. One of them—the boy who'd helped tear off the roof and then roll out the vegetable oil—Ivan Petrovich snatched out of the inferno when he could no longer comprehend anything. He snatched him out and hauled him down to the road, where the boy settled in for a night's sleep on the flour sacks. Another one, a roughneck in a burnt quilted vest, somebody tumbled outside like a sack, and while he was rolling around among the sacks, having trouble getting to his feet, Ivan Petrovich noticed that he was wearing new felt boots that hadn't been broken in.

They were throwing the sacks right by the door, throwing them just to get them out, to snatch them from the fire. But there was no salvation for them there either, two steps away from the warehouse. The roof would cave in, and they'd still end up in the flames. Ivan Petrovich set about dragging them toward the fence. He no longer hoisted them onto his shoulders but pulled them up onto his weak stomach and then threw them down the slope with an awkward run. There somebody was picking them up again and carrying them to the road. And from the way the person lifted them, clumsily scooping them up against his side, Ivan Petrovich concluded that this was One-Armed Savely.

A robust guy, this One-Armed Savely, tenacious and not all worn-out from work despite his age. And today he'd been constantly moving heavy objects, working quickly and without a lot of fuss, and his claw-like good arm didn't lose its grip when he grabbed the sacks.

Somebody was calling Ivan Petrovich in a drunken voice. If the voice reached him, that meant it wasn't coming from the fire, and that meant the person wasn't burning up, so Ivan Petrovich didn't turn around. They were now down to the final minutes.

For some reason he needed to know whether it was morning or night. His need to know this was greater than his desire to fall down and catch his breath. He looked up suddenly toward the hill where daybreak appeared and it seemed to him that the darkness there might be growing damp and acquiring a dull moistness. So it must be close to morning. While looking away, he tripped and almost fell.

And wasn't it strange? First everything around him would suddenly grow silent and Ivan Petrovich would be deserted, left in complete stillness. Then sounds would spring up and people would start rushing around nearby. And then each shout would resound in him abruptly, as if it were aiming right for him and subsiding in him. And then, without looking, he'd see the whole compound with the warehouses now engulfed in flame, with the sides wide open where the fences had been and a disorderly whirl within.

In the corner where the fire had started, the low embers were burning out. That was where a draft seemed to have fanned the flames. From there the fire had traveled outward along the two shoulder pieces of a wide, curving yoke. At the ends of the yoke, the farthest warehouses still shone darkly through the flames as though hanging from hooks. Little by little the men had taken apart half of the warehouse that lay in the path to the store. Kozeltsov's voice was giving orders over there again. People were colliding and rebounding, colliding and rebounding, and the searing heat brushed them away like mosquitoes.

The dominant sound in the uproar created by the fire was not a hum, not a whistle, and not a howl, but a crackle, a mighty crackle—as if the blaze were breaking away from the wood and ripping the sky apart as it leaped upward.

And everybody in the compound kept shouting and shouting.

Valya the storekeeper was demanding that Vodnikov not waste any time in setting up a committee to take inventory of the salvaged goods. Boris Timofeich's voice cracked as he coughed up the words.

"What do you mean 'committee'?! Are you nuts?! What good is a committee now! Just take a look!"

"No, you take a look!" Valya spread her arms in a wide circle. "Just take a look—here's what's left! Those crates were all counted." She was pointing at some stacked crates of vodka. "I counted sixty-eight crates— where are they now, those sixty-eight?!"

"To hell with your crates! Who dragged them out? I didn't give any instructions to drag them out! Let 'em burn."

"No, to hell with your workers! These crates are a millstone around my neck!"

And when it hit the storekeeper that there were countless other millstones around her neck and that a red-hot band was tightly squeezing this slender neck, Valya began to sob again. And when she took her hands away from her face, Vodnikov was no longer there, but Uncle Misha Khampo was standing around nearby trying somehow to look after the poor woman.

"Keep an eye on things, Uncle Misha, keep an eye on things," she asked for the tenth time through her tears. And, with Uncle Misha's help, she began dragging the scattered and strewn items into a single mound.

The people in the flour warehouse began shouting more loudly and swearing more foully—they couldn't do the job without yelling, without something to jolt them and to urge them on. And as they threw the sacks outside, the men began to pause more and more often—to grab some air. Ivan Petrovich continued to stand at the crossroads. He had no feeling in his arms and legs, and his heart had grown weak from the driving pace and was no longer kicking. He remembered only one thing: hoist, hold, and drop, and these three simple movements, repeated countless times, divided each run into three breaths.

As he let a sack slip out of his hands, he sensed that amid the general commotion and disorder something in particular was out of joint. He seemed to sense rather than see that something was wrong and only afterward did he take a look. Sure enough, once again a figure had gone farther away than the disorder required, and it was heading for the bathhouse. It was heading in that direction and carrying a sack. Ivan Petrovich went down to the road. On its way back the figure noticed that someone was waiting, gave a start, and then quickened its pace. Savely was not one to lose his nerve.

"What do you think you're doing?" Ivan Petrovich confronted him. "Are you starving?"

"You saw me?"

"Yes, I did."

"You didn't see a damn thing. You've handed in your resignation. So just keep your mind on that. Got it?"

And he dropped his solitary, heavy hand on Ivan Petrovich's shoulder.

Why is it that when people want you to do something bad, they clap you on the shoulder?

They made it. They picked up everything that was left in the last warehouse and came tumbling outside—yelling, frenzied, and totally spent. Even Afonya Bronnikov, always a calm, cool-headed guy, shouted in a savage roar and looked like a full-grown devil with his mouth wide open, all covered with flour and soot. Ivan Petrovich watched them with surprise and felt guilty, as if he'd been standing there twiddling his thumbs. Something inside the empty warehouse fell with a thud and something began to howl and to pull the flames upward, with one last effort connecting the whole row of food warehouses in a single, tall, roaring blaze.

Someone completely overcome by fumes wrung out of himself with a desperate wheeze:

"We'll ne-ver sur-ren-der our proud 'Vi-king' ship!
No-bo-dy is as-king for me-r-r-cy!"

Although he'd seen his fill of everything imaginable in this hot tur-
moil, Uncle Misha Khampo still rubbed his eyes to make certain: two
guys were playing ball. Squashed, ragged, and resembling a big, loose
bundle, the ball would fly from one guy's foot to the other guy, zigzag-
ging its way with kicks and throws toward the toppled fence. Uncle
Misha looked around to show somebody, but no one happened to be
close by. Meanwhile the ball had plopped down on the fence, and something had fallen out of it. Without giving it any more thought, Khampo
rushed over to the players. One of them grabbed the ball with his hands,
tossed it into the street, and jumped into the street himself. Uncle Misha
jumped after him. And when the guy bent down to pick up the ball,
Uncle Misha overtook him. Grabbing him by the collar with his good
hand, he jerked him up off the ground like a child and managed to make
out that the "ball" really was a bundle, with colorful fancy clothes coming out of it like a fan. And the guy picking it up was Sonya.
    Khampo had just made out who and what this was when a blow
struck him from the side. He managed to change his grip, swing Sonya
around by the neck, and pull him toward himself. Sonya began squealing like a pig and jumping up and down, trying to knock Uncle Misha
into the tormentil. And they hit him again and again—not with their
hands but with some heavy object. Uncle Misha tried to turn his head to
see who was beating him, but he couldn't lift his head at all and merely
held out his right arm, the one he couldn't control, trying to defend himself. And they kept beating and beating him, beating and beating . . .

◢◤   This is how they looked when Ivan Petrovich saw them afterward: they were lying on the trampled snow locked in an embrace—
little Sonya all hunched up and Uncle Misha Khampo on top of him with
his head twisted awry. And five steps away lay the wooden mallet.

Eighteen

There comes an end to everything. Even this terrible night passed,
and morning rose. By the light of day the fire dwindled and subsided,
wearily finishing off what was left. The morning rose warm and damp,
and acrid smoke, hanging low, enveloped the town and wouldn't leave.
Smoldering chunks of wood shone darkly along the riverbank and on
the ice, giving off smoke. The muddy compound, smashed to a pulp and
sharply outlined on two sides by the wide, smoking strip where the fire

had been, represented something terrifyingly hopeless and final. And the little green store, still intact, provided no comfort whatsoever; on the contrary, it added bitterness and pain and a flood of emotion by standing out from its surroundings.

The supply department's salvaged goods lay right in the middle of the compound under a huge new tarpaulin. And Uncle Misha Khampo and Sonya were also lying under a tarpaulin, still unseparated. Guards stood over the tarpaulins in both places, talking with no one and allowing no one to approach.

They were waiting for the police and an investigator. They were waiting for a commission—the first one, and the second one, and the third one, for there would be no end to them now . . . They were waiting for their own bosses and for the higher-ups from outside. Telegrams had been sent to all quarters at the start of the working day. All work had been abandoned and it was quiet on the streets and in the garage. Not a sound came from the lower landing. They were waiting.

They were waiting to see what would happen next.

After returning from the fire, Ivan Petrovich did not lie down. The stove was lit when he got there—Alyona wouldn't have forgotten to look after the household even during a bombing raid. She threw something together in a jiffy and set it on the table. But, after serving the meal, Alyona began to sob with great bitterness and then fell into bed.

Ivan Petrovich sat there for a while, just sat there without touching the food, then changed his boots, looked out the window and saw how the smoke was drifting away from the riverbank, and went outside. He went to Afonya's house, hoping to get there before Afonya collapsed into bed and fell asleep. But Afonya wasn't planning to go to bed either. His daughter was cleaning and rubbing something into two cuts on his forehead and his chin that were as deep as wounds and caked with dried blood. Whenever his daughter took her hands away, he would sip tea from a huge metal mug.

Ivan Petrovich asked, "What are we going to do, Afanasy? Do you know what to do now or not?"

"We'll go on living," said Afonya, wincing either from his disturbed wounds or from his disturbed soul. "Living in this world, Ivan Petrovich—it's a tough thing to do, but still . . . we still have to live."

And after taking a sip from his mug, he also asked, "And what've you decided to do?"

"Go on living is what we'll do," replied Ivan Petrovich, merely putting the same words in a different order.

Nineteen

The earth lay in the loose snow, hiding quietly and sadly as if it, too, were suffering from the night's misfortune. It slid gently down the hill into an open field, through a scattering of young pine, and then under the ice. The hill contained some woods, next to which two dark patches of wasteland jutted into the field. Dark forest also rose in the direction Ivan Petrovich headed while leaving the town, but it was extremely sparse over there, and the bay began just beyond it. Right up against the first patch of wasteland, separating it from the road, was the cemetery, where in a couple of days they would lay to rest a long-suffering Yegorovka man and an unknown and forever nameless wretch. They, the living, would determine where to lower each of them, but it was up to the earth—to the one that brings forth the righteous and the guilty, its own folk and strangers—it was for the earth to decide, to judge by its own rules, what would eventually become of each one.

It was very still all around—like sediment in which new movement is building to a head. The smoke from the town didn't reach this far, and you could see clearly and for a long distance in the softened light of dawn. The heavy sky, more wan than white, just like the slightly thawed field below it, receded in a long slope beyond the Angara, where the sun set. The forest was dark over there, too, and there, too, it wasn't dense.

But by now the young pine trees on the riverbank were stretching responsively, yielding to the first feeling of warmth, and the air smelled slightly scorched. By now the sticky snow was settling underfoot and the distant span of the river was growing soft. Spring had found even this earth—and the earth was waking up. Now it would take roll call to see what had died off and what had survived, what had increased through people's doing and what had diminished. It would gather what had survived and not died off into one living mass and prepare it for birth. The sun would warm up—and once again, just like every spring, the earth would bring forth all its green and flowering wares and present them by agreement for human toil. And it wouldn't remember that human beings don't keep the agreement.

No land is ever orphaned.

Ivan Petrovich kept walking and walking, leaving the town and, as it seemed to him, leaving himself, pressing farther and farther into the solitude he'd found. And it felt like solitude not only because there were no other people around him but also because he sensed emptiness and monotony in himself, too. Whether this was consent or fatigue, a brief trance or the beginning of solidification—how could he tell! But his steps were light, free, and even, as if he'd hit his stride and found his breathing rhythm by accident, as if he'd finally been carried off down the right road. It smelled of pitch, yet it wasn't the man in him that perceived this smell but something else, something that merged with the scent of pitch. A woodpecker rapped on a dry tree trunk, yet it wasn't a woodpecker rapping but his heart responding to something with gratitude and impatience. He saw himself from a long way off: a little man who'd gotten lost was walking across the spring earth despairing of ever finding his home, and now he'd disappear behind a thicket and vanish forever.

Half meeting him, half seeing him off, the earth was silent.

The earth remains silent.

What are you, our silent earth, and how long will you remain silent? And are you indeed silent?

1985

AUNTIE ULITA

Memories sometimes appear right out of nowhere, without any external cause, it would seem, and they take on a certain life all their own.

Often, very often, I remember an August evening long ago when the air was thick, numb, and drenched with sunlight. I recall our unpretentious household, now located in the new village, which had been moved away from the Angara River before they built the dam, and two old women on the back stoop. I had already gone off and found a job by then, and I loved to come back in August—to pick berries and mushrooms. One of the old women is my grandma, a person of stern and upright character with Siberian ways inherited from ancestors whose roots, once firmly grounded in the soil of Northern Russia before their migration across the Ural Mountains, grew even stronger out here in these unfettered forests. Grandma, who was usually both affectionate and didactic, had a special knack for sniffing out a guilty conscience and would immediately bristle. And God forbid that anybody should try to calm her down—this only fanned the fire. She would calm down by working and by being left alone, having edified herself on what suited her temperament and what didn't.

The second old woman is our neighbor from across the road, Auntie Ulita, Ulita Yefimovna. She and Grandma are some sort of distant relatives, not just distant but really only shirttail relatives, a relationship they couldn't even figure out themselves. No one, indeed, could have gotten along in our villages of old without common kinship, and although the villagers lived in family clusters, threads still ran from one cluster to another both in former and in recent times. Yet it is not this kinship that keeps the old women side by side but their long-standing habit of getting together each day, if only for a moment, even when their work is at its peak, to chew the fat.

Today this moment has dragged on for a long time. The warm, quiet August evening, somehow especially attentive to all living things, is very gentle and fine. You get the feeling that evening itself does not want to leave the earth, so now it has come to a halt as it ponders what more equally fine deeds it might do to make things a little easier for the coming day. The old women are sitting on different steps, Grandma on a higher one and Auntie Ulita on a lower one, and I am off to one side of them on the low earthen insulating wall. Having nothing better to do, we are all watching the birds feed—chickens, sparrows, pigeons. From time to time Grandma tosses them some grain out of the skirt of her dress—they flutter up and quiet down, unafraid. In the midst of this harmonious communal operation a rooster, inexplicably remembering his dignity, rushes after a hen and overtakes her following a brief chase. Only after this did Grandma, raising a threatening fist at the rooster, sing out sarcastically, "Oh, Andriyasha! Oh, Andriyasha!"

This made me laugh.

"Why 'Andriyasha'?"

"Well, now, just look at how he tore up that pullet! Take a look. Pecked out her tail and her comb both. As to how come he's Andriyasha, just ask her, ask Ulita."

Auntie Ulita did not reply. And she pretended she didn't know what we were talking about.

"Don't you remember Andriyan, the town chairman from Krivolutskaya?" This is Grandma addressing me. "Don't you remember what he was like? That's just the way he lorded it over the women after the war. Once he laid eyes on one—better just clear out of town. He'd fluff up his tail feathers, his eyes would bulge out, and he'd be off—with nary a look back. I'm telling it right, aren't I, Ulita?"

"You didn't live there—you went there about once a year, so you should know!" Auntie Ulita replied evenly, both admitting it and denying it. "You oughta know our affairs better'n anybody!"

"Oh, in them days even the dogs quit yelping over it."

"So don't you go yelping lies either."

"To tell you the truth, they really loved him, their Andriyan, their town chairman," said Grandma, not letting herself get sidetracked by mockery. "Don't matter what damn thing they found out about him, they still loved him. It's like this—he was their defender and their bread-winner, and the only man in the whole village. All the men, you see, got beat to a pulp. Vasily, he come back, but not for long . . . He come back that way, all battered and bruised . . . but he didn't even live a year, did he?"

"He might've lived a bit longer'n that, but what's the use? He never got out of bed."

"But this ataman, oh, this ataman! Where'd that one ever come from?! They'd go flying away from him like arrows when he lined 'em up in the morning for work. Manka—over there, Sanka—over there, Ulita—over here—"

"How come you know all this?! As if you were there, at our line-ups! As if you heard the shouting that went on! 'They'd go flying away like arrows.' Those arrows weren't flying away from him but right at him. Fighting us off, though . . . that was even livelier than the other war."

"So then, make war all day, make war all night—"

"Now I don't know nothin' about that."

Grandma threw Auntie Ulita a meaningful look out of the corner of her eye.

"And then he sits 'em on horses, these troops of his . . . I hear 'em three versts* from my place. It's Mamai† on the rampage! Oh, you got to save yourself any way you can—Mamai's on the rampage with his troops! And they're all howling at the top of their lungs. It was these holidays— what do you call 'em, these new ones? These shoving-in ones?"

"What do you mean 'shoving-in'?" I didn't understand.

"Why, when they shove these things, these scraps of paper, into cracks and make a holiday out of it . . ."

"Voting, is that it? Elections?"

"Yeah, yeah, elections. They put up these boxes in our village, at the town hall, and they rounded up folks from the other villages. They all come riding over full of pomp and circumstance, from Filippovka, and Yeryominskaya, and Baranovskaya, but that one swooped down on us a-whooping and a-hollering and hooves a-clattering. Weren't enough

---

*Verst—a pre-Revolutionary Russian measure of distance equivalent to about two-thirds of a mile.

†Mamai—a Tatar chieftan who invaded Russia during the thirteenth century.

horses for the kids, and they come busting in afterwards in a separate horde. But the women, they're all around him on horses, all on horseback. Ulita, I bet you still got one place on you that never did heal—they galloped around without saddles! Weren't enough saddles for everybody."

"Cut it out!"

"Oh, they're on the rampage, all right! And seeing as how I didn't have time to lock up and make it past the garden, he rears up his horse, and that horse dangles its front legs over the fence while he himself runs some kinda lash across the windows and yells, 'Marya-a!' They all go 'Marya-a!' after him at the top of their lungs. 'If you don't offer the people of Krivolutskaya three liters of moonshine right this minute, we're gonna level your cottage down to the bare timbers and set you loose to roam the world.' And they all holler the same thing."

"And did you offer them any?"

"Sure I did. Two or three times. What can you do?! They probably wouldn't have leveled the cottage, but they wouldn't have given up, you see. They'd have scared all the cattle, all the livestock, half to death, and you can wait all you want but there won't be any wool or milk after that. Here she sets, the meekest of the meek, but you should've seen this meek one back then. Eyes blazing, hair crackling, smoke coming out of their noses and ears, and she's all tensed up herself, like any second she'll turn into something else. And they're all like that, not a one is any better'n the others. Sure I offered 'em moonshine—how could I get around it? You wanna stay alive."

"Just listen to her." Auntie Ulita brushed everything aside with mild irritation. The recollection, even though spiced up in someone else's version, had made her grow warm, and instantly her face had somehow smoothed out and become flushed. "Listen to her drag us through the mud. She's the one come out the gate flaunting her wares. And our man, he loved to go on a spree during a holiday, and he pulls his horse around closer—"

"So I flaunted my wares, did I?"

"Well, it wasn't me . . . I didn't live in Atalanka. I came to you as a guest."

"You'll get treated like a guest all right if you demand it like that. You'll be yelling from the bottom of the Angara."

"We were just yelling for fun. And you had everything all ready at your house. You'd been waiting around since morning."

"Don't that beat all!" Grandma exclaimed, turning to me for support. "My family was starving, but I was s'posed to cook up a storm for them, for their whole army. Don't that beat all!"

"You were always that way."

"What way?"

"Simpleminded."

Grandma was silent for a while, unable to decide whether it was worth it to become indignant, and, having gotten sidetracked, she wound up her story, cutting it short.

"And they trotted home just as fast as they come, without losing a one. He was pretty tuckered out, his head was drooping, but they were all around him, they were all around him . . . Somebody held him by the arm, somebody else by the leg, and they propped up his horse on all sides. They would've tore out each other's hair, though, if he'd've fell off."

"And we were right. He couldn't. He was the town chairman."

"Around him they didn't act the least bit like normal women. I sure don't know who they acted like, but they didn't act like themselves."

"Around him we worked. I tell you, Marya, we worked like I myself never worked since and never saw anybody else work either. Years on end without a break. But what come after that? Afterwards it wasn't work, just . . . farm production and business. Life sure cooled off after that . . ."

And this was Auntie Ulita speaking, a woman who hadn't spent a single day in her whole life without good hard work, who didn't give up her cow until the last hour of her seventy-odd years, who put up all the hay for it without any help, and who tended a sizable garden in order to send potatoes and all the rest to her sister and nephews in the city each fall, running down to the riverbank a dozen times and finally reaching an agreement with the folks on the barge. She'd lug down the sacks, bent over double, she'd help others who were also sending things to somebody by the same barge, and, after seeing the barge off and making the sign of the cross after it, she'd hurry on to the next task. And as if that weren't enough, she also took a job baby-sitting in order to earn a few kopecks, because you couldn't get stylish boots for the niece studying in the big city if you were living on a farmer's pension, which was barely enough for salt and matches. The way Auntie Ulita baby-sat was truly a sight to behold. I saw it, being her neighbor, and I'll never ever forget it. After dragging the little guy away from his young parents—he looked less than a year old—Auntie Ulita pulled off his pants so he wouldn't ruin the fabric, prepared some bread by chewing it up (recalling her own childhood), stuffed this mush into his mouth, stuck a frying-pan handle into his hands, and ran off to tend the cattle. His crying rousted me out of my house across the way—at first it was strong and angry, and then it turned more and more into a pathetic whimpering. I crossed the road, glanced into the cottage, and ran into the little guy right at the doorstep, which he couldn't get across only because he'd grown too weak from crying. After dragging him back from the doorstep, I tried to quiet him down—forget it! I found Auntie Ulita in the cow shed, where she was fixing something.

"Auntie Ulita, don't you know he's crying? How come you abandoned him? Some baby-sitter!"

"He's crying?" She straightened up and listened. "Just go close the door. Close it and you won't hear him no more."

"But he's crying!"

"Well, so what? Let'm cry a little. It'll do him good. He'll sleep better."

The next day the little guy cried somewhat less, and on the third day, when I glanced into the cottage again out of curiosity, having noticed that Auntie Ulita was rooting around in her garden, he was moving the frying-pan handle in front of him like a probe and screeching with delight from time to time whenever he discovered something with it. And of course, needless to say, he slept extremely well.

And I also remember this. Auntie Ulita and I were running to the meadow at haying time, and for some reason we were running in the middle of the day, in the heat, because I had apparently gone down into the village for bread and waited around at the bakery for it to finish baking while Auntie Ulita had been delayed because of her cow. And now, passing the river, I sighed, "Ah, if only we could take a dip . . . You probably haven't been swimming in a long time, have you, Auntie Ulita?"

"Boy, I never been swimming in my life," she replied.

I was amazed.

"You've never been swimming? Why not?"

"No time for it. Once the girls shoved me into the water just like I was, clothes and all, but I jumped out in a flash and got right back to my sickle. When did we have time to float around in the water?!"

Then I asked, "And why didn't you get married, Auntie Ulita?"

"Who to? There wasn't anybody around to marry after the war, then the young fellows grew up, but I was too old by then. And I didn't want to go off to some strange village."

◢ One summer when it was a good year for mushrooms, my neighbor and I would row across the river twice a day to gather saffron milk caps. They were especially plentiful out there, in the abandoned fields among the unspoiled pine forests near Krivolutskaya. One day, toward evening, after filling my container to the brim, I came quietly out of the woods into a clearing. The cove where our boat was gleamed on the other side. I had apparently emerged without making a sound, and Auntie Ulita, who was sitting on a log facing in my direction, or rather in the direction of the Krivolutskaya fields, didn't have time to wipe away her tears. She didn't even try to wipe them away, and she said to me, "When I die, you think I'm gonna be lying in the graveyard? No, boy. I'm gonna be wandering around out here."

"With no work to do?"

"I daresay some kind of work'll turn up."

Auntie Ulita died that winter. I had arrived in the village three days earlier and had gotten the stove going, and after the smoke began to rise Auntie Ulita was the first one to look in on me. We didn't talk long; she was rushing off somewhere, as usual. "How are you, Auntie Ulita?" "Well, now, what's there to say about me? Still up and around." She invited me to come over and "chew the fat." And that very evening she took to her bed. They told about how she had tried to roll a barrel of frozen water into her yard (the water truck had filled it, but she hadn't noticed that the water had frozen). She gave it a shove to knock it loose and "something happened in her chest." She lay in bed for two days. But she didn't actually stay in bed. I went to see her just before evening, when two guys were cutting up some logs with a chain saw outside her gate. Though ill—nobody knew just how ill—she still moved around and got them something to eat. When they left, she closed the door behind her, lay down, and never got out of bed again.

And so they lie not far from each other—Grandma in one of the middle rows of that densely populated and becalmed village and Auntie Ulita in one of the upper ones. The graveyard is high up, as if it has ascended above everything that surrounds it. There's a good view of the Angara from there, in all its overflowing expanse, and, if you stand facing the water, you can see the clearings in the Krivolutskaya forest to the right, while to the left are Grandma's, the clearings near Atalanka.

1984

ESSAYS

YOUR SIBERIA AND MINE

What is Siberia?
This time let's not talk about the expanses and distances that stagger the imagination, or about the harsh natural conditions that are supposedly impossible to endure very long, or about the resources, old, new, and eternal—in other words, everything that immediately springs to mind and formed the first common conceptions about this region. Let's get to the heart of the matter and try to understand Siberia's place in our feelings about our Native Land and perhaps even about the entire world on an abstract level, as it were, by perceiving it as a part of the whole—part of our lives and fate, part of the path already traversed by the human race, and part of our confidence in tomorrow. What is Siberia in relation to humankind, or rather what is their mutual relationship? What does Siberia hold that has the power to influence and affect us? Why do people who have lived here only two or three years, or sometimes even one, then pride themselves for the rest of their lives on the period they spent in Siberia? All right, let's flatter them by presuming that they withstood ordeals, tempered their spirits, or completed some professional school . . . But surely there is more to it than that. Even those who didn't

pass the test, who weren't tempered or educated here, pride themselves on merely having been to Siberia, the way people used to pride and congratulate themselves on a trip to Mt. Athos. It is thus a question not only of material, professional, and physical gains but also of something else that defies immediate classification and yet exists and constitutes no small part of the concept of "the Siberian attraction."

We recently celebrated the four hundredth anniversary of Yermak's expedition* and the beginning of Siberia's annexation to Russia. As is customary for commemorative publications, many figures were cited reflecting the past, present, and future condition of Siberia, and many comparisons and forecasts were made in reference to Siberia's growth spurts, mainly in the economic area, showing what this land has become today and what it hopes to become tomorrow. Not everything, however, lends itself to comparison. Some things cannot be compared; they are inexplicably self-contained and evolve according to their own particular laws. They can even be found in the commonly held notions about Siberia if we do not regard it solely from an economic point of view.

Along with the two types of people who inhabit Siberia—indigenous Siberians, for whom this land is home, and occasional residents, for whom it is a place of temporary refuge, a hunting ground, or a work site—differing views have also long been noted, including attitudes and approaches that differ even though they appear to coincide. One need not be a confirmed mystic to believe that Siberia, like every other living land, senses the potential contribution and the particular need of every visitor and meets and greets him accordingly. Having long been a place for mass punishment and having become practically an open door for various kinds of profiteers, Siberia ought to possess a special sensitivity. Through the centuries it has had ample opportunity to gain experience in distinguishing predators from workers and settlers.

This is precisely the distinction: predators, who are impatient and foolhardy, the most harmful type for Siberia, true thieves posing as benefactors, prospectors, and reformers; non-native workers, who have done and continue to do a considerable number of good and useful deeds for Siberia, builders by nature who in their work treat this land as though it were their own; and local inhabitants, whether indigenous Siberians or people who have put down roots here, who are linked to Siberia through the whole structure of their existence, spanning several generations. There is probably more truth in this division into those who contribute to its well-being and those who do not than in a division into

---

*Yermak Timofeevich (d. 1594)—Cossack leader of an expedition of 840 men that set off in 1581 to conquer the indigenous Siberian tribes, during which he drowned in the Irtysh River.

natives and outsiders. Even having to turn to such a division and to spell it out is painful, however, for the simple reason that Siberia has not yet firmly established itself as an immense and vigorous domain and has not set a straight course toward what it will finally become, which in fact is still unclear. But because it needs a work force, it unintentionally attracts a considerable number of opportunists who count on making quick and easy fortunes, as did their predecessors one and two hundred years ago, and who look on Siberia as a malicious deceiver if for some reason the fortunes they crave do not come easily.

While needing a work force, Siberia has a hundred times greater need for inhabitants who could become sons, caretakers, and patriots, who, as they transform it, would do so not with a cold heart as though for someone unknown but for their own children and grandchildren.

In due time Siberia became a part of Russia with surprising ease. It was like a gift from heaven—there is no other comparison. Nowadays one simply cannot imagine how it could have happened any other way. As it was, Siberia seemed to have been kept waiting too long for the desired reunification while Russia, blind to its main interests, was preoccupied with wars against Turkey, then against Lithuania and Poland, and continued to chatter about what kind of creatures lived beyond the Ural Mountains and whom they most resembled—man or beast. There was no need to dispatch huge armies to this region, and not a single commander succeeded in becoming renowned here for his skill as a military leader, with the exception of Yermak, and even he headed across "the Rock"* unbeknownst to Moscow, following the trails blazed by the free Cossacks. The annexation of Siberia required a different sort of skill, one that nobody displayed to a greater extent or employed with greater talent than the Russian, with his exceedingly patient body and spirit—it required the skill of the pioneer.

Russian Cossacks reached the shores of the Pacific Ocean less than sixty years after the arrival of Yermak. We who are now accustomed to all manner of miracles accept this fact as historical reality and nothing more, as a certain primordial given; we are incapable of fully comprehending what this meant in those times, with those means of transportation, with that sort of equipment, in that Siberia . . . No, this was something supernatural; those people were somehow different, somehow special, for they felt an unusual urge and knew a wonderful passion. And if we now call it a feat, and probably not without good reason, when someone builds a new railroad, then what should we call the roads and byways, the labors and deeds of Semyon Dezhnyov, Yerofey

*The Urals.

Khabarov, Vasily Poyarkov, Pyotr Beketov, Vladimir Atlasov, and their many, many comrades who crossed great expanses as though flying through the air, traveling along rivers and portages, through taiga and tundra, and along the paths of wild animals so that Siberia would always have the smell of Rus?* History ruled with impudent justice: the hordes of Genghis Khan came out of the East and three and a half centuries later small detachments of Cossacks would cover the same distances back to the East again.

Russian Siberia began with them, and they also laid the foundation for the Siberian character type, a topic of debate to this day: which is greater, the human influence or nature's, social conditioning or that which is acquired spontaneously? Perhaps dominant in the Siberian type is the individuality that belongs to it alone.

What do we mean by *individuality*? It is a unified plurality, an enlargement of one's possibilities and their subordination to the principal purpose that determines all. Without a purpose, individuality does not exist. I would give a lot to learn how much Yerofey Khabarov and Semyon Dezhnyov thought about profit and how much they thought about Russia during their terrible ordeals, during the months and years of walking side by side with death—freezing in flimsy winter huts with no bread or salt, encountering starving wild animals, dodging the arrows of indigneous peoples, losing consciousness when tortured by the voivode's† executioners as they conducted inquiries into anonymous crimes—and what the concept of Russia included back then. It is possible and even likely that self-interest was linked to higher intentions; if they had been motivated only by self-interest, their names would not have been allowed to shine with immortality. To achieve this they had to choose something quite different to lead and protect them, something that, like the Star of Bethlehem, would also be a guiding force—this was their Native Land, which they were extending eastward. They surrendered completely to this Providence, which could see far ahead, and it helped them accomplish things that we find incredible.

To serve Russia by way of Siberia was no small feat, and it could not be entrusted to just anyone.

Thus Siberians contained a mixture of individualistic qualities from the very start. Siberia was settled by desperate people, by those who had reason to seek refuge in a bleak and distant land, who hoped to live here

---

*Rus—the most venerable, and now largely poetic, name for Russia.

†Voivode—the title given to Siberian provincial governors-general, who were responsible, though not always completely accountable, to the political authorities in European Russia.

amid the freedom and justice denied them in their previous homeland, who, acknowledging the rectitude of the newly revised law of collectivity, clustered in communal groups and established villages unsullied at first by worthless people, and who, relying only on themselves, went off to remote parts to live in solitude. In all cases this required an indomitable spirit. The unbridled freemen, who sprang from the common people and who had settled and continued to settle in Siberia, were later reinforced and partially ennobled but partially damaged and corrupted by the huge number of banished criminals, so that in discussing Siberian individuality one does not necessarily have its best features in mind. Individuality can also have an ugly side. In order for it to develop properly, a social climate, even a barely tolerable one, is essential, as is confidence in the social structure, which Siberia could not claim to have. Here, out of the tsar's sight, there very quickly developed a lawlessness and corruption quite unprecedented, which took hold more quickly, firmly, and relentlessly than anything else in young soil that had dreamed of completely different shoots. Hopes for a promised land had to be abandoned; Siberians retreated into themselves against their own will and there erected a fortress into which outsiders could not easily gain admittance. A host would check ten times to see what kind of guest had come and what he brought with him before opening up and letting him in. This gave rise to a reticence, distrustfulness, and wariness that appear in Siberians more often than in anyone else, that one way or another have been handed down to us, too, and that must not be judged harshly: you should have tried to survive here, amid the unrestrained human lawlessness stemming from Siberia's position as a land for correction and exile and one given to arbitrary rule. You should have tried to survive here very long with a soul laid bare to all!

But this also gives rise to another aspect of the Siberian character, obviously not its worst—powers of concentration that bespeak dignity and close attention to what is happening all around. Siberians never retreated so far into themselves that they remained there exclusively. A glance sharper and livelier than theirs has yet to be found, and their keen minds were constantly trying to fathom the primary cause and the essence of things, choosing the shortest possible route and guided by two basic questions: how was something made and why did it exist? With typical practicality, they tried to apply these questions even when they were inappropriate. Not strongly inclined toward abstract contemplation, they nonetheless possessed powers of concentration that focused on a broader span of life than the one allotted them; and, looking around at the visible world, scanning the years that their own memories could encompass, they were inclined to measure themselves against an inherent standard that allowed them to see further and remember more. In this respect the position of the Russian Siberian may be viewed as advantageous: countless generations did not stretch behind him, he could still trace his ancestry back to the pioneers who had brought his family name here, and, standing on the same spot as the ones who arrived first, he could easily imagine his forebears' initial difficulties and thoughts. Such things are inaccessible to the person who does not delve into himself.

Every now and then I recall the "philosophy" of one old man, Grandpa Yegor, from my own native village, which still stood on the banks of the Angara River back then but was already preparing to move: the Bratsk Dam under construction farther down the river would wipe out all the old settlements in one fell swoop. The impending resettlement gave rise to Grandpa Yegor's "philosophy," which was not exactly depressing but not very cheerful either, casting a glance as it did at death. Because I left the city to visit my parents only in the summer, I found myself in the position of merely half-belonging to the village, and this alone disposed the villagers to abstract revelation in my presence, for holding such conversations among one's own people was generally not done.

Illuminated by the sunset that caressed the Angara, we were sitting on some logs on the riverbank when Grandpa Yegor said: "You know, there must be a reason for this." He nodded vaguely toward the river— before us unfolded a scene of rare beauty, which those who remember the former Angara will confirm. "There must be a reason for my being here . . . eh? All right, I'm going to die pretty soon, and others will come. And everything will be done differently around here. But all the same, I've carried on the things that meant a lot to my father." And he added (these words are clearly engraved in my memory), "If you want to know, I never harmed my own land."

What saintly simplicity! How could he harm it, he, a true toiler and guardian who had now already become a part of this land and had added to it a considerable portion of human warmth? But to his way of thinking, he could. He could cause harm even with a bad feeling, but he did not permit himself any feeling that would have shown disrespect for the labors and graves of his forefathers, for the choice they had once made, out of the vast sequence of broad expanses and horizons, to carve out a new homeland on this particular spot. Just as the center of life shifts to each person's "I," the center of the universe shifts to our "small" homeland, and there is nothing wrong with such egocentrism or whatever you call it—nothing wrong with it at all. I cannot say that the Siberian's feeling for the land of his forefathers is more intense than that of a European Russian, but it is undoubtedly fresher and more self-engrossed, more tangible, it would seem, and more personal; besides emotion, it contains the power of distinctiveness and of vested interest.

It was also enhanced by the sparseness of population, which compelled Siberians to value the worker in themselves twice or thrice as highly, and by the very spirit of this far-flung land, proud and majestic, which seemed prepared to accept not just anyone who came along but only those who were somehow chosen, who conformed to it in some way.

The extent to which Siberians conform to Siberia is a separate issue. This trait was apparently still just developing as human nature unconsciously sought ways of matching the serene might of the country that gave it refuge when, one must assume, Siberia ran out of time to shape its inhabitants after its own fashion and a new force appeared—technology, which swiftly elevated the human race and yet unintentionally destroyed its ties to the natural world.

What is the reason, you ask, for this excursion into Siberia's past, into the history of its inhabitants? It is not to show that we Siberians were not born yesterday, that we're not pushovers. And it is not to attempt to prove that the Siberian breed is something special, the sturdiest and most reliable. Much as we would like to flatter ourselves with such a view, it would be untrue. Siberians today are ceasing to exist as the composite of their former stable features and are outliving their distinctiveness, wearing it out like old clothes. Everything that was formed by nature, by remoteness, by self-sufficiency, and even by a certain conservatism is gradually finding common expression and is being recast in a single mold. Whether for better or worse is another matter, but such is the reality you must reckon with whether you want to or not. Siberia has ceased to be a remote, unknown land, and the Siberian has donned all the armor of a person of the twentieth century, and not without a certain satisfaction.

And yet . . .

Our sense of a particular region has its own logic and does not always conform to factual analysis. Whatever Siberia might have become, however it might have been transformed today, it continues to be seen as a sleeping giant by many, many people both knowledgeable and ignorant of Siberian affairs, a continent of immense, untapped strength, a land held in reserve. In the old days the tsarist government let itself rush headlong into questionable ventures and, running short of money, traded away Alaska: Russia still had its Siberia. Even had this not been written about and discussed openly, it would have gone without saying. Siberia stood as a fortress where shelter could be found, a storehouse that could always be opened in case of need, a force that could be mustered, a rock that could repulse any attack without fear of defeat, and a glory destined to ring out someday. In short, for a long time Siberia remained firmly entrenched in human consciousness as a spearhead for the future, to which people looked with confidence: whatever they might use up, wear out, or squander in their own economic sphere today, they would find something to replace it with tomorrow in Siberia. Everything there was abundant; there lay in essence a virgin land just waiting to be exploited. How this exploitation would take place and what path the further development of Siberia would follow were still vague concepts to the Russian as little as one hundred years ago, and even with the construction of the Trans-Siberian Railroad, which completed Russia's actual assimilation of Siberia, the gaze he cast beyond the Urals remained clouded. Siberia continued to loom in the distance as an unmovable and back-breaking weight.

And, one must assume, that is what it was. To annex Siberia proved far simpler than to develop these vast expanses. The first wave of "development" after Yermak was the most rapacious: they killed off the sable and the polar fox, took out all the mammoth ivory, and plundered the precious metals, hurriedly grabbing what lay close by and was easy to obtain. In essence, they behaved as if this land were in imminent danger of falling to the enemy forever, and thus they had to take out everything the enemy might be able to use. Then they came to their senses. They found that vast Siberia, larger than any continent, became much less large and bottomless if they did nothing but scoop everything out. It must be generally acknowledged that during the development of Siberia the periods of sobering up and of attempting to learn something about it, to ennoble and to improve it, continually gave way to renewed bouts of intoxication and feverish pillaging in the wake of new discoveries. Having long been our native land, our own land, Siberia nevertheless continued to serve as someone else's appendage or rental property—to satisfy immediate needs and fancies. Consequently Siberia is a land that gives and is capable of giving even more, but, no matter what you call it, this land does not give readily, for it demands effort and sacrifice. The very word *Siberia* suggests contradictions: wealthy impoverishment, broad narrowness, exultant inhospitableness, a land that belongs either to the past or to the future but not to the present. Its day is either over or not yet begun, and it has just barely created the first minimal conditions for the support of life.

As is only fitting, the most important and firmest steps in the development of Siberia were taken by those who came here as permanent residents. They were tillers of the soil who made not a fortune but a living from Siberia, who obtained their daily bread, literally, through hard work. As we conceive it, this hard work consisted first and foremost of the struggle against the surrounding natural world, from which the first settlers had to win every clump of tillable ground through unbelievable effort. So it was indeed, and we should question not the amount of labor but the extent of the struggle between humankind and nature, the antagonism between them that is now exaggerated. We must not forget that in such cases the outcome of the struggle is always decided beforehand in favor of the human race, and for that reason our ancestors tried not to take more from the taiga than they needed. Naturally, the axes they wielded then were not bulldozers or LP–19 tree-harvesting machines, which today's woodsmen use to fell timber in a matter of seconds, but even with an axe it was possible, figuratively speaking, to lose one's head and cut too much firewood. This, of course, did happen here and there throughout Siberia's open spaces—the world is not without evil people—but even then the land did not forgive those who mocked it, and after thirty, forty, or fifty years had elapsed, or even after one hundred or one hundred and fifty years, a village would be forced to move away from the place it had long occupied and migrate to an unspoiled part of the country. Or it could eke out a meager existence when crops suffered year after year from drought, floods, or insects appearing out of nowhere. As a rule, Siberians moved into the taiga cautiously and with moderation, not with the devil-may-care "Step aside, taiga!" attitude that is our manner, clearly recognizing that the taiga provided no less food than the fields did.

I well remember how in my early years my grandfather had an educational "talk" with me when I once burst into the house with an armful of broken currant branches, wanting to show how lushly the berries had ripened on the islands in the Angara. By today's standards those currant bushes were extremely plentiful. And I recall the feeling of helplessness and numbness that seized me one recent autumn when I saw trucks loaded with buckthorn bushes driving one after another along the Tunkinskaya Valley beyond Lake Baikal; the bushes had been cut down so that the berries could be picked somewhere else, in a quiet remote spot. And this in spite of prohibitions, public warnings, and policemen at their posts. I must admit that even Siberians, especially city dwellers, have now grown lax in their attitude toward their native land, and they attack the autumnal taiga with as much greed as if tomorrow they will have to retreat or advance, as in a military campaign, rather than remain here to the end of their days.

However Siberia may have been viewed in the past, one still cannot help but notice that it is changing more and more from a stable land awaiting us in the future into a land of the present. And at times one can hear them scrape bottom as they remove the natural resources. Siberia is now poised at that inevitable balance point at which the spoils are slowly but surely beginning to tip the scale in their favor. This does not mean, of course, that the development of Siberia has been completed and now we must leave it alone. The mere fact that barely one tenth of the country's population lives here permanently, in the great expanses from the

Urals to the ocean, suggests that Siberia is, if not a deserted wilderness, at least underpopulated. The guest-worker system, no matter how many people it gives us, does not count: it might be suitable for the moon, but not for Siberia. Siberia is ready to accept people, to give them refuge, to provide work that is useful to the fatherland, and to feed at least twice as many people as live here today. But if Siberia had its own voice with which to articulate its true attitude toward its fate, it would say, "Yes, I am ready, but don't subjugate me any longer—I was subjugated long ago and belong to you—and don't look on me in the old way as a region unfit for life; rather it is time to accept me as a part of your native land without which all the rest of the country could not exist and to treat me like your native land, with love and concern. Come to me, but with these things—faith, love, and protectiveness."

Rational utilization, comprehensive development, responsible treatment of Siberia's treasures large and small—now is the time for these principles of theoretical economics to finally become the law of life and action. *Sturm und Drang* in Siberia's development is no longer acceptable; otherwise the blushing bride, as people continue to regard Siberia, could easily turn into a feeble old woman. Its properties of self-preservation, in which we intentionally or unconsciously place our trust—hoping that the natural resources will gradually be renewed by themselves, that everything will be absorbed and diluted in the vast surroundings, that everything will be healed and restored on fresh soil—these intrinsic recuperative powers at the sites of massive industrial intervention are no longer coping with the heavy tread of humanity and should be counted on only to the extent that they can provide an auxiliary thrust to accompany our precautionary measures.

Siberia is large, but we cannot allow a single meter of ground to be treated carelessly, and we cannot permit another tree in its forests to be felled without urgent need. Siberia is large, but we can claim no credit for its largeness. We will deserve credit if we preserve nature's primordial grandeur side by side with the grandeur of our own deeds.

So what exactly is Siberia and why does it draw people here with an irresistible and disquieting attraction? This attraction is often vague and not fully identifiable, but it will persist until people head across the Urals and plunge into Siberia, whether carrying out an ancient, forgotten pledge or filling an aching emptiness inside that demands "something like this"—it is like plunging into a dream that has surfaced and become reality. And if in real life this dream does not fully correspond to their vision of Siberia, we have only ourselves to blame. And if it does correspond, all the better. In both instances things become easier for them, no matter how much time they spend in Siberia: they acquire a palpable sense of being filled with the special qualities that are found only here and that then help them understand themselves and others. Perhaps these are merely idle conjectures and nothing of the sort happens in Siberia, but then how do you explain the self-confidence and tranquillity, akin to clarity of expression and self-discovery, that are so often encountered in people who have been to Siberia, qualities that were not there before? How do you explain the unintentional, innocent flash of joy on someone's face when he hears that you are from Siberia and then springs at you: "And I've been there, too, you know!" It is possible that he left nothing good here except for random impressions in someone's memory, but he was here, he was here and proud of it, which means that Siberia left a profound mark on his soul, however aimless and unsteady it may be. And why at the mere mention of the word *Siberia* do people living farthest from it, somewhere in the country's western extremities, who have never made it to Siberia, involuntarily perk up and pay attention: what's it like out there, in Siberia? What is it in them that responds to this word? Which is it—joy or sorrow, hope or disappointment, expectation or compassion? What has Siberia's all-pervasive vitality breathed into them? Don't they, with their vague notions and feelings, believe that we may commit errors in remaking nature anywhere we please, only not in Siberia? Don't they believe that, having learned from the experience of other times and continents and as proof of our common sense and good will, we are obliged to treat this huge land with devotion and concern, a land in a position to prolong our hopes for clean air, water, and tillable soil for a long time?

We have only one Siberia. Each land belonging to us is unique in number and kind, and in this regard Siberia does not constitute an exception for any of us. It is an exception in being a wilderness preserved intact until recent times, one currently experiencing the immense, unprecedented influence of our economic activity. Here the human race is now being tested to see what it has become in the present and what can be expected of it in the future.

Isn't this still another reason why people are drawn here, to feel in themselves the boundary between the temporal and the eternal, the inconstant and the true, the ruined and the preserved?

1984

HOW DID THEY END UP

IN IRKUTSK?

When a casual visitor drops by the Irkutsk Art Museum for the first time during a spare moment, perhaps out of curiosity, expecting to discover nothing more than a collection of limited merit embellished by a few noteworthy canvases, he is usually stunned. To his great amazement he will find himself among the very best "company" of Russian and Soviet artists: Ilya Repin, Vasily Surikov, Vasily Perov, Vladimir Borovikovsky, Dmitry Levitsky, Orest Kiprensky, Vasily Tropinin, Viktor Vasnetsov, Ivan Ayvazovsky, Isaak Levitan, Boris Kustodiev, Konstantin Korovin, Ivan Shishkin, Konstantin Somov, Arkhip Kuindzhi, Fyodor Bruni, Vasily Vereshchagin, Mark Antokolsky, and many more of their no less famous contemporaries, along with Kuzma Petrov-Vodkin, Arkady Plastov, Martiros Saryan, Sergey Gerasimov, Nikolay Romadin, Konstantin Yuon, Tatyana Mavrina, Sergey Konyonkov, Anna Golubkina, Ivan Shadr, Yevgeny Vuchetich . . . Even a selective list of the best Soviet masters would take up too much space.

This essay was written as a foreword to *The Art Treasures of Irkutsk* by Aleksey Fatyanov. The translation omits a few phrases referring exclusively to the book.

But this kind of surprise, on "discovering" the Irkutsk Museum, can happen, we repeat, only to a newcomer because it is not the specialists alone who are aware that today it houses the richest collection of art treasures beyond the Ural Mountains, a collection that continues to increase and to expand with every passing year.

Inevitably the question arises: How did they end up in Irkutsk? By what special and fortuitous circumstances were these tremendously significant pieces of valuable fine art brought together here? If Irkutsk seems entitled to be a huge and remarkable depository of Eastern art on the basis of its location, of its proximity to this art, then the rare collection of medieval Russian paintings cannot be explained by the age of our city;* we must look for different reasons as to why the heart of Siberia received icons of the Moscow, Yaroslavl, Novgorod, Pskov, Palekh, Stroganov, Northern, and Southern schools as well as specimens of Byzantine and Mt. Athos iconography that have now become unique.

And what about the Western European section, ranging from the Middle Ages to recent times! And Siberia's own ancient and contemporary art!

And all this has occurred only since the Civil War,† when the museum became public property, a State-run art gallery. Thus it has attained its present richness and scope within only a few decades, an astonishing feat for a museum of this size. And, indeed, many of its outstanding exhibits have unusual histories. The fate of some, like that of the Kazantsev family's Urals Collection, for example, which was brought to Irkutsk by the storms of the Civil War, is even filled with adventures worthy of a master of the detective story.

There were times when the museum was extraordinarily lucky, especially at first, but later on this "luck" cost its curators and contributors a great deal of work and superhuman effort. Then evidently the law by which treasures attract other treasures went into effect; that is, they began to find their way by every possible intricate route to those who knew their true worth and who acted unselfishly for the benefit of their home town.

And here it is necessary to make one fleeting digression. Even at the end of the nineteenth century, Siberia was considered a land of well-preserved, unimpeded, and flourishing ignorance, a land with an impenetrable lack of culture. Endless evidence and countless examples appear in the reactions of foreign visitors as well as in the sad acknowledgments of our fellow countrymen. The exceptions merely seemed to confirm the general rule. Moreover, the Siberian was often not given

---

*Irkutsk was incorporated in 1686.
†Russian Civil War, 1918–1921.

credit for having any poetic sensibility; his soul was portrayed as a stone from which it was difficult to extract even the slightest murmur of aesthetic appreciation. None other than Nikolay Yadrintsev,* a Siberian and patriot of Siberia, writes about the Siberian:

> Terrifying ghosts with shaggy paws surround him in the woods. He has no time to daydream, for he is laying down a road through dark thickets, and he is seized with superstitious fear. In the evening he makes himself a lean-to. When the slanting rays of the sun penetrate the woods at dusk and a golden ray streams down amid the black tree trunks while the glowing, crimson sky blazes between the branches, the poor trapper will kneel in front of his lean-to with his hands folded and say a wordless prayer: a one-syllable sound might escape from his breast . . .

And, continuing in this vein, Yadrintsev cites a Kirghizian proverb: "The Goddess of Song flew low over the steppe but passed high above the forest."

There is a measure of accurate observation here, to be sure, but only concerning the external aspects of the Siberian's difficult life. The severity of nature left its mark on man, of course, and fettered his lyrical sensibilities, but only until he came to grips with the new conditions and until severity ceased to be severe for him and became his customary native habitat. During that time his soul could not possibly become hardened or closed to fear, which was why during those first years, when the settler was still learning to recognize the alarming sounds around him and still adjusting to unfamiliar conditions, he most needed the sustenance of popular beliefs and songs, of the rhythmic, storytelling voices of his ancestors, which were brought from his original homeland and which structured the harmony of his soul. And there is no need to demonstrate that in the isolation of the taiga the hunter looked to himself for salvation; if the community felt nostalgic for the land they had left behind, they would get together to sing and to reminisce. And things continued in this fashion until new words and new elements of poetry in tune with the new way of life entered naturally and imperceptibly into the old poetic structure.

The Siberian's outer gloominess, which he acquired involuntarily from the spirit of the natural world around him the way one acquires a suntan, was perceived by outsiders who did not know him well as com-

---

*Nikolay Mikhaylovich Yadrintsev (1842–1894)—Russian ethnographer, archaeologist, explorer of Siberia, and Siberian "regionalist" (*oblastnik*). In an earlier version of this article the author referred to Yadrintsev as someone who had "labored tirelessly for its [Siberia's] scientific and cultural development."

plete muteness, as an inability of his soul to produce an artistic echo. Even his fellow Siberians, who left behind an unflattering opinion of this aspect of their fellow countryman's life (here Shchapov* may also be cited along with Yadrintsev), even they proceeded by comparing the Siberian with the inhabitant of European Russia, a comparison that could not favor the Siberian and that depressed those who responded to it more than it should have. It is well known that forty years after Shchapov's death Mark Azadovsky went to the Lena River, to Shchapov's native region, and recorded folk tales and songs remarkable for their artistic value and for their state of preservation. Russkoe Ustye, located on the Indigirka River in the far north of Yakutia, is one of the most fertile spots for poetry in Siberia. And what about the "family" villages in the Trans-Baikal region! And the folk art of the Old Believers in the Altai Mountains! A curious pattern can be discerned: the harsher the conditions in which the Siberian lived and the more physical effort he expended on acclimation and survival, the richer was his poetry. It is not, then, so much a matter of physical hardships stifling ritual and song as it is the community's strength and cohesion being unable to do without them.

Folklore as popular art is far removed, of course, from the classic forms of art, but at the same time a serious creative artist cannot realize his full potential without folklore, without it permeating the fiber of his soul from the very outset. Were it not for this, there would have been no poet named Pyotr Yershov, no painters named Vasily Surikov and Mikhail Vrubel, no composer named Aleksandr Alyabev, nor many other great masters native to Siberia, in whom Siberia rightfully takes pride and who captured the voice and spirit of the land while exploring the possibilities of its mighty artistic strength.

Consequently, it would be unfair to claim that the Siberian of the past had no exalted temperament or poetic streak. Further proof can be found in the multivolume edition of Siberian folklore now under preparation. It is quite another matter, however, that great numbers of Siberians were deprived of education and that their creative instincts usually atrophied, unable to develop in an unsuitable milieu. It is no wonder that, fearing a milieu that even in the major cities was preoccupied as a rule with the physical struggle for survival, a milieu unburdened by nonmaterial concerns and one in which artistic tastes remained in an embryonic state or took ugly forms, Siberians with talent went away to study at the metropolitan universities and academies in European Russia and were afraid to come back: they could not expect to find an

---

*Afanasy Prokofievich Shchapov (1831–1876)—Russian historian, publicist, and Siberian "regionalist" (*oblastnik*).

environment favorable for creative activity in their native land. A phenomenon characteristic of Siberia appeared and took hold—absenteeism, that is, the pursuit of one's occupation outside of one's homeland, an involuntary exodus of the best talents and minds.

The educated and patriotically inclined people of Siberia naturally refused to resign themselves to this situation. They needed to form their own cultural community consisting not only of exiles and sojourners but also first and foremost of native inhabitants, who were backward in the arts and sciences not because they were coldly practical at heart but because of the Russian government's established policy regarding this region: to take as much as possible and to give as little as possible. Siberians could not count on Imperial pronouncements of good intent—the time had come for Siberia to look after the building of its own cultural and spiritual life.

By the second half of the last century, the prerequisite social conditions had grown ripe. The three hundredth anniversary of Siberia's annexation to Russia was drawing near, which Siberia was preparing to commemorate by recognizing the full-fledged role it played in the nation and by displaying all the best it had to offer. At that time things began to move forward noticeably in the cultural sphere. Many cities were opening libraries and museums, building theaters, creating learned societies and music salons, and organizing art exhibits. It became fashionable among wealthy Siberians, who had been viewed until quite recently, and not without some justification, as tightfisted moneybags, to loosen their purse strings at art auctions in the major cities of European Russia.

Transported at first by wagon and then also by means of the newly built railway, meticulously packed parcels and crates of canvases and sculptures, of books and educational materials began hastening eastward one after another. More and more often, benefactors would donate art objects to the high schools and colleges of their choice rather than give farewell speeches and rhetorical blessings. We may aptly recall that in the hallways of the Irkutsk Boys' High School there were several paintings by Ayvazovsky, a sculpture by Antokolsky entitled "Ivan the Terrible," and pictures by Western artists, all presented by one Sibiryakov. (Fate sometimes works in amazing ways: these valuable pieces, which were acquired by the art museum in due time, recently returned to their old paternal home, as it were, when the former school building was given to the museum!) The same Sibiryakov bought Vasily Zhukovksy's* library and donated it to Tomsk University at its open-

---

*Vasily Andreevich Zhukovsky (1783–1852)—the founder of Russian Romantic poetry and tutor of the future Emperor Alexander II.

ing—this enormous treasure seemed to raise Siberia's cultural level overnight, allowing it to look out across the Urals if not on an equal footing
with Central Russia then at least with a gladdened and reassuring gaze.

The Irkutsk Art Museum, as is well known, grew out of the picture
gallery owned by Vladimir Platonovich Sukachyov, who had been the
city's mayor for many years and was a man of considerable education and
patriotic endeavor. His collection, which included paintings by Repin,
Vereshchagin, Klodt, Makovsky, and other "Wanderers,"* and also an
unexpected rarity by Nicolas Poussin, "The Selection of the Apostles,"
was precisely one of these vivid manifestations of Siberia's artistic self-
assertion. Sukachyov bought up pictures and transported them to Irkutsk
not out of a rich man's vanity but out of a desire to sow the seeds of
beauty and inspiration in the souls of those fellow countrymen who
were artistically unsophisticated. His collection was accessible to everyone; children were urged to visit and were admitted free of charge. Even
before the Revolution, Sukachyov dreamed of turning over his collection
to the city of Irkutsk, and only the sluggishness and ignorance of the
municipal authorities and then the beginning of World War I prevented
him from carrying out his intention. [. . .]

While acknowledging that our museum was born under a lucky star,
we must seek its greatest good fortune and success in the people who
devoted themselves to it. Immediately after the Sukachyov collection became nationalized, the curator of the gallery was a sculptor named K. I.
Pomerantsev, who had a subtle and professional grasp of art that did not
betray him during the troubled times of formalism and imitation and
that prevented him from pandering to those who held the ill-considered,
devil-may-care views that prevailed. At the end of the 1920s, Pomerantsev
was replaced as the museum's curator by B. I. Lebedinsky, a nationally
renowned artist whose prestige in the art world enriched Irkutsk with
many first-rate exhibits of Russian and Soviet classics.

Then came Aleksey Dementievich Fatyanov . . . Fatyanov is one of
that inexplicable breed of people who not only work in the field of art
but also live and breathe it, as if they are operating in the realm of ultimate values. Even astonishment grows timid before people this fanatically devoted to a certain cause and finds it impossible to fathom their
secret, the mainspring of their activity, which never slackens. It is not
enough simply to reiterate the well-known aspects of Fatyanov's life,
such as his being an ardent patriot of his city and region, a severe critic
and inspired apologist for art, both its manual laborer and its scholar.

---

*The Wanderers ("Peredvizhniki")—a group of nineteenth-century Russian painters
who organized traveling exhibits to bring serious art to the common people.

Regarding him, all these notions must be raised to the next power and elevated in quality to a rare degree. [. . .]

One cannot help but be startled by a certain fact. Over the course of two years (1948–1949), our museum received more exhibits from State archives than all other museums in the country put together!!! No amount of exclamation points can convey our rapt excitement at such adroitness. And what exhibits! Kramskoy, Savrasov, Tropinin, Petrov-Vodkin, Surikov, Makovksy, Malyavin, etc. Unfortunately, it is impossible to calculate how many "degrees" the cultural level of Irkutsk rose after that, but there can be no doubt that the spiritual magnetic field essential for such a rise intensified significantly. And continues to intensify.

In recent decades and during the past few years, one of the principal sources for the museum's acquisitions has been private collections. Now and then donors present gifts that are truly greater and more valuable than those of royalty. In the span of twenty years, a man from Moscow named N. K. Velichko turned over to Irkutsk more than one thousand works representing the most widely varied genres and schools of the fine arts, including dozens of medieval icons. But as everyone knows, an art collector is highly discriminating and will not present such generous gifts to just anyone off the street. One must win him over not only to oneself but also to one's city and must succeed in proving that a remote Siberian museum will put his property to appropriate and widespread use. All it took was one sigh at the apartment of another donor, F. E. Vishnevsky, at the sight of a masterpiece that Fatyanov longed for: "And Irkutsk doesn't have a Kiprensky!" The sigh escaped of its own accord, [. . .] won a Kiprensky for Irkutsk with its noble despair, and filled a gaping "hole" in the collection of the best masters of the past with "Portrait of a Soldier." A donor might seem to give gratuitously and unselfishly, but it is not that simple and not for nothing. He needs to receive or, better put, to feel assurances that he is being of the greatest service to others, in which he sees a continuation of his own life.

Art endures and develops not through a campaign whose well-meaning but superficial goal is the acquisition of culture by physical means but rather through creativity and selfless devotion. Spirit, including the spirit of sublime art, as they say, breathes where it will, but it lives and breathes most easily among dedicated people, in an atmosphere of kind-heartedness and understanding.

1984

BAIKAL

One of the first rapturous testimonials about Lake Baikal ever made by a Russian comes down to us from Archpriest Avvakum.[*] On returning from exile in Dauria,[†] the "frenzied" archpriest had to sail from the eastern shore of the sea/lake to the western shore in the summer of 1662, and he writes of Baikal:

High hills and exceedingly high rocky cliffs are all around it—over twenty times one thousand versts and more have I dragged myself and nowhere seen any like unto these. Atop them are bed chambers and sleeping benches, gateways and pillars, stone fences and courtyards—all wrought by God. Onion groweth upon them and garlic—larger than the Romanov onion, and exceedingly sweet. There, too, doth grow God-cultivated hemp, and in the courtyards beauteous grasses both colorful and

[*]Avvakum Petrovich (1620/1621–1682)—leader of the Old Believers, a conservative sect that split away from the Russian Orthodox Church under his guidance, for which he was banished to northern Russia and Siberia and eventually burned at the stake.
[†]Dauria—the region of Siberia just east of Lake Baikal.

surpassingly fragrant. Exceedingly many birds, geese, and swans swim upon the sea covering it like snow. It hath fishes—sturgeon, and salmon, sterlet, and omul, and whitefish, and many other kinds. The water is fresh and hath great seals and sea lions in it: when I dwelt in Mezen,* I saw nought like unto these in the big sea. And the fishes there are plentiful: the sturgeon and salmon are surpassingly fat—thou canst not fry them in a pan, for there will be nought but grease. And all this hath been wrought by Christ in heaven for mankind so that, resting content, he shouldst render praise unto God.

"The sacred sea," "the sacred lake," "the sacred water"—that is what native inhabitants have called Baikal from the beginning of time. So have Russians, who had already arrived on its shores by the seventeenth century, as well as travelers from abroad, admiring its majestic, supernatural mystery and beauty. The reverence for Baikal held by uncivilized people and also by those considered enlightened for their time was equally complete and captivating, even though it touched mainly the mystical feelings in the one and the aesthetic and scientific impulses in the other. The sight of Baikal would dumbfound them every time because it did not fit their conceptions either of spirit or of matter: Baikal was located where something like that should have been impossible, it was not the sort of thing that should have been possible here or anywhere else, and it did not have the same effect on the soul that "indifferent" nature usually does. This was something uncommon, special, and "wrought by God."

Baikal was measured and studied in due course, even, in recent years, with the aid of deep-sea instruments. It acquired definite dimensions and became subject to comparison, alternately likened to Lake Tanganyika and to the Caspian Sea. They've calculated that it holds one fifth of all fresh water on our planet, they've explained its origin, and they've conjectured as to how species of plants, animals, and fish existing nowhere else could originate here and how species found only in other parts of the world many thousands of miles away managed to end up here. Not all these explanations and conjectures tally even with each other. Baikal is not so simple that it could be deprived of its mystery and enigma that easily, but based on its physical properties it has, nevertheless, been assigned a fitting place alongside other great wonders that have already been discovered and described, as well it should. And it stands alongside them solely because Baikal itself, alive, majestic, and not created by human hands, not comparable to anything and not repeated anywhere, is aware of its own primordial place and its own life force.

*Mezen—a city in northwest Russia near the White Sea, to which Avvakum was exiled in 1664 and where he remained until 1665.

How and with what can its beauty actually be compared? We won't insist that nothing in the world is finer than Baikal: each of us regards his own region as beloved and dear, and, as everyone knows, the Eskimo or the Aleutian considers his tundra and icy wilderness the crowning glory of nature's richness and perfection. From the time we are born we drink in the air, the salt, and the scenes of our homeland; these influence our character and shape our vital makeup to no small degree. For this reason it is not enough to say that they are dear to our hearts—they are a part of us, the part that is formed by the natural environment, and that part speaks inside us with an ancient, eternal voice and cannot help but make itself heard. It is meaningless to compare the ice caps of Greenland with the sands of the Sahara, giving preference to one or the other, or the Siberian taiga with the Central Russian steppe, or even the Caspian Sea with Baikal; we can merely convey our impressions of them. All these have their own splendid beauty and their own amazing vitality. More often than not, an attempt at comparison of this type arises from our unwillingness or inability to see and to feel the singularity and the intentional design of a particular scene, of its tenuous, uneasy existence.

Yet Nature as the sole creator of everything still has its favorites, those for which it expends special effort in construction, to which it adds finishing touches with special zeal, and which it endows with special power. Baikal, without a doubt, is one of these. Not for nothing is it called the pearl of Siberia. We will not discuss its natural resources at present, for that is a separate issue. Baikal is renowned and sacred for a different reason—for its miraculous, life-giving force and for its spirit, which is a spirit not of olden times, of the past, as with many things today, but of the present, a spirit not subject to time and transformations, a spirit of age-old grandeur and power preserved intact, of irresistible ordeals and inborn will.

I recall taking a long walk with a colleague of mine who had come for a visit. We followed the old Baikal Shoreline Railroad for some distance along the seacoast, one of the most beautiful and striking spots at the southern tip of Baikal. It was August, the best, most bountiful time of year at Baikal, when the water warms up and the hills are a riot of multicolor, when even the rocks seem to blossom, blazing with many hues; when brilliant sunlight delineates the newly fallen snow on the distant, bare peaks of the Sayan Mountains, which the eye perceives as many times closer than they actually are; when Baikal has already built up its water supply with glacial runoff, holding it in reserve, and is sated and often calm, gathering strength for the autumn gales; when fish play in lavish abundance near the shore, accompanied by the cries of seagulls; and when all along the railroad tracks you encounter one kind of berry after another—now raspberries, now red and black currants, now honeysuckle . . . And what's more, it turned out to be an uncommonly fine day: sunny, windless, and warm, the air reverberating, Baikal clear and frozen still; rocks sparkling way out in the water and colors playing across them; and the smell of warmed air, bitter from the various maturing grasses, coming down the hill and reaching the tracks as it alternated with the cool, sharp breath wafting carelessly from the sea.

By this time my colleague had been overwhelmed for nearly two hours by the lush, wild beauty pouring down on him from all sides and creating a lavish summer celebration the likes of which he had not only never seen until now but also never even imagined. I will repeat that this beauty was in full bloom and at its peak. Add to this scene mountain rivers running noisily down into Baikal, to which we descended time after time to taste the water and to see with what mystery and self-sacrifice they flowed into the common maternal water and abated in oblivion. Also add to this the frequent tunnels that appear to occur naturally, with neat and tasteful finishing touches. Here there are practically as many of them as there are kilometers on this route, and cliffs tower above them, solemnly and sternly in some places and playfully in others, as if displaying the freedom of just having ended a game.

Everything we have for gathering impressions became overloaded very rapidly in my colleague, and, by now in no shape to be further amazed and delighted, he fell silent. I kept on talking. I told him about how I'd been fooled by the water's transparency the first time I came upon Baikal during my student years and tried to reach out of the boat and pick up a pebble, which, when we took a sounding, turned out to be over four meters away. My colleague accepted this incident apathetically. Somewhat hurt, I informed him that you can see more than forty meters through the water in Baikal—and I kept laying it on thick, but he didn't react to this either, as if such things are fairly common in the Moscow River, which he regularly drives past in his car. Only then did I guess what was wrong with him: tell him that in Baikal we can read the date on a two-kopeck coin at a depth of two to three hundred meters and, having passed the point of amazement, he will no longer be amazed. He was filled, as they say, to the brim.

I remember that what finished him off that day was a freshwater seal. They rarely swim right up to shore, but here one was luxuriating in the water quite close by, as if on command, and when I noticed it and pointed to it, a loud, wild cry burst from my colleague, and he suddenly began to whistle and beckon to the seal as if it were a dog. It immediately went underwater, of course, and my colleague, in utter amazement at the seal and at himself, lapsed into silence again, this time for quite a while.

I present this recollection, which has no significance in itself, merely to create an opportunity to quote a few words from my colleague's long, enthusiastic letter, which he sent me soon after returning home from

Baikal. "My energy level has risen—that's normal, that's happened before," he wrote. "But now my spirits have been lifted, and that comes
from out there, from Baikal. I now feel that I can accomplish a great deal,
and I seem able to determine what needs to be done and what doesn't.
It's a good thing we have Baikal! I get up in the morning and, bowing in
your direction, toward Father Baikal, I begin to move mountains . . ."

I understand him . . .

But you know, my colleague saw only the tiniest edge of Baikal, and
he saw it on a marvelous summer day when everything all around was
showing its appreciation for the tranquillity and the sunshine. He doesn't
know that on just such a day, when the sun is shining and the air is practically motionless, Baikal can rage for no reason, it would seem, as if
whipped up from inside. You look and can't believe your eyes: stillness,
no wind, and crashing water. This is a swell that has traveled from the
site of a gale a great many miles away.

My colleague did not end up in a *sarma*, or a *kultuk*, or a *barguzin*.
These are the names of the winds that can instantly swoop down out of
the river valleys with insane force and are capable of causing no small
amount of trouble on Baikal, sometimes raising waves four to six meters
high. Unlike in the song, a Baikal fisherman is not about to ask, "Hey,
Barguzin, stir up a swell . . ."

He did not see northern Baikal in all its stern, primordial beauty, in
whose midst you lose both your sense of time and your yardstick for human achievements, so bountifully and regally does radiant eternity hold
sway there over the pure waters of the distant past. In recent years, however, human beings have been rushing to catch up there, too, in·their
usual manner, diminishing the regality and eternity and peacefulness
and beauty.

He didn't go to Peschanaya Bay, where there are many more sunny
days per year than in the famous southern resort towns, and he didn't
swim in the Chivyrkuysky Gulf, where in summertime the water is just
as warm as the Black Sea.

He doesn't know Baikal in winter, when the transparent ice, swept
clean by the winds, seems so thin that the water beneath it is alive and
stirring, like under a magnifying glass; you're afraid to step on it, yet all
the while it might be over one meter thick. My colleague hasn't heard
the rumbling and cracking in spring when Baikal, quivering from time
to time, breaks up this ice with wide, bottomless cracks that can't be
crossed on foot or by boat and then, pushing them back together, erects
magnificent masses of light blue ice walls.

He didn't find himself in a fairy tale: now a sailboat rushes straight at
you with its snow-white sail unfurled; now a castle, a medieval beauty,
hangs in the air, smoothly descending and apparently trying to maneu-
ver into the best possible landing place; now swans swim in a broad line

with their heads proudly held high and then charge you, coming very close . . . These are mirages on Baikal, a common occurrence here, which are linked to a good many beautiful legends and superstitions.

There is a lot that my colleague didn't see, hear, or experience. Rather he saw, heard, and experienced practically nothing. And we who live near Baikal cannot boast that we know it well, because to know and to understand it completely is impossible—that's what makes it Baikal. It is always different and never repeats itself; every moment it changes its colors and hues, its weather, movement, and spirit. Oh, the spirit of Baikal! This is something special, something living, something that makes you believe in the old legends and ponder with mystical apprehension the extent to which people in some places feel free to do anything they please.

And although he was here for a very short time and saw precious little, my colleague still had the opportunity to get a feel for Baikal, if not to understand it. In such situations, getting a feel for something depends on us, on our ability or inability to allow the spiritual seed to take root inside us. And when my colleague describes what Baikal was able to give him during one walk, I understand him.

Baikal, it would seem, ought to overwhelm a person with its grandeur and its dimensions—everything in it is big, everything is large-scale, enigmatic, and free—yet on the contrary, it is uplifting. You experience a rare feeling of elation and spirituality at Baikal, as if in the face of eternity and perfection the secret stamp of these enchanting notions has touched you, too, and an all-powerful presence close at hand has breathed on you, too, and a share of the magic secret of all that exists has entered you as well. Merely by standing on this shore, breathing this air, and drinking this water you seem to have been singled out and marked. Nowhere else will you have the sensation of such a complete and welcome merging with and penetration of nature: this air will stupefy you, make you dizzy, and carry you away across this water so quickly that you won't have time to recover your senses. You will visit untouched wilderness beyond your wildest dreams, and you will return with ten times the hope you had: there, up ahead, lies the promised life . . .

And the purifying and inspiring and encouraging effect of Baikal on our intentions and our souls! . . . To make a list, to write it all down, is impossible; again, you can only feel its effect inside, but the mere fact that it exists is enough for us.

After returning from a walk one day, Leo Tolstoy noted, "How, in the midst of nature's charms, can feelings of malice and vengeance or the passion to destroy others like himself possibly remain entrenched in man? It seems that all evil in a person's heart should vanish when it comes into contact with nature, this spontaneous expression of beauty and goodness."

Our old primordial disharmony with the land we live on and with its heavenly abundance is an old misfortune of ours.

Nature by itself is always moral; only human beings can make it immoral. And how do we know that nature itself isn't what keeps us to a large extent within those more or less still rational limits that define our moral condition, that nature isn't what reinforces our good sense and good deeds?! It is nature that looks into our eyes day and night with entreaty, hope, and warning, gazing at us through the souls of the dead and of the unborn, of those who went before us and will come after us. And don't we all hear this summons? In times past the Evenk* standing on the shore of Baikal as he was about to cut down a birch tree out of necessity would repent for a long time and ask the tree's forgiveness for being forced to destroy it. Nowadays we are different. And yet aren't we in a position to stay the indifferent hand that is no longer raised against a birch tree, as it was two or three hundred years ago, but against Father Baikal himself precisely because we can thus pay back a miniscule part of what nature, including Baikal, has invested in us?! Favor for favor, one good turn for another—this is in accordance with the primordial circle of moral existence . . .

Baikal was created as the crowning glory and mystery of nature not for industrial requirements but so that we might drink from it to our heart's content—water being its primary and most priceless resource—admire its sovereign beauty, and breathe its cherished air. It has never refused to help human beings, but only as long as its water remained pure, its beauty unsullied, its air unpolluted, and the life in and around it unspoiled.

This is imperative above all for our own sake.

Baikal, Baikal . . .

Long ago it became the symbol of our relationship to nature, and now too much depends on whether or not Baikal will remain pure and intact. This would have been not just one more boundary that the human race conquered and crossed but the final boundary: beyond Baikal there would be nothing that could stop people from going too far in their efforts to transform nature.

It is hard to refrain from repeating after my colleague: it's a good thing we have Baikal! Mighty, rich, majestic, beautiful in many, many different ways, regal and self-contained, unsubdued—it's a good thing we have it!

1981

---

*Evenks—a nomadic people indigenous to the taiga of eastern Siberia who live principally by reindeer herding, hunting, and fishing.

WHAT WE HAVE

A

Baikal

Prologue

Without

an

Epilogue

Morality and *spirituality* may well be the most over-used words today. And yet we are forced to invoke them again and again as we seek reasons for things that have no other explanation. And the same with patriotism, which so often serves as a rhetorical device; it, too, takes hold not when it has been grafted onto us but when it results from a genuine sense of our native land. *Genuine*, accordingly, means proceeding from the moral and spiritual foundations that are common to our people. These are indispensable. Any substitute turns into the same serious disease that Dostoevsky spoke of: "You know, a great many people are afflicted with their very health, that is, with being too sure that they are normal." We may add: "And with having no doubts in cases where they should look before they leap."

Somewhere inside each person there is a wellspring bubbling out of the earth on which he, grateful for his origins, was born (and don't let it bother anyone that a spring can bubble out of the earth inside a person). But while some people live by drawing from this wellspring, others have filled it in and made it dry up. Some use it to gauge every action on earth; others calculate its material advantages (whether to them personally or to the government agency they work for is unimportant). And more and more often, current conditions put us at cross-purposes in our public activity, causing sporadic confrontations in various fields of endeavor that can only be compared with the most famous military battles.

For many years we struggled over reversing the flow of several rivers in Siberia and Northern Russia.* The stakes were extremely high—and this was no game, for the physical map of the country was in jeopardy: millions of square miles of Russian land would have been altered permanently. In such instances people call it "the land we inherited from our ancestors." Someday the property rights of the various generations will have to be adjudicated. Those who own the present do not necessarily own everything, both past and future. We don't inherit the earth so that we can test our legendary strength, to see if the human race has accumulated enough power to turn the world upside down. In this case no test is needed: we have. And by now it is becoming somehow awkward to ask whether we truly understand to what sort of life we condemn our grandchildren if our children don't also resolutely abandon the practices we have instilled in them. It's awkward because the ones to whom the question is addressed don't hear it while those who do hear the question repeat it endlessly without finding either an answer or any consolation.

"What's frightening is that nothing is frightening," Ivan Turgenev once said in a moment of bitterness. Some things, like the meter or the kilogram, should remain constant regardless of circumstances and disagreements. What ought to frighten us the most is that both sides—both for and against the reversal of the rivers—justified their actions by using the exact same rhetoric, appealing to the Fatherland. They certainly made strange bedfellows, for they had completely different, even opposite, goals. Whenever desperate for arguments, they chanted the praises of patriotism. Demagoguery wasn't born today or even yesterday, but until now people with a cause kept their distance from it. An unjust cause led to the distortion of sacred concepts, reducing them to demagogic noise. Dozens of planning institutes and tens of thousands of people were pressed into serving the river-reversal machine, hundreds of millions of rubles were spent—and all this was done irrationally, in haste, without adequate technical expertise and economic justification. An embezzler is prosecuted for taking only a thousand rubles, yet here there were hundreds of millions of rubles and, after the government passed a resolution curtailing work on the project, there were tens of thousands of corrupted souls who considered themselves cheated

*A project conceived in the 1930s to divert northward-flowing rivers to arid regions in the southern part of the Soviet Union to provide water for irrigation and other purposes.

and wronged for no reason. And what came of it? Was anyone punished for this gigantic boondoggle, for this record-breaking act of lawlessness? Was a single hair on anyone's head ever harmed? No.

Before talking about responsibility assumed on threat of punishment, don't we need to recall the concept of responsibility as accepting the specific consequences of the role we choose to play? But in this case we must turn again to our moral foundations, because they are what stand between the role one adopts and its consequences. Without moral foundations, a role is adopted too casually. With them, the results that one's role might lead to in the present and future will be taken into consideration from the start. "I put the harness on wrong but rode off like that anyway" was never a good motto, and here we're talking not about an ordinary household errand but about something a bit more complex. We are not owners of the nation's soil but merely its tillers, reaping nourishment and prosperity; the land is the mother and nurturer of the people, their eternal refuge, their sole dwelling place, to which nothing more can be added from the outside. And when out of this populace individuals appear who believe that the earth is put together wrong and must be rearranged, what's dangerous is not that they appear but that we allow ourselves to follow their lead as though they were prophets. It is no accident that the alarm has gone off in our time: those who come after us will not forgive us. In Russia they will not forgive us for ruining Lake Baikal and the Volga River, in Belorussia for the Pripet Marshes, in Armenia for Lake Sevan, in the Ukraine for the Dnepr River and Chernobyl, in Latvia for the Western Dvina River—everywhere, everywhere, everywhere . . . Future tillers will not forgive us for our wastefulness and intemperate actions. Regardless of whether the expansionism of government agencies is blown out of proportion or stifled, sooner or later it will burst, and what good are its regurgitations?

In light of the various evaluations of what is beneficial and what is harmful to our homeland (we'll assume that they have all mingled in the house of national interest), let's take a closer look at how the participants in these bold, nature-reversing projects operate. Means and methods of action, as a rule, tell us a great deal. We aren't dumb enough to draw conclusions that will leave us open to attack. Work begins on these projects even before they receive official approval, before the government has given its "okay," and before all the "pros" and "cons" have been thoroughly examined. Work not only begins but is hurried along, speeded up, and expanded in breadth and depth; funding, staffing, and materials are acquired—faster, faster, before they come to their senses, before they suddenly figure out what's going on—in order to mire the government in expenses, after which they will have no choice but to throw up their hands in despair. That's what happened with the "project of the century," the reversal of the rivers, and that's what is happening right now in the Altai Mountains, where the Ministry of Energy is continuing the construction of hydroelectric power plants on the Katun River without waiting for official sanction of the project. The Baikal Cellulose and Paper Plant was built in 1966, but its final design specifications were not approved until years after the enterprise began production. The list of examples could go on and on.

The Lake Baikal drama is so much like a cleverly and boldly contrived plot that one can only marvel at the skill of its performers. Each time it seems that the picture is finally becoming clear, that the matter is heading toward a resolution, toward disclosure of the whole truth, this fails to happen—time after time new characters appear on stage, there are new court appeals and new arguments, and the action again reaches a heart-stopping climax. And Baikal continues to suffer. In February 1986 a State commission was created to draft proposals for the protection of our "glorious sea." N. V. Talyzin, the head of this commission and head of the State Planning Committee of the U.S.S.R., put aside unnecessary diplomacy during one discussion of the Baikal problem that took place in Irkutsk and stated, "Even a fool can now see that a cellulose plant should never have been built on Baikal." Meanwhile, the fate of Baikal was being influenced once again by someone who had appeared before Talyzin at a session of the previous commission, an academician named N. M. Zhavoronkov, the persistent and chief defender not of Baikal, as one would expect of a scholar, but of both industrial plants, the one already mentioned and the one on the Selenga River,* which uses cellulose to make cardboard. There is no need to explain what he recommended, despite the obvious consequences.

The fact that Baikal is no place for industrial plants was clear even then, in the 1960s, when they were trying to make a final decision on how to utilize Baikal. Hardly anyone, even among the plant managers, actually believed the "scientific" arguments suggesting that boiling the cellulose would only improve Baikal's water because it allegedly contained too few minerals in its natural state and was harmful to drink. But as the bureaucratic wheel gathered speed, it seemed determined not to turn away from Baikal. Lining up advocates presented no special problem, for you can always find experts willing to support anything whatsoever. But now it is the easiest thing in the world to pin the blame for the industrial plants on bureaucratic intransigence. No, it was back then, as I recall, that another force appeared for the first time, one far

---

*Selenga River—a river rising in the Mongolian People's Republic and flowing 897 miles to Lake Baikal.

more formidable and extensive than the parties with a vested interest in what the plants produced. Their output, by the way, actually inhibited the development of the tire industry; when tires are made from Baikal cellulose rather than from synthetic materials, the State loses money.

In the early 1960s, like everywhere else, our society felt the effects of the scientific and technological revolution and reflected what was probably an entirely predictable division between "reactive" and "vestigial" thinking.* Traditional humanistic forms of expression were naturally relegated to the category of vestigial thinking, which supposedly employed worn-out truths and didn't keep up with the pace of modern life. The debate between physicists and poets, which seemed destined to bathe the physicists in spiritual light, to reveal to the poets the realities of a changing world, and to end in universal benefit, in reality moved from the auditorium to the workplace and changed from a hypothetical point of view into a modus operandi. Disagreement between the "old" and "new" ways of thinking has undoubtedly always existed in every age, and these ways of thinking were tolerant of each other because out of their disagreement came dynamic social truths. But this time the human race, standing at the conveyer belt of technological progress, used the advantage of its position to obtain not just a moral victory but also a complete and final one. In less than twenty years the friendly "physicist," who had once resembled a hussar, grew into a dangerous and autonomous technocrat maneuvering skillfully among duty, purpose, advantage, and morality. Concerning morality, it has become the stepchild in the family, allowed to sit at the table when guests are present but banished to a corner when no outsiders are around.

Twenty years ago, P. Katsuba, then a Party official in Irkutsk, publicly accused Baikal's defenders of aiding the cause of imperialism. Precisely that; no more and no less. That was about as far as you could go, and anything less would have fallen on deaf ears. This logic was quickly adopted on the eastern shore of Baikal: whoever opposed the cellulose plant was an enemy of the Buryat people. Such arguments immediately immobilize the hands and the tongue; the Russian language in general adapts poorly to this kind of long-range firing back and forth. As we look back now, we can only frown in disgust; and yet all this actually happened; it all happened and took its toll. They didn't mince words. With each side asserting its own concept of civilization, the two forces locked horns as though they were on foreign soil rather than on the one and only land belonging to them. And if nature itself had not intervened

---

*"Reactive" (*reaktivnoe myshlenie*) in the sense of flexible, dynamic, appropriate for current conditions; "vestigial" (*ostatochnoe myshlenie*) in the sense of rigid, static, anachronistic.

in the debate, presenting evidence here and there of the fruits of mechanized "enlightenment," we have no idea what heights the discussion might have reached. Now they are forced to change the tone of the discussion, but demagoguery and rhetoric cannot change the essence of their aims and deeds. Today the candid technocrat is like an alcoholic who understands perfectly well that he shouldn't touch a drop, that it's an either-or proposition, but he reaches for the glass anyway to get temporary relief, and after that the whole world can go to blazes.

In early 1986, M. I. Busygin, Minister of the Wood Pulp and Paper Industry, agreed to meet with me at the request of the newspaper *Izvestia*. We talked about Baikal and the Baikal Cellulose Plant, which has long been a stumbling block, the talk of the town, a "Trojan horse"—indeed, what hasn't it become in the struggle over Baikal? But the plant still stands. During our conversation the minister cited a fact that was supposed to demonstrate his agency's concern for Baikal: during its twenty years of operation, the PDK* (the allowable maximum concentration of pollutants) in the waste water from the plant has been changed six times. I didn't know that and took his statement at face value, but the minister could not help knowing that by no means have the standards always been changed in Baikal's favor; they have simply been adjusted to fit the purification capabilities of the plant. Under the present policy of glasnost, much that once remained confidential is now being disclosed, but the agency machine in its dialogue with public opinion continues its custom of relying on two kinds of information—open information for publicizing successes and closed information for concealing areas in which it has "flunked."

As far back as 1974, Galina Suslova, who formerly worked for the Energy and Paper Industry and is now retired, wrote to me that she had been instructed to calculate the depletion of mineral salts in the soda-regenerative boilers at the Baikal Plant. After making the calculations, she looked at the final report and saw that the figure for the depletion of alkalies had been reduced—by a factor of ten. The report had been compiled at the plant, but then it went on to the ministry and has probably been used there more than once to show that its factory is harmless.

After this we should not be surprised at the innocent figure claiming that the Baikal plant is responsible for only a little more than one percent of the lake's pollution. Even Academician Pyotr Kapitsa used to caution us about such bare quantitative statistics. Speaking in 1966 at a joint meeting of the boards of directors of the State Planning Committee and of the State Committee on Science and Technology and the Presidium of

---

*PDK—*predel'no-dopustimye kontsentratsii.*

the Academy of Sciences, he stated, "As can be seen from data cited by a commission of experts, the polluted water discharged into Baikal from a cellulose plant has a completely different chemical composition from the water entering through the rivers that flow into the lake. . . . Thus even a small concentration of toxic pollutants from cellulose plants can utterly destroy the favorable balance of nature and totally ruin the lake's purity."

We are close to that now. More than one hundred government-agency scientists working for the Institute of Environmental Toxicology form a wall of support around the plant, but, no matter how tenaciously they may try to prove the opposite, there is overwhelming factual evidence that the plant is not the innocent child they portray. The destruction of the Epischura, the zooplankton that forms the basic biological purifier of Baikal's water, and of other endemic species (like the famous omul salmon, which now grows to only half its former weight and length) and the tens of thousands of hectares of forest that are drying out from the atmospheric wastes and hundreds of thousands of hectares already damaged—all this is the handiwork of the cellulose plant.

Beginning in 1987, Baikal will breathe more easily. The government is formulating a far-reaching and comprehensive program for the preservation of its water and forests. But the ministry is putting up a fight for its plant. They have got to retool it sometime, but the deadlines are being pushed back into the next Five-Year Plan and, according to calculations made by Baikal's defenders, still further and further into the future. Diverting the waste water through a pipeline into the Irkut River is being proposed as a temporary measure. It's not hard to see through these plans; the temporary measure will become permanent. Is it economical to spend millions of rubles on a life preserver? Isn't it better to say once and for all, "We made a mistake—let's correct the mistake," and do without interim measures, expensive crutches, and rationalizations? Our times have already shouldered this heavy burden, for Baikal is worth whatever effort it takes to defend it. Diverting the waste water is not a permanent solution to the problem; the atmospheric wastes remain, and, according to the experts, they cannot be made completely harmless.

And besides, how can we believe a ministry that long ago adopted the practice of reneging on its promises to protect the environment? Reneging on its promises—pure and simple. The closed system of water utilization that was planned for the year 1980 at the Selenga Cellulose and Cardboard Plant is still circulating in a paper chase. Way back when the State Commission on Baikal was still functioning, the Baikal plant received orders to stop producing yeast in August 1986, but only recently has it halted production, and then only after an uproar.

Oh, all in the name of national interest! This is the phrase they bandied about during construction of the plants, this is what they put forward year after year in defense of the plants, and this is what they're resorting to even now. The State Planning Committee insists that the nation can't get along without cellulose from the Baikal plants, that it's practically doomed to destruction without it. But according to information from V. F. Yevstratov, a tire expert and Corresponding Member of the Soviet Academy of Sciences, the Soviet tire conglomerate Soyuzshin had planned to use only sixteen thousand metric tons of viscose cord in 1990, but eighty thousand tons are being forced on it. And what if we scour other branches of the economy? Don't we have enough evidence to go out tomorrow and stop an operation that is fatal to Baikal? Or to distribute its quotas among other enterprises?

Let's remember that at the beginning of World War II all our vitally important industries, on which the nation's very survival depended, were moved from west to east in a matter of months. I permit myself this comparison because in the very near future the pure waters of Baikal could turn out to be no less a lifesaving asset.

"We neglect what we have, then cry when it's gone." This old Russian proverb never even suspected how global and universal its truth would become. It is now in the national interest above all else to restore people's faith in the common sense and moral origin of everything we undertake.

And, finally, I'd like to quote a few lines from a letter sent to me by Vasily Zabello, a worker at the Baikal Cellulose Plant:

> They call it "the surrounding environment"—how's that for heartless officialese! They shouldn't talk about Baikal that way. Baikal is our national shrine. And now we're threatening the existence of this beauty of nature. How could we even think of raising a hand against it?! And no matter how much I hear about the need for this plant, no matter how much they tug at my shirt, which is made from viscose rayon, and ask me what I would be wearing right now without it—neither my mind nor my heart can accept the notion that we need viscose fiber more than we need Baikal. I would be very happy to wear a shirt made of linen.
>
> Granted, not all my fellow workers put the question the way I do, but deep down inside each of them feels the same way. Something to the effect that here we are working, getting paid for our labor, earning awards and pensions, and in the final analysis all our energy, all our labor leads to the destruction of Baikal. This kind of labor can't bring any satisfaction.

Who says that workers can't think in terms of the nation as a whole?

March 1987

YOUR SON, RUSSIA,
AND OUR PASSIONATE BROTHER

On

Vasily

Shukshin

"Morality is truth," wrote Shukshin. "Not simply truth but Truth. For it is courage and honesty; it means living the joy and pain of the common people and thinking as they think, because the people always know the Truth."

And just as in the folktale "Before the Cock Crows Thrice," in which Ivanushka the Fool—that ancient, eternal fairy-tale character in Russian folklore and the Russian people's own flesh and blood—sets out to search the world over for proof that he is by no means a fool, so, too, beginning with Vasily Shukshin's very first stories, does the "oddball,"* his invariable protagonist, set out on a long and difficult quest for the true answer to the questions, Who are "the people" and what is truth? [. . .]

This translation contains minor omissions, mainly long quotations from Shukshin's stories.
*In Russian, *chudik.*

The appearance of Shukshin's protagonist in the early 1960s was somewhat unexpected. By then, of course, our literature had already strayed quite far from its customary path—according to which protagonists were created and positioned strictly along positive and negative lines for the convenience of teachers and for effortless comprehension—but somehow the "oddball," or rather his predecessor, did not blend very well into literary society even then. One assumes that Shukshin himself was aware that his protagonist stood out like a sore thumb, and, either to rationalize or to defend him, he entitled his first books *Rural Residents* [*Sel'skie zhiteli*] and *Eccentrics* [*Kharaktery*] and his first film "There Lives This Guy" [*Zhivet takoi paren'*]. Let's also add the title of the novella *Out There, Far Away* [*Tam, vdali*] and, although this approach may not be entirely reliable, we are tempted to surmise that in this way Shukshin seemed to be cautiously saying that these strange characters are possible out there, far away in some Siberian village, and that a guy like this might live there, too. But very shortly thereafter the author quite correctly brought his protagonist closer to himself and to all of us by emphasizing our direct kinship and moved him to center stage: Shukshin called his next film "Your Son and Brother" [*Vash syn i brat*], one of his books *Fellow Countrymen* [*Zemliaki*], and a novella *My Brother* [*Brat moi*]. It's not hard to understand Shukshin, who, after gaining strength as a writer and film director and after winning an audience, then felt ready to demonstrate with all his inherent fervor that there is nothing strange about his protagonist; that, unlike many of us who are materially well off, mentally frigid, and spiritually slippery, he is a living person capable of suffering and of taking action. If his soul is in pain, if his actions are generally viewed as absurd, then you just try to figure out why this has happened and ask yourselves whether you don't envy him.

So who exactly is he, this "oddball," as the critics have generally chosen to label Shukshin's protagonist? What is it about him that arouses alarm and a sense of conscience in us and calls forth a nostalgic sympathy, once nearly lost, for someone who clearly lacks high principles and standards of conduct?

Monya Kvasov (in the story "Stubborn" [*Upornyi*]) doesn't believe that it's impossible to come up with a "perpetual-motion machine" and spends his time trying to build one. Styopka, from a different story also entitled "Stubborn," escapes from a prison camp, from confinement, three months before he would have been released because, as he explains it, "I was tormented by dreams. I dreamed about my village every night." He escapes and, after carousing for one single evening at home, goes back into captivity for years. "That's all right. Now I'm fortified. Now I can serve time." [. . .]

The list of these "oddballs" could go on forever. They appear in the majority of Shukshin's short stories, which one reads sometimes with laughter, sometimes with sadness, but most often with alarm, and which, when taken together, create a motley, yet consistent, impression. For all of them describe the individual traits, the individual features, of one character, whom Shukshin sketched from start to finish and whom he essentially succeeded in portraying. This character is free and independent by nature, [. . .] someone who uses every possible means and all his eccentricities to defend his natural right to be himself, to have his own opinions, and to apply his intelligence and experience to everything under the sun. Strongly influenced by uncontrollable forces and chance circumstances, harrassed, impulsive, organically incapable of enduring any kind of hypocrisy, no matter what its ultimate objective, torn by contradictions, and suffering from the inadequacy of reality and from the unattainability of his dreams, Shukshin's protagonist, despite all this, is a fully human and integrated personality, for he doesn't let anyone confine him to the general ranks but lives separately and independently, the way people should. And by this alone he wins our favor and makes us feel uneasy about ourselves. [. . .]

The sense of individuality, the sense of his own worth in Vasily Shukshin's protagonist can be called a raging passion.

Alyosha Beskonvoyny,* who gets his way and spends Saturdays heating up his bathhouse,† lights the stove, looks at the flaring fire, and thinks, "You folks out there want all people to live alike. Even two logs don't burn alike, but you want people to live their lives alike!"

Thus a passionate, feverish sense of individuality streaming over the edge of prudence is the first and perhaps main characteristic or "peculiarity" of Shukshin's "oddball" protagonist, making him an "oddball" according to the accepted view. Before him no one in our literature had ever claimed his right to himself with such impatience, and no one had succeeded in making us listen to him concerning such a private matter. Concerning the suffering soul.

Now the word has been uttered, one of Shukshin's fundamental and most resounding words. The soul . . . And what is the soul? Why is it that more and more often literature is taking both the liberty and the responsibility of tormenting people with the idea of the soul, which must be in them somewhere, in some unknown depths, and

*Literally, "unescorted."
†Instead of working on the collective farm.

without which nothing, no amount of well-being, it is believed, will bring relief? Isn't the soul exploited mercilessly because, having neither flesh nor a location, it is unreachable, and appealing to it is the same as calling into a void from which no response can be expected, which suits us precisely because there will be no response, for then we cannot be found guilty of false morality? And let people search for the soul; they probably won't find it because so far no one has managed to find something that doesn't exist, but while they're occupied with this quest they will be distracted from worse and even more frivolous pursuits that could only bring them harm. Isn't this how experts on the soul reason, referring to it willy-nilly, right and left? Isn't this in fact how it is?

No, it's not. Don't refer to it right and left, for nothing good will come of this. But there can be no doubt that the soul, which has no sides or anything else to grab, means a great deal to people. Its significance is not as an unknown quantity but as something valuable that exists in a person from the beginning yet is not always identified and brought to life; as a force that transfigures him, that turns him into something different from the person without a soul, something more on the march, let's say—in the sense that a person must make unswerving progress toward his high aims and ideals; as the fulfillment of his calling to be an individual; as a sign of welcome self-discovery. The soul, one must assume, is really the essence of an individual personality, an extension of the life of a permanent, historical being that is not broken by temporal misfortunes.

Thus we come back once again to individuality, autonomy, and self worth. These are impossible to avoid when considering the soul. Sidestepping it won't work either, because that would mean pretending to be deaf, pretending not to hear and to understand Shukshin. Rarely does any story (and not only his stories) contain no mention of the soul, no feeling of discord with the soul, no wish to recover that which would have established his protagonist firmly in life and revealed its meaning. [. . .]

"But it aches, you know, the soul does. When teeth start aching at night, we run like crazy . . . But where can you go when your soul aches?" ("Nighttime In the Boiler Room" [*Noch'iu v boilernoi*]). [. . .]

Some people view life with astonished confusion: What is this? Where am I? Why am I here? Others are tormented and tear around, tear around and are tormented, and their torments never seem to end. Still others, like Yegor Prokudin in "The Red Snowball Tree" [*Kalina krasnaia*], periodically organize a "celebration for the soul"—going out on a binge—as when Yegor goes to a little local restaurant and throws away a bundle of money on a stupid, vengeful party (taking vengeance mainly on himself). A lot of drinking occurs in Shukshin's stories, which is also a weak, useless, but well-worn attempt within people's reach to soothe the hungry cavity and to somehow free themselves, even temporarily, from its exacting pull. [. . .]

A life that is not sustained by the idea of the soul is a haphazard existence. Shukshin's protagonist has no desire to resign himself to such haphazardness—he is above it—but he also senses that he is too inadequate and unstable to lead a purposeful life. This torments him and forces him to commit acts that seem to happen outside himself and that are usually harmful to him. Unpredictability, uncontrollability, consistent illogicality of action, and the qualities that Russians in general secretly love about themselves are completely unrestrained in the "oddball" and reach a rapturously destructive degree when he is both his own executioner and his own victim.

But isn't it strange? Nothing in Shukshin's works would seem to speak directly to his protagonist's imminent discovery of his soul, and yet the reader almost becomes convinced that this will happen. The pain and passion with which he tears around in dismay and yearns for his soul transform it into something almost material, something with a location where it can be found. Not to respond to this desperate appeal seems impossible.

As to the place where the soul resides, this is not terribly difficult to surmise. It is a person's homeland, the land of his birth, which at the outset gave him everything essential for stability in life.

One can't help but notice: to the extent that the "oddball," that unstable and unhealthy character intuitively striving for wholeness and health, arouses our sympathy and support, the women in Shukshin's stories (especially in his short stories) are to the same extent undeserving of sympathy as a rule, and the traits of a great many female characters add up to a figure far from endearing to any of us. If it were merely a matter of liking them or not, this subject wouldn't need to be raised, for one way or another it wounds women's self-esteem. But there is a larger issue here: the state of the feminine personality and even the direction in which it is headed, whether toward itself—what a person should be—or away from itself—what a person should not be. At issue, in the final analysis, are the results of this movement.

Not much in Shukshin's works is accidental or beyond the bounds of his observations and firm views, especially in this area—here his attitude is all the more mature, all the more a product of suffering, because over the years it not only did not become attenuated, as they say, but, on the contrary, grew stronger, acquired a serene explanation, and led to a definite philosophy. The story "Alone" [*Odni*] was written at the very beginning of the 1960s, and Marfa, the wife of a harness maker named

Antip who begrudges him six rubles for a balalaika, is an angel from
heaven compared to Venya's wife and mother-in-law in "My Son-in-law
Stole a Truckload of Firewood!" [*Moi ziat' ukral mashinu drov!*] and even
more so in comparison to Kolka Paratov's wife in "A Wife Saw Her Husband Off to Paris" [*Zhena muzha v Parizh provozhala*] (both of these stories
were written ten years after the first one). Kolka Paratov, driven to despair by the accusations and nasty fights in his family, by the constant
degradation of his human dignity, turns on the gas in the kitchen and
leaves his little daughter a note: "Sweetheart, Papa went away on a business trip." "The trouble all started when Kolka soon discovered his
wife's immense, astonishing greed for money."

Greediness for money and possessions, spiritual deafness and mean-
ness, the lack of desire and the inability to understand anything at all
about the man living beside her, shrewishness, even an unnatural kind
of aggressiveness—these qualities are not simply observed but, with
few exceptions, stand out boldly in the fairer sex as she appears before
us in Shukshin's world. After the protagonist of "How the Bunny Flew
on Balloons" [*Kak zaika letal na vozdushnykh sharikakh*] leaves a village in
the Altai Mountains and goes to the city to visit his brother, he tells his
sick niece a fairy tale and says in fairy-tale style: "Ye-es, if it's a woman,
then it's Baba Yaga."* Shukshin makes no distinction between the city
and the countryside—this occurs everywhere.

One contradiction in Shukshin's view of women can be perplexing.
Everything said so far applies to women as wives. He has a completely
different, almost opposite, attitude toward women as mothers. For him
a mother means love, kindness, the ability to understand and to forgive,
natural gentleness, and spiritual steadfastness. Aleksey Khomyakov[†]
wrote:

> Feats can occur in battle,
> Feats can occur in strife,
> The highest feat is in patience,
> Love, and a prayerful life,

And the mothers in Shukshin's works perform this "highest feat" to
the highest degree. Examples can be found in the stories "A Mother's
Heart" [*Materinskoe serdtse*], "A Mother's Dreams" [*Sny materi*], "Vanka
Teplyashin," "At the Cemetery" [*Na kladbishche*], and others, as well as
in the image of Yegor Prokudin's mother in the film "The Red Snowball

---

*Baba Yaga—an evil, ugly sorceress in Russian folktales.
†Aleksey Stepanovich Khomyakov (1804–1860)—Russian Romantic poet, Slavophile
theoretician, and lay theologian.

Tree." But in that case, where do mothers come from if not from wives, and by what means can good spring from evil or understanding and acceptance from rejection? Isn't this view of wives still slanted and isn't it the result of an arbitrary, illogical division whereby mothers are one thing but wives another?

But it is not difficult to find logic and causality here, too. It's all a matter of age. Mothers are older than wives, and this difference in years has a detrimental effect on the essence and character of women. Lured away, displaced from their eternal moral foundation by the light promises of high ideals, women have not, however, become firmly established in their new place in society because, one can't help but think, it doesn't quite mesh with their feminine nature; and they have risen so awkwardly and find themselves in such an unnatural and unstable position that they can go neither forward nor backward. Forward, where they instinctively sense danger, is impossible, while backward is shameful. And to retreat is no longer a simple matter; movement has occurred in all directions, and, what's more, this new position does have its temptations and its charms, which flatter their pride. The seducer has turned out to be cruel—this time women have been unfaithful to themselves. The result is that women, once the permanent moral bastion of the family, the educators and spiritual teachers of their children, the peacemakers and peacebringers, now find themselves on morally shaky ground, and while they have not exactly transformed these qualities into their opposites (things haven't gone that far, of course), they have deviated from them to a considerable extent.

Naturally this accusation, referring to women as a whole, to their social and moral character, cannot be directed at all women indiscriminately, but we seem to be nearing the point at which it can be said that what had formerly been the rule is becoming the exception and what had been the exception is turning into the rule. In our general moral displacement, women have moved out ahead because their personalities are more agile and sensitive than men's, less hardened and less cautious when it comes to external change, and this alienation, insignificant in itself but palpably dangerous, has taken a bitter toll on their nature. The toga of lofty social standing, long a temptation to women, was hastily put on inside out and has had a grievous influence on their natural human qualities. Our concern, of course, is not that women should know their place and never leave their kitchens and families—that would be excessively crude and incorrect—but that they should not forget their main and irreplaceable importance in society in holding families together and in bringing up children and that they should not perform these functions haphazardly. [. . .]

Women themselves, one must assume, sense that they've ended up separated from themselves, that they are not who they intended to be or where they intended to go with the freedom given them. A natural feel for such things, which was always more highly developed in women than in men, cannot help but suggest this to them. And here is where we should seek the reason for their nervousness and nonchalance, in which it is easy to discern perplexity and a fear for their fate as well as for the fate of that heavy load women have pulled for ages and have now unhitched. Looking back at it, they can't help but suffer from its neglect—from the loneliness and coldness in their families, which have decreased both in size and cohesion and to which they come running sporadically only to leave again after some hasty shouting and caressing, with hurried instructions until the next foray.

While striving for the significant and elevated role that they are ready to play in life, women haven't taken into account that this new role is possible only in combination with and in subordination to their former role, which forms the basis for their humanity, and not in liberation from it—not in a logical solution to the problem, which says that point B can be reached only after abandoning point A.

No one attempting to discuss Shukshin can escape the following question, Shukshin's last question, which rang out like a moan, like a desperate cry, in the story "The Scandal" [*Kliauza*] after he'd reached the limit of his physical and moral strength: "What is happening to us?" Shukshin passed away a month after "The Scandal" was published, and this question has remained with us; it has not only remained unresolved but has also intensified during recent years and, so to speak, matured.

There is no need to retell "The Scandal." It is a documentary account of what happened to the author in the hospital when a woman janitor, a person with a lowly job and with rights corresponding to that position, soared to such heights in her demanding, brutish behavior and acquired such strength and power that it was impossible either to restrain or to understand her through any arguments concerning Christian humility. For Shukshin this seemed to be the limit, and he writes, "I don't know what happened to me there, but suddenly I felt that everything had come to an end. I couldn't figure out what sort of 'end' or an 'end' to what—I don't know even now—but the premonition of some very simple, mindless end was distinct." But we now know from the heights—or is it from the depths?—of today's experience, both as those who endure brutish behavior and as those who permit it, that this was by no means the limit, that after surpassing the limit brutish behavior has gone on to new horizons.

Shukshin exposed the main purveyors of brutish behavior for more than ten years in a row, calling them by their names with amazing consistency: bureaucrats, sales clerks, and street toughs, the latter being hoodlums, criminal brutes whose very appearance bears the stamp of a seemingly innate brutishness elevated to the one and only law of life. Shukshin didn't really expose them—this is not the right word, for as a true artist he never directly exposed anything—but each time he encountered circumstances in his work in which he could not honestly overlook brutish behavior, he would tense up like a fighter meeting his arch enemy, he'd "get all worked up," to use his language,* and he'd neither want nor be able to sidestep it calmly. He also considered himself a fighter when sitting at his work table, and there he endured a state of conflict and battle until the end—this is easy to sense from the tension and incandescence of his prose where the lines pulsate like bare wires with the overloaded current of human pain. He certainly did not agonize over these lines, and it's even less likely that he found them while wandering around in that precious corner we call "inspiration." Instead, they were the ones who controlled him and directed his hand, hurrying as they demanded a way out and a voice to bear witness.

Thus the bureaucrats, sales clerks, and street toughs:

"The oddball respected city people. Not all of them, it's true: he had no respect for hoodlums and sales clerks. He was slightly afraid of them" (from the story "The Oddball" [*Chudik*]).

"I'm scared of bureaucrats, sales clerks, and types like that gorilla over there . . . that maniac with the long arms and narrow forehead . . ." ("Borya").

"Why is this? How long are we ourselves going to aid and abet brutish behavior? Why this habit? Why this cursed desire to please a brutish sales clerk, a bureaucrat, or a plain old brute—and please them at all costs! For we're the ones who produced these brutes, we ourselves! Nobody delivered them to us, nobody dropped them here with parachutes" (from the story "The Insult" [*Obida*]).

Here Shukshin is offering an explanation—not a complete one, of course, and possible only in the context of artistic narration, but not a trivial explanation either—of why brutish behavior thrives.

And we really can't pin the blame on its being a remnant of the cursed past, as we usually do. This doesn't work. True, brutishness was always present in the rich bouquet of traits that make up the Russian national character. Brutish behavior did exist, but in former times it was inhibited by restrictive limits, it cropped up outside morality and the law, and it represented a kind of moral deformity. But now, while continuing outwardly to be beyond morality and the law, it has actually sunk its roots into the foundation of these concepts by taking advantage of permissive-

---

*In Russian, *vzvinchivalsia*.

ness, has expanded beyond a mode of individual existence, and is flourishing. It has begun to speak on equal terms with other human qualities and has become an excusable weakness, a commonplace phenomenon.

The brutishness of bureaucrats . . . This stems above all from the spiritual disparity between the person and his official post, from the distortion of the letter and spirit of his official position when service turns into self service and subservience, from civic inferiority, and from the unevenness and lack of firmness in society's directives and the mildness of society's punishments. Skilled in bureaucratic paperwork and well aware of the power of the information he dispenses, the bureaucrat grows in his own eyes into an enormous figure free to chastise or to favor, to stamp some trivial document today or to make you come back for it over and over again for a whole month. One stipulation must be made: the brutishness of bureaucrats is not necessarily the crudeness, mockery, and insults that we customarily mean by brutishness. No, it is frequently well-bred, moralizing, and even seemingly friendly in these offices. It is brutishness simply because of the humiliating position in which people are placed.

And brutish behavior has now taken a giant step out of the office and into the big wide world, where it has found someone dear to its heart standing behind the counter—sales clerks. Obviously the term *sales clerk* means our society's entire service sector, but since sales clerks are the very members of this sector whom we must encounter most often and from whom we must endure the most, they are named as the specific purveyors of the average and most widespread form of brutish behavior. And it's true that in sales clerks it has found ideal conditions, the whole range of conveniences: first, a very low level of general culture and a distorted concept of our relationship to them, which sees only our dependence on them; and second, the crowd on the other side of the counter, a crowd that is often agitated and demanding, the victim of shortages, and not always capable of using its common sense in time—an immense field with rich soil for brutish behavior.

Everything can be explained in the end, everything has its reasons—the brutishness of bureaucrats, the brutish behavior of sales clerks, and street brutality—and we can concur with these reasons, but it is impossible to condone the phenomenon itself. No amount of strength or imagination is enough to condone, to accept, and to keep repeating with malicious satisfaction this phrase from the repertoire of service-sector brutishness: "You ain't seen nothin' yet!"

Brutish behavior is a means of asserting one's individuality. That's how it has always been regarded. And it leads to the destruction of individuality. When a person doesn't know how to prove himself an individual any other way, he turns to his bestial origins and, despite the protesting voice of his conscience, apparently finds some sort of satisfaction in this. In other words, brutish behavior is a sign of backwardness, of stunted or degraded individuality. And yet this occurs when brutishness manifests itself in one person or in individuals.

No, Shukshin's question is not simple: "What is happening to us?"

Gleb Kapustin in the story "He Cut Them Down" [*Srezal*] is a wonderful example of how the lessons of demagoguery and empty rhetoric can be mastered. He turned out to be an able pupil, and in an argument with some city folks, who until recently had held a monopoly on eloquence, he displays true aerial acrobatics in the verbal duel that he himself forces on them, in which words are completely ravaged. This seems to be the last straw: a so-called simple person has mastered demagoguery.

Acting not on anyone's orders but on his own initiative, Shurygin, the foreman of a work crew (in the story "Tough Guy" [*Krepkii muzhik*]), destroys the beautiful ancient church that stood in his native village. He destroys it despite objections, despite the persuasive arguments and the tears of his fellow villagers, his mother and wife among them, and despite threats of punishment in heaven and on earth. Nothing has any effect: Shurygin, a "tough guy," tears down the poor church with the help of today's mighty machinery, gets on his motorcycle, and rides off singing to celebrate this event.

And here the limit has been reached. Shurygin also turned out to be an able pupil with a good memory. The code of behavior changed, but he had mastered an earlier one for life, absorbing it as an immutable law to be implemented.

And we'd imagined that all this was still far off, that it wouldn't happen any time soon. It turned out that we got what we deserved. It turned out to happen in our lifetime. The boomerang has come back with ten times its original force.

That's what is happening to us.

And now, on this sad note, it is time to return to the words of Shukshin that have already been cited: "Morality is truth. Not simply truth but Truth. For it is courage and honesty; it means living the joy and pain of the common people and thinking as they think, because the people always know the Truth."

But perhaps there is no basis for such certainty. Who are the common people nowadays and what is truth? Haven't these concepts already been washed away, obliterated by tears of emotion, and don't they encompass far too many things, some of which are occasionally incompatible? Do the people really and truly know the truth?

Worshiping the common people is also a Russian trait, but a cold, heartless deification of the people has never added any consolation to its fate. Shukshin had to have known this, and he wouldn't have offered the monument yet another amorphous, elevated figure created out of laudatory words—especially when the monument is already overcrowded with similar figures—if he had been uncertain of their truth. On the contrary, he would never have uttered such words in honor of Gleb Kapustin, Shurygin, and the multitude of others like them whose sheer numbers seem to make them inseparable from the body of the people.

For this reason, when discussing the people it is essential to immediately separate two concepts. There are the PEOPLE as the physical, moral, and spiritual basis of a nation who exist within each generation in an objective and real sense; they constitute the nation's root system, which preserved and continues to preserve its health and intellect, carries on and develops its best traditions, and nourishes it with the juices of its history and genesis. And there are the people—"in the broad sense of the word, the entire population of a specific country," as we read in the encyclopedia. The first concept enters the second and exists and operates within it, but it is not the same thing. And when Shukshin says with certainty that "the people always know the truth," he means the heart and soul of the people, the healthy part that gives it direction, but when Fyodor Abramov* addresses his fellow villagers in his famous letter, accusing them of careless farm management, he is aiming his just accusations not at the PEOPLE but at the population that constitutes the life and labor force of his native town. And that constitutes, moreover, a part of all the people—as population.

Shukshin is right a thousand times over: "The people always know the truth." For the people are those who live by the truth, however heavy this burden may be; truth is what forms the first principle and fundamental meaning of "the people" as well as the true essence of each person and his life, which is not subject to spiritual amputation. One's true essence is not naked, of course, not absolute and formal; instead it corresponds to the times—such is its nature.

Naturally this is not a complete definition of "the people," only a moral one, the moral unknown quantity of its essential being. But the moral component is now the most important. A definition of truth can be nothing else but moral. One must assume that the people not only

*Fyodor Aleksandrovich Abramov (1920–1983)—Russian novelist who wrote about village life; his letter appeared in 1954 in the journal *Novy mir*.

live by the truth even today but also are inclined toward the truth in their strivings and wanderings, that they crave it and receive it over the course of time, and that with anxiety and doubt they hesitantly decipher the spiritual symbols imbedded in their hearts and memories by many generations.

"Don't love us—love what we stand for. That's what the people will tell you if they want to be convinced of the sincerity of your love for them"—these are the well-known words of Dostoyevksy.

Alyosha Beskonvoyny would seem to have achieved no great accomplishment, no great victory—all he got was saunas on Saturdays! He achieved not freedom so much as the satisfaction of a whim, if one takes a sensible view, but look how changed and ennobled the man becomes: "Recently Alyosha had begun to notice that he was completely aware of loving. He loved the steppe beyond the town, sunsets, summer days . . . That is, he fully realized that he loved them. His soul began to feel at peace—he began to love."

The victory is small, but hand it over anyway and it will prove useful in preserving the person within and in saving the soul. Movement, albeit small, blind, and instinctive, has occurred—movement in a direction that is beneficial and dear to humankind.

Monya Kvasov, the same Monya who tries to invent a perpetual-motion machine (in the story "Stubborn"), leaps up in the middle of the night, makes a sketch, and, certain that it will work, that he's got what he wants, is seized by a rare mood: "Nothing seemed to have changed, but life had become so precious and cherished. Ah, how in the world can you end up not noticing that everything here is splendid, simple, extremely precious!"

And out of a seemingly wrong-headed impetus (a perpetual-motion machine) comes the beginning of movement toward the best in him, toward finding spiritual freedom and spiritual beauty.

And Genka Proydisvet in the story with that title badgers his uncle not because the uncle's belief in God bothers him but because he is not convinced of the sincerity of this faith and fears that his uncle might run from the rejection of one lie to another.

"Uncle Grisha, my friend, what do you need this lie for? You're a man, after all, a peasant, a hard worker—what do you need this lie for? How can people live like this?!' Genka grimaced and began to cry . . . But he wasn't angry at his tears, they were merely a hinderance, and he hurriedly wiped them away with the palm of his hand. 'How can we live like this?! If you lie even once, nothing is worthwhile! What? You condemn me, everybody condemns me: why did I leave the institute? I didn't want to lie! Once I felt that this wasn't all that necessary for me, why should I pretend? I find life interesting without a diploma, too. But why . . . Ha! I thought you weren't capable of lying—why should any man need this? Aren't there enough phony people in the world already? Where do you want me to go now? To whom? Shameless people, this is the example you set . . . Everything can collapse this way, you see!'"

And after their fight:

"'This makes me sick,' said Genka, spitting out ichor. 'Oh, this really makes me sick! We were talking about Rus.* And this . . . this wheeler-dealer started pretending. Dumb outsider. He started violating his soul . . . he wanted respect. He started lying! If I clown around when I'm on the road'—Genka forcefully thumped himself on the chest and his wet eyes flashed—'I know that Rus stands behind me: I won't be lost, I'll still be a person. I've got somebody to turn to!' Genka began shouting as if he were at the market, as if he were yelling at a greedy, unscrupulous sales woman after people had already gathered around and there was no longer anything shameful about yelling. 'We'll go under this way!'"

This comprehension, these golden words about a man having no reason to lie, about the perniciousness of taking part in a lie, this devout belief in Rus—all this offers the greatest hope for the fate of our homeland and our people. And because these words are spoken by such an outwardly worthless, reckless guy, by someone as unsettled in life as Genka, we can be all the more confident that the spiritual bastion of the people is located there, in the depths of the people's consciousness, and has as much strength and validity as ever.

Freedom is one of Shukshin's favorite words and favorite concepts and is found almost everywhere in his works. Not the official-sounding "liberty"[†] but the precious Russian "freedom"[‡] that is dear to each person. "I have come to give you freedom" is how the novel about Stenka Razin begins.[§] He put his most important ideas about Russia and its fate, ideas gained through deep suffering, into this novel and dreamed until his final days of putting them into a film in order to make them vivid and visible. Shukshin's folk hero and defender, Stenka Razin, is defeated because he doesn't completely trust the peasants and begins to fear them, then betrays them near Simbirsk, and repudiates the truth told by Matvey Ivanov, a peasant philosopher and wise man.

---

*Rus—the most venerable, and now largely poetic, name for Russia.

[†]In Russian, *svoboda*.

[‡]In Russian, *volia*.

[§]Stepan Timofeevich Razin (d. 1671)—leader of a major Cossack and peasant rebellion in southwestern Russia in 1670–1671 that ended in defeat, after which he was tortured and executed.

Matvey Ivanov, Frol Minaev, and Stepan Razin are three hypostases of the Russian character: in Frol Minaev we find reasonable protest within certain limits, which is actually reasonable obedience expressed through long suffering; in Stepan Razin there is constant readiness for self-sacrifice, uncontrollability, and even aggression directed at oneself; and in Matvey Ivanov we have the basis of the people and popular truth, which have suffered long and painfully at the hands of their own kind as well as at the hands of strangers and which have preserved and continue to preserve Russia in spite of all its overt and secret enemies.

A memorable conversation takes place between Frol Minaev and Stepan Razin at the end of the novel when the latter is being taken to Moscow with his hands and feet bound.

" 'So what was it you wanted, Stepan?'

'I wanted to give people freedom, Frol.'

'And what came of it?'

'What came of it? I gave them freedom,' said Stepan with conviction.

'How's that?'

'I gave them freedom. Let them take it.' "

There can be no doubt that he is talking about spiritual freedom, about inner emancipation, about driving the slave out of oneself and realizing one's individuality. In this sense, Stepan Razin fulfilled his task completely; he really did give people freedom. The scope of the Cossack and peasant revolt he raised demonstrated the possibilities of the power of the people and instilled in the people a great faith in themselves despite the failure of the insurrection. If the people sang the praises of the dear tsar before this without daring to lift their eyes, then afterward they even lay down under the lash with proud hearts.

For Shukshin "the people" are, above all, the sharing of a common blood that has the same components as that of other peoples but in different proportions; each nation differs from others in its historical and ethnic features and in the spirit of the land that gives its people birth. During the long and complicated course of its fate, a nation's people inevitably goes through illnesses as well as through doubts and ordeals, and in a certain sense all these can even contribute to their moral purification and to the arousal of their civic feelings. There are no misfortunes on earth that a people cannot overcome if they are properly organized and directed in accordance with the whole flow of their historical progression and their spiritual commonality. And only the following can have extremely serious, even irreparable consequences for any people: the complacency of a generation or of several generations, obliviousness to their roots, and a conscious or unconscious break with the centuries-old experience of the past, all of which lead, through subsequent phases, to the loss of national feeling and historical memory, to fragmentation, depersonalization, and homelessness. Then the people are a population and their homeland a place of residence and registration; then we stop hearing the currents of shared blood in another person and remain alone. Deafness to those near us threatens us with general deafness and total permissiveness; a person views himself as an act of chance and puts his trust in chance, and chance becomes his fate.

Shukshin's "oddball" is that very character, that very person who can't stand homeless solitude and who searches blindly, uncertainly, and unsystematically for ways to be close to the people, to return from a cold concept to their living flesh, and, not being content with the value of physical existence, to obtain spiritual meaning. The liberty that humankind so ardently fights for leads to ugliness in those who don't have a common, time-honored goal. Individuality is properly free and autonomous only among one's people, for only there does it have space and freedom, and it finds its meaning and eternity among them, in their straight and continuing path.

Not long before his death Shukshin wrote, "During its history the Russian people have selected, preserved, and elevated certain human qualities to a degree of respect, qualities that cannot be improved: honesty, diligence, conscientiousness, goodness . . . Believe at last that all this was not in vain: our songs, our folktales, the incredible difficulties of our victory,* our suffering—don't let it all go up in smoke. We knew how to live. Remember this. Be a human being."

"Be a human being" . . . Everything Shukshin did in the world of art is anointed with this exacting conception of his, with this passion and pain, which he forced everyone to hear whether they knew how to listen or not. In recent decades we have not had another artist like this, one who would burst into any human soul so mercilessly and with such certainty and require it to take a good look at what it was, at what open spaces and distant spots it had become lost in, at what temptations it had yielded to, or, on the contrary, at what had helped it stand firm and remain true and pure. Everyone in Russia, from the loftiest mind to the most fallen soul, was and remains a reader of Vasily Shukshin and an admirer of his films; his talent lies in the alarm, despair, and faith of an all-penetrating conscience that seeks traces of itself in each person.

And in this respect—regarding the utmost intensity of words and their uniting force—we writers apparently failed to give Shukshin adequate support. We also discuss the same things but more calmly and with greater detachment, and we are read, but our readers are gourmets. Literature after Shukshin has returned to its usual channel; he,

*In World War II.

however, succeeded in taking it to the level of propagandistic sharpness and alarm, to the summit of strength that destroys all indifference, to Avvakum's* height of passion, without losing the beauty and feeling of art.

We badly needed Shukshin—and he came, he did his job with talent and honesty, without sparing himself, and, overstrained by this neglected work, he departed prematurely after demonstrating that it is essential for an artist to live, work, and think in the name of the people and of truth.

1984

* Avvakum Petrovich (1620/1621–1682)—leader of the Old Believers, a conservative sect that split away from the Russian Orthodox Church, who was noted for his zealousness.

THE TRUTHS OF

ALEKSANDR VAMPILOV

With the premature deaths of poet Nikolay Rub-
tsov, prose writer Vasily Shukshin, and dramatist Aleksandr Vampilov,*
Russian literature seems to have lost at the same time its hopes for the
future and its very soul. And our literature's very conscience seems to
rest with them forever, in their works.

Our people are amazingly sensitive to talented artists. A similar sensitivity is unlikely to be found anywhere else, in any other people.
When it comes to literature, this aptitude is even linked to our readers'
personal aspirations. They don't regard a talented writer as a phenomenon that has appeared and exists independently of the reader. No, they
have been waiting and hoping for him, they seem to have sacrificed a
part of their own destiny to facilitate his birth, and their patience has
been rewarded. The writer with talent may not be acclaimed yet, he may
still be gathering steam as a literary figure, and there may as yet be no
audible signals to distinguish him from the writer without talent, but

---

*Rubtsov—1936–1971; Shukshin—1929–1974; Vampilov—1937–1972.

our readers are following their own instincts, which are extraordinarily well developed and receptive to the truth, and they already know about this writer through some kind of mysterious impulses and underwater currents. They eagerly latch onto his every word, because there they discover the truth about themselves and about their times—that straightforward and sacred truth that people need, along with their work, in order to live healthy and moral lives. And our readers and viewers respond to the loss of a talented writer, to his death, as though it were a personal tragedy.

Because the artistic gift of the talented writer is drawn from many, many people and his heart seems filled to overflowing with goodness and understanding, we unfortunately tend to forget that during his own life he clutches his heart more often than anyone else and that this heart has throbbed with the pain of all those people from the very start.

Aleksandr Vampilov's heart stopped beating only a few yards from the shore of Lake Baikal when he was trying to swim to safety after his boat struck a submerged log and capsized. The following day he would have turned thirty-five. He and a friend had gone to the lake the evening of 17 August 1972 to catch a mess of fish for his birthday celebration. His friend survived, but he did not. Now, as the years go by, I believe more and more firmly that his tragic death, which was accidental in the sense that it happened precisely then and in that way, was in effect not so accidental. This raises a tough question, one that we run out of breath trying to answer: why don't we assess a talented writer at his true worth while he is still with us? We seem to be punished for this oversight by some outside force that cruelly pronounces a higher form of justice. Fortunately, Vampilov had time to write *Duck Hunting* [*Utinaia okhota*] and to create in the character of Zilov "a hero of our time."* Let's not be modest: Zilov is not simply a protagonist, a character in one of Vampilov's plays; he is a type, a figure by no means unique or innocuous. Far into the future we'll still be locked in a struggle with the deeply rooted social phenomenon of "Zilovitis" and suffering immeasurably from its effects. It may be Vampilov's greatest achievement as a playwright that he was among the first to recognize and to depict this, and he depicted it so vividly, with such artistic power, that only now can we timidly bring ourselves to watch it on the stage. "The artist is an artist only because he sees things as they are rather than the way he wants to see them" (Leo Tolstoy). And whatever the critics may say about Zilov being obsolete, essentially a corpse, believe me, this corpse still has a lot of life in him.

---

*A reference to Mikhail Lermontov's 1840 novel of this title, whose chief protagonist, Pechorin, was one of Russian literature's first antiheroes.

And what's more, Zilov lives in almost every one of us, nudging our sincerity toward cynicism. Why we have let him in, why we allow him to take over, is something we must keep trying to understand.

Critics are no longer reluctant to write at length about Vampilov. They argue incessantly over his characters and reach such diverse conclusions that a phrase has even been coined: "the ecstatic misunderstanding of Vampilov." This misunderstanding stems from their presumptions about art rather than from the presumptions about life that form the basis of Vampilov's art. Night after night his characters mount the stage of many theaters in our country, and it is also his characters who, though not always perceiving their own mirror image, watch themselves from the audience and laugh. It would not be enough, however, if they just laughed. Vampilov certainly did not write plays so that the audience could sit back and relax with their souls at peace; he did not acknowledge any art that is created purely for entertainment. He began to address this issue in "The Incomparable Nakonechnikov" [*Nesravnennyi Nakonechnikov*], a play that remains unfinished, but unfortunately he didn't have time to develop his views fully. An audience arriving at a theater to see one of Vampilov's plays automatically faces a difficult moral test, a kind of confession. It is the audience's confession that sooner or later, one way or another, draws in all the spectators during the performance and stays with them for a long time after the play is over. This constitutes the unobtrusive but amazing power and passion of his talent. And when we speak about "the theater of Vampilov," we obviously should take into account not only what is presented to the audience but also what happens to the audience, the profound psychological effect of his plays, which the trappings of the theater actually seem to intensify rather than to diminish. Moreover, Vampilov's plays themselves appear to dictate how they should be staged and do not allow for variant readings.

Vampilov brought goodness and sincerity to the theater—feelings as ancient as bread and just as essential to art as bread is to our existence. I can't say that the theater before him was totally without these qualities. They were present, of course, but they evidently lacked the same degree of persuasiveness and proximity to the audience. In *The Older Son* [*Starshii syn*], the pure, naive soul of Sarafanov is laid completely bare before us and groans deeply as he asserts that "all men are brothers"—an age-old truth that is becoming a ridiculous paradox in our daily lives. In *Last Summer in Chulimsk* [*Proshlym letom v Chulimske*], Valentina walks onto the stage and everything base and filthy automatically steps out of her way. This is not simply the entrance of a heroine who possesses virtuous traits but the entrance of suffering virtue itself. These are powerless people, unprotected and unable to defend themselves against the prosaic side of life, but look at what staunch, absolute inner conviction they have about the most important and sacred laws of human existence. Even in tears or in despair, they fanatically maintain their belief in human nature at its best and remain blind to it at its worst. One can only guess what will happen to Valentina later on, beyond the framework of the play, how her destiny will unfold on a daily basis. But this is certain: she will not lose her faith, and her virtue will neither weaken nor surrender. Vampilov leaves us convinced beyond the shadow of a doubt.

The old familiar truths appear in Vampilov's short stories as well as in his plays (and even in his feature articles when he was a newspaper reporter). He didn't try to think up new ones, for there aren't any new ones; he simply placed these truths in a contemporary context and they began to sound new. They are the eternal themes of art, which, like day and night, do not fade or age and will never cease to stir up humanity—life and death, love and hatred, happiness and grief, conscience and duty. Each new age adds its own distinguishing features to these concepts, and these then become the signs of the time; but the concepts themselves, with all their complexity and durability, remain unchanged. One person loving another means the same now as it did a thousand years ago. But how is one to love? What does this most sensitive and primary feeling include? How does it enrich us? What makes us lose it? How long-lasting is it? As long as at least one person remains alive, he will love and hate in his own way, he will both fear and wish for death as no one else before him feared and beckoned it. Human feelings are unique.

These truths are old but also eternal; they don't wear out either physically or morally with the passing of time. And in Vampilov's works they have still another important quality: they produce a certain personal, individual illumination in each reader and member of the audience. It remains a mystery how he manages to convince each of us that his plays are relevant to us (to us and, therefore, to me), that they are of primary concern to us and are aimed straight at our feelings, but a direct appeal on the one hand and a personal response, a personal involvement, on the other are always present. And after reading a play or seeing a performance, more than one of us will catch ourselves wishing like naive children to become, say, that older son of Sarafanov so that we can help this good man who, even in the midst of today's complicated and hopelessly muddled life, has preserved his radiant soul into old age. To produce this kind of reaction is the dream of every artist.

The main question that Vampilov seems to be constantly asking is, Will you, the human race, remain human? Will you manage to overcome all the falsehood and evil that await you in those many daily trials in which it has become hard to tell the difference between opposites like love and betrayal, passion and indifference, sincerity and phoniness, well-being and servitude? Here again we invariably think of Zilov, who, not having the strength to resist, allowed all these positive qualities in himself to be replaced by their antitheses.

Yet as you read Vampilov, you come back again and again, filled with hope, to Dostoevsky's age-old conviction: "Beauty will save the world." He means the beauty and power of natural spiritualness that have become the beauty and power of human spirituality, for whose preservation art is obliged to toil.

1977

Appendix

Guide to Word Stress in Russian Names

Abrámov, Fyódor Aleksándrovich
Afanásy, Afónya
Alexándra
Altái Mountains
Alyábev, Aleksándr
Alyóna
Andriyán, Andriyásha
Angará River
Ánna
Antip
Antokólsky, Márk
Arkhárov, Nikoláy Petróvich
Arkhárovtsy
Astáfiev, Víktor
Atalánka
Atlásov, Vladímir
Avdótya
Avvakúm Petróvich
Ayvazóvsky, Iván
Azadóvsky, Márk
Bába Yagá
Bábushkin
Baikál
Baikál-Amúr Main Line
Baránovskaya
bargúzin
Bekétov, Pyótr
Belóv, Vasíly
Berezáy Station
Beryózovka
Beskonvóyny, Alyósha
Borís Iványch
Borís Timoféevich/Timoféich
Bórka, Bórya
Borovikóvsky, Vladímir
Brónnikov, Afónya
Brúni, Fyódor
Buryát
Busýgin, M. I.
Chernóbyl
Chitá
Chivilíkhin, Vladímir
Chivyrkúysky Gulf
Chulímsk
Dál, Vladímir
Dárya
Daúria

Dezhnyóv, Semyón
Dikánka
Dnépr River
Dostoévsky
Dviná River
Evénk
Fatyánov, Alekséy Deméntievich
Fédka
Filíppovka
Gálya
Gerásimov, Sergéy
Gógol, Nikoláy
Golúbkina, Ánna
Golyánushkin
Góshka
Grísha
Guskóv, Andréy
Ilyá
Indigírka River
Irkút River
Irkútsk
Irtýsh River
Iván Petróvich
Ivanóv, Matvéy
Ivánushka
Kacháev
Kalíningrad
Kapítsa, Pyótr
Kapústin, Gléb
Katsúba, P.
Katún River
Kátya
Katyúsha
Kazántsev
Khabárov, Yeroféy
Khabárovsk
Khampó, Mísha
Khomyakóv, Alekséy Stepánovich
Kiprénsky, Orést
Klávka
Koltsóv, Semyón
Konyónkov, Sergéy
Kopylóva, Anastasía Prokópievna
Koróvin, Konstantín
Kozeltsóv
Kramskóy
Krasnoyársk

Krivolútskaya, Krivolútskies
Kubán River
Kuíndzhi, Arkhíp
Kultúk
Kustódiev, Borís
Kvásov, Mónya
Lebedínsky, B. I.
Léna River
Lérmontov, Mikhaíl
Levitán, Isaák
Levítsky, Dmítry
Lídia Mikháylovna
Likhachyóv, Dmítry
Lyókha
Lyóshka
Makóvksy
Malyávin
Mamái
Mánka
Márfa
María
Marína
Márya
Matyóra
Mávrina, Tatyána
Mezén
Mináev, Fról
Mityáy
Nádya
Nakonéchnikov
Nástka, Nástya
Nastyóna
Natálya
Nikoláy Ivánovich
Nizhneangársk
Nóvgorod
Pálekh
Parátov, Kólka
Pechórin
Peredvízhniki
Peróv, Vasíly
Peschánaya Bay
Pétka
Petróv-Vódkin, Kuzmá
Plastóv, Arkády
Pochiválova, Nádya
Podkámennaya Street
Pomerántsev, K. I.
Poyárkov, Vasíly
Prípet Marshes
Prokúdin, Yegór
Proydisvét, Génka
Pskóv
Pyótr
Raspútin, Valentín Grigórievich
Razbórov, Pétya
Rázin, Stepán Timoféevich

Répin, Ilyá
Romádin, Nikoláy
Románov
Rubtsóv, Nikoláy
Rússkoe Ústye
Sánka
Sánya, Sanyók
Sarafánov
sárma
Saryán, Martíros
Sáshka
Savély
Savrásov
Sayán Mountains
Selengá River
Sergéy
Seván, Lake
Shádr, Iván
Shchápov, Afanásy Prokópievich
Shíshkin, Iván
Shukshín, Vasíly
Shúra
Shurýgin
Sibiryakóv
Simbírsk
Sólodov, Andréy
Sómov, Konstantín
Sónya
Sosnóvka
Soyuzshín
Strigunóva, Klávka
Stróganov
Styópa, Styópka
Sukachyóv, Vladímir Platónovich
Súrikov, Vasíly
Súslova, Galína
Svetlána
Sýrniki
Talýzin, N. V.
Tánya
Teplyakóv
Teplyáshin, Vánka
Tíshka
Tíshkin
Tofalár
Tolstóy, Leo
Tómsk
Tropínin, Vasíly
Tunkínskaya Valley
Turgénev, Iván
Ulíta Yefímovna
Ust-Ilím
Ust-Udá
Vádik
Valentína
Válya
Vampílov, Aleksándr

Ványa
Vasilísa
Vasíly Andréevich
Váska
Vasnetsóv, Víktor
Velíchko, N. K.
Vénya
Véra
Vereshchágin, Vasíly
Vishnévsky, F. E.
Vódnikov, Borís Timoféevich
Volódya
Vrúbel, Mikhaíl
Vuchétich, Yevgény
Yádrintsev, Nikoláy Mikháylovich
Yakútia

Yaroslávl
Yegór
Yegórov, Iván Petróvich
Yegórovka
Yermák Timoféevich
Yershóv, Pyótr
Yeryóminskaya
Yevstrátov, V. F.
Yuón, Konstantín
Yúry Andréevich
Zabéllo, Vasíly
Zalýgin, Sergéy
Zhávoronkov, N. M.
Zhigulí
Zhukóvsky, Vasíly Andréevich
Zílov

Bibliography of Major Works
by Valentin Rasputin

Krai vozle samogo neba: ocherki i rasskazy (A land next to the sky: essays and short stories). Irkutsk: Vostochno-Sibirskoe knizhnoe izd-vo, 1966.

Chelovek s etogo sveta: rasskazy (A person from this world: short stories). Krasnoiarsk: Krasnoiarskoe knizhnoe izd-vo, 1967.

Den'gi dlia Marii: povesti i rasskazy (Money for Maria: novellas and short stories). Moscow: Molodaia gvardiia, 1968.

Poslednii srok: povest' i rasskazy (Borrowed time: a novella and short stories). Irkutsk: Vostochno-Sibirskoe knizhnoe izd-vo, 1970.

Vniz i vverkh po techeniiu: povesti (Downstream and upstream: novellas). Moscow: Sovetskaia Rossiia, 1972.

Zhivi i pomni (Live and remember). Moscow: Sovremennik, 1975.

Proshchanie s Materoi (Farewell to Matyora). In *Povesti* (Novellas). Moscow: Molodaia gvardiia, 1976.

Vek zhivi—vek liubi: rasskazy (Live and love: short stories). Moscow: Molodaia gvardiia, 1982.

Izbrannye proizvedeniia v dvukh tomakh (Selected works in two volumes). Moscow: Molodaia gvardiia, 1984.

Pozhar (The fire). In *Poslednii srok; Proshchanie s Materoi; Pozhar: povesti* (Borrowed time; Farewell to Matyora; The fire: novellas), pp. 327–83. Moscow: Sovetskaia Rossiia, 1986.

Chto v slove, chto za slovom?: ocherki, interv'iu, retsenzii (What's in a word, what's behind a word?: essays, interviews, literary criticism). Irkutsk: Vostochno-Sibirskoe knizhnoe izd-vo, 1987.

"Tetka Ulita" (Auntie Ulita). In *Vek zhivi—vek liubi: rasskazy, ocherki, povest'* (Live and love: short stories, essays, a novella), pp. 203–10. Moscow: Molodaia gvardiia, 1988.

"Sibir', Sibir' . . ." (Siberia, Siberia). *Nash sovremennik* (Our contemporary) 5 (1988): 3–40, 8 (1988): 3–54, and 7 (1989).

Works in English Translation

Live and Remember. Translated by Antonina W. Bouis. New York: Macmillan, 1978.

Farewell to Matyora. Translated by Antonina W. Bouis. New York: Macmillan, 1979.

Money for Maria and Borrowed Time. Translated by Kevin Windle and Margaret Wettlin. London: Quartet Books, 1981.

"Downstream." Translated by Valentina G. Brougher and Helen C. Poot. In *Contemporary Russian Prose*, edited by Carl and Ellendea Proffer, pp. 379–430. Ann Arbor: Ardis, 1982.

You Live and Love and Other Stories. Translated by Alan Myers. New York: Vanguard, 1986.